The Historic Landscape
of the Quantock Hills

The Historic Landscape
of the Quantock Hills

Hazel Riley

with illustrations by Elaine Jamieson

ENGLISH HERITAGE

Published by English Heritage, Kemble Drive, Swindon SN2 2GZ
www.english-heritage.org.uk
English Heritage is the Government's statutory adviser on all aspects of the
historic environment.

© English Heritage 2006

First published 2006

ISBN   10-digit   1 905624 29 8
         13-digit   978 1 905624 29 4

Product Code 51199

British Library Cataloguing in Publication Data
A CIP catalogue record for this book is available from the British Library.

The National Monuments Record is the public archive of English Heritage.
For more information, contact NMR Enquiry and Research Services, National
Monuments Record Centre, Kemble Drive, Swindon SN2 2GZ; telephone
(01793) 414600.

Application for the reproduction of images should be made to the National
Monuments Record.

Edited and brought to publication by David M Jones, Publishing, English Heritage, Kemble Drive, Swindon SN2 2GZ.

Proofread by Diana Smith
Cover design and page layout by Mark Simmons
Indexed by Alan Rutter
Printed by CPI Bath Press Ltd

Contents

Illustrations   vi
Foreword by Lady Gass and Chris Edwards   vii
Acknowledgements   viii
Summary   ix
Resumé   x
Zusamenfassung   xi

Introduction   xii

1 A special place?
The landscape of the Quantock Hills   1

Cheerful beauty: the natural landscape   1

The man-made landscape   6

The English Heritage archaeological survey
of the Quantock Hills AONB   14

2 A ritual landscape?
The early prehistory of the
Quantock Hills   15

Handaxes and early humans in the Lower
Palaeolithic period   15

The ice was all around: climate change and the
Middle and Upper Palaeolithic periods   15

Hunters in the forest: the Mesolithic period   18

Landscapes of death and life in the
Neolithic period   19

The Bronze Age: funerary and mundane
landscapes   28

The funerary landscape: Bronze Age burial
monuments   30

The mundane landscape: Bronze Age
settlement   43

3 A defended landscape?
The Quantock Hills in Iron Age
and Roman times   51

Beyond the pale of civilisation: the Iron Age   51

Business as usual? The Roman occupation   72

4 A managed landscape?
The Quantock Hills in the
medieval period   77

The migration and early medieval periods:
Britons and Anglo-Saxons   77

The later medieval period: lords of
the manor   85

5 A Romantic landscape?
The Quantock Hills in the
post-medieval period   115

A changing landscape: enclosure,
improvement and industry   115

Gardens bright with sinuous rills: designed
landscapes on the Quantock Hills   115

A working landscape: farms, farming and
industry in the Quantock Hills   127

6 A remembered landscape?
The Quantock Hills in the
20th century   152

A rural idyll? The Quantock Hills in the
early 20th century   152

The Second World War and the Cold
War: the Quantock Hills in the later
20th century   153

A changing landscape? The historic
landscape of the Quantock Hills in the
21st century   159

Appendix 1: Site gazetteer   162

*Appendix 2: English Heritage Quantock project
survey reports*   163

References   164

Index   168

Illustrations

i.1   Time-line
1.1   The Quantock Hills
1.2*   The Quantock Hills: location map
1.3*   The Quantock Hills: topography and relief
1.4   The Quantock Hills: geology
1.5   Cottages, Over Stowey
1.6   Medieval buildings, Kilve
1.7   The foreshore, Kilve
1.8   Heath and woodland
1.9   Swaling on Quantock common
1.10   Quantock commons
1.11* The Quantock Hills: land use and historic commons
1.12** Crowcombe Court
1.13   'The Old Gate', Halsway Manor
1.14   Surveying the Trendle Ring

2.1   Doniford and West Quantoxhead
2.2*   The Quantock Hills: Palaeolithic and Mesolithic artefacts
2.3   Palaeolithic handaxe
2.4*   The Quantock Hills: Neolithic artefacts and sites
2.5   Neolithic stone axe
2.6   Norton Fitzwarren
2.7*   Battlegore barrow cemetery
2.8   Battlegore, portal dolmen
2.9*   Pit circle, Langford
2.10   The Long Stone and Triscombe Stone
2.11   Westleigh urn
2.12* The Quantock Hills: Bronze Age sites and artefacts
2.13   Hurley Beacon
2.14   Barrows
2.15   Cairns
2.16* Barrow groups
2.17   Platform cairns
2.18   Beacon Hill
2.19   Ring cairns and embanked platform cairns
2.20* Black Hill barrow cemetery
2.21   Black Hill barrow cemetery: detail plans
2.22   The western scarp of the Quantock Hills
2.23* Wills Neck barrow cemetery
2.24   Wills Neck: cairn enclosure
2.25   Reconstruction of Bronze Age funeral pyre
2.26   Greenway: prehistoric settlement
2.27   West Hill: prehistoric settlement
2.28* Linear earthworks
2.29* Linear earthworks, barrows and cairns

3.1*   The Quantock Hills: Iron Age and Roman sites
3.2*   Ruborough Camp: earthwork plan
3.3   Ruborough Camp: the ramparts
3.4   Dowsborough Camp: the hillfort
3.5*   Dowsborough Camp: earthwork plan
3.6   Dragon, Crowcombe Church
3.7   Bicknoller Hill: the hilltop enclosure
3.8*   Bicknoller Hill: earthwork plan
3.9   Cropmark complex, Yarford
3.10* The Trendle Ring: earthwork plan
3.11* Plainsfield Camp: earthwork plan
3.12   Rooks Castle: enclosures
3.13* Rooks Castle: earthwork plan
3.14* Higher Castles: earthwork plan
3.15   Higher Castles: the enclosure
3.16   Reconstruction of Iron Age life

3.17* Cropmarks, Dene Cross
3.18* Cropmarks, Upper Cheddon
3.19* Hillslope enclosures, Broomfield
3.20* Cropmarks, Clavelshay
3.21* Multi-phase cropmarks, Goathurst
3.22   Excavations at Volis Hill
3.23   Roman forts and roads
3.24   Excavations at Yarford
3.25   Mosaic at Yarford
3.26   West Bagborough hoard

4.1   Stoneage Barton post-Roman cemetery
4.2*   The Quantock Hills: Anglo-Saxon sites
4.3   St Decuman's Church
4.4   Anglo-Saxon coins from Watchet mint
4.5   Rooks Castle: enclosure and quarries
4.6   Coastal settlements
4.7   Stogursey Castle
4.8   Sir Matthew de Stawell, Cothelstone Church
4.9   Kingston St Mary Church
4.10   Medieval door surround, Court House
4.11* The Quantock Hills: medieval sites
4.12   Nether Stowey
4.13   Nether Stowey Castle: earthwork plan
4.14   Nether Stowey: 1750 map
4.15   Manorial earthworks
4.16   Adscombe Chapel c 1903
4.17   Adscombe Chapel: window surround
4.18   East Quantoxhead: medieval landscape
4.19   East Quantoxhead: deer park and rabbit warren
4.20   Pillow mounds
4.21   Cothelstone: the medieval landscape
4.22   East Quantoxhead: 1827 map
4.23   Manor Cottages, Cothelstone
4.24   Manorial enclosures
4.25   Medieval gatehouse, Court House
4.26   Reconstruction of medieval manor, Kilve
4.27   Deserted farmsteads
4.28   Holcombe and Aisholt Common
4.29   Higher Aisholt Farm
4.30   Domescombe
4.31   Deak's Allers: earthwork plan
4.32   Middle Halsway Farm
4.33   Bicknoller: enclosed strip fields
4.34   Nether Stowey: strip fields in 1750
4.35   Windmill mound
4.36   Miller, Bishops Lydeard Church
4.37   Stock ponds
4.38   Withyman's Pool
4.39   Textile worker, Spaxton Church

5.1   Cothelstone Manor: gatehouse
5.2   Cothelstone Manor: early post-medieval layout.
5.3   Cothelstone Manor: formal gardens
5.4*   The Quantock Hills: the designed landscape
5.5   17th-century formal gardens
5.6   Crowcombe Court: 1767 map
5.7   Crowcombe Park
5.8   Crowcombe Park: Gothic folly
5.9   Fyne Court: folly
5.10   Terhill House: 1778 map
5.11* Terhill Park
5.12   Terhill Park: grotto

5.13   Grotto on 1778 map
5.14   Weacombe: tree ring enclosures
5.15   Tree ring enclosures
5.16   Beacon Tower, Cothelstone Hill
5.17   Conifer plantations, Smith's Combe
5.18* The Quantock Hills: agriculture and mining
5.19* Relict field systems
5.20   Lydeard Hill: shelters and cairns
5.21   Beacon Hill: relict field systems
5.22   Court House: farm buildings
5.23   Outbarn, Deak's Allers
5.24   Combe Farm: 1797 map
5.25   Deserted farmsteads
5.26* Broomfield: deserted settlements
5.27   Ivyton Farm
5.28   Catch-water meadows, North Stream
5.29   Lime burner's shelter, Hawkridge Common
5.30   Lime kiln, Aisholt
5.31   Merridge: limekilns
5.32   Oak woodland, Holford Combe
5.33* Holford Combe and Hodder's Combe: charcoal burning platforms
5.34   Charcoal burning platforms: plans
5.35   Charcoal burning in Slaughterhouse Combe
5.36   Nether Stowey tan yard
5.37   Tom Poole's bark house
5.38   Hayman's Pool
5.39   Drying loft, Tanyard Farm
5.40   Marsh Mills
5.41   Marsh Mills silk factory
5.42   Dye house, Holford
5.43   Openworks
5.44   Engine houses and shafts
5.45   Beech grove engine house
5.46   Rural industry

6.1   Oil retort, Kilve
6.2   Communication post, West Kilton Farm
6.3*   Tank training range, West Kilton Farm
6.4   Blast-proof shelter, Lilstock
6.5*   PoW camps
6.6   Searchlight battery, Crowcombe Gate
6.7   Wooden toy made by PoW
6.8   Bunker, Cothelstone Hill
6.9   ROC post, Holford
6.10   Stable block, Friarn

Images (except as otherwise shown) © English Heritage

* These maps are based upon Ordnance Survey maps, drawn by English Heritage with the permission of the Ordnance Survey on behalf of The Controller of Her Majesty's Stationery Office, © Crown copyright. All rights reserved. Unauthorised reproduction infringes Crown copyright and may lead to prosecution or civil proceedings. Licence Number GD030859G.

** Every effort has been made to seek permission to reproduce this image from the copyright holder.

Foreword

Somerset's Quantock Hills form a richly complex landscape that has been shaped by human activity over many thousands of years. In 1956 the Quantocks became England's first Area of Outstanding Natural Beauty, in recognition of their very special qualities, and it is appropriate in this fiftieth anniversary year that the hills should be recorded and interpreted in a splendid new archaeological survey.

The survey has been undertaken by English Heritage and is published at a moment when the hills face great pressures and challenges. English Heritage and all those involved are to be congratulated for bringing the survey to completion and for making the information it contains widely accessible and in so attractive a form.

There is much to discover and to learn from this important book. It deserves to be widely welcomed and appreciated both within the county of Somerset and beyond.

Having known and loved the Quantocks all my life it is a particular pleasure to be writing this foreword.

Elizabeth Gass
Lord Lieutenant of Somerset
June 2006

On a late February afternoon in 1798, three people – brother, sister and friend – climbed an Iron Age hillfort in the Quantocks and looked down on 'a magnificent scene, curiously spread out for even minute inspection'. Many times during her research for this outstanding book Hazel must have stood in Dorothy Wordsworth's footsteps on Dowsborough Camp and looked out, seeing the history in this special landscape. That the Quantocks still have extraordinary crystal clear days, and that they retain an unspoilt landscape the Wordsworths and Coleridge would instantly recognise, is a source of great satisfaction to many.

More than 400,000 recreational visits are made to the Quantock Hills each year, indicating a remarkable focus of attraction. The Quantock mix of wooded slopes and open hilltops creates a natural-feeling sense of wildness in a scale of landscape found unthreatening by most people. All British landscapes are historic but here the casual walker enjoys almost prehistoric environments of heath, birch and oak alongside medieval farmland, 1000-year-old hedgerows and 18th-century designer deer parks that still echo with the roaring of stags during the autumn deer rut. Beyond purely aesthetic appreciation and potential wildlife encounters, this historic landscape gives a satisfying sense of consistency and permanence to the visitor. Geology is the canvas, but the historic landscape is the image constructed by millennia of varied land use. This book is the story of that still-evolving relationship between people and the Quantocks.

The Quantock Hills Area of Outstanding Natural Beauty (AONB) is recognised internationally as a Category V Protected Area, highlighting the extent to which human land use has created and continues to maintain the landscape's distinctive appearance and wildlife interest. The Quantocks were the first area in England to receive AONB designation, in May 1956, making 2006 the 50th anniversary of this event. Fifty years is a small step in the development of this landscape, however it is a conscious step to understand and protect the natural and cultural elements that give the Quantocks their special status. Understanding the historic significance of this AONB informs appropriate management and inspires greater awareness and support in both resident and visitor.

I hope the work of the AONB Service helped attract English Heritage to the Quantocks, and special mention goes to Somerset County Archaeologist Bob Croft who was instrumental in setting up the project. The Somerset County Council Historic Environment Service continued to support the project throughout its duration. I further hope the result achieved here strengthens the Historic Environment Accord signed by the National Association of AONBs and English Heritage in December 2004. All credit for the archaeological survey, research and writing goes to Hazel with the support of Elaine Jamieson and other English Heritage staff. Jane Brayne was commissioned by the AONB Service to paint images of the Quantocks in the Bronze Age, Iron Age, medieval and post-medieval periods, which put people in the foreground of the historic landscape. Thanks are also due to the supporting partnership. This level of research requires decent financial support, and while English Heritage provided the majority of funds a significant contribution came from a range of funding partners including Somerset County Council, the National Trust, the Friends of Quantock organisation, the Fairfield Estate and the AONB Service. The AONB Service is itself funded by a partnership between West Somerset District, Sedgemoor District, Taunton Deane Borough and Somerset County Councils, and the Countryside Agency.

Despite a changing population and the information age many Quantock people still have an unconscious sense of historical connection, which was picked up in a 1934 Somerset guidebook published by the Great Western Railway Company. Author Maxwell Fraser wrote: 'In no part of England is history a more living, vital thing than in Quantoxland, where the thrilling stories of battles which took place a thousand years ago, and the romances and scandals of as far back as the sixteenth century, are remembered, retold and commented upon by villagers ...as though they were of recent occurrence...'

The Historic Landscape of the Quantock Hills, and the research from which it has been distilled, adds fundamentally to the sum of understanding of this precious landscape, ensuring that the story of these hills will continue to be told with increasing accuracy. I thank English Heritage and specifically Hazel Riley and her colleagues for the two and a half years of all-weather effort and commitment it has taken.

Chris Edwards, Manager
Quantock Hills Area of Outstanding Natural Beauty
October 2005

Acknowledgements

The Quantock Hills archaeological survey project and this book would have been very different were it not for the timely appointment of Elaine Jamieson to English Heritage in 2001. Elaine not only shouldered the burden of half the fieldwork for the project but she also designed and produced the figures in this book, completed most of the archive plans, undertook the design and illustration of the survey reports and somehow found the time to carry out extensive research on sites at Kilve, Court House, Fyne Court, Plainsfield Camp and the landscapes around East Quantoxhead and Crowcombe. I am also grateful for Elaine's careful reading of sections of the book at draft stage, and for her many helpful comments and suggestions throughout the project.

The Quantock Area of Outstanding Natural Beauty (AONB) Service have been unfailingly helpful during the course of the project. Chris Edwards was instrumental in instigating the field survey and the publication, never tired of discussing things Quantockian and read through the draft text. The whole team helped with access arrangements, site clearance and, in particular, the section on Bronze Age settlement on the hills would have been very short were it not for the co-operation of the Rangers and their willingness to be shown 'a series of small walls' so that their annual programme of swaling (controlled heather burning) could be co-ordinated with our fieldwork on the commons. I am especially grateful to Andy Harris and Ella Briens who arranged several events on the hills, which gave me the opportunity to engage with both local people and visitors about our survey work. The Quantock Hills office at Nether Stowey provided a welcome refuge from rain, snow and sun. The Quantock Hills AONB, Somerset County Council and the Friends of Quantock financial contributions to the field survey and to this publication are gratefully acknowledged here.

Taunton lies on the southern edge of the Quantock Hills, it is also the repository of a huge amount of published and unpublished information about Somerset. I would like to thank David Bromwich of the Somerset Studies Library and staff in the Somerset Archive and Record Service for helping me to find my way around the books and documents. Chris Webster of the Somerset Historic Environment Service supplied all of the material from the Somerset Historic Environment Record needed at the beginning of the project and helped with the interpretation of some of the military archaeology. Steve Minnitt of Somerset County Museums Service facilitated access to the collections at Taunton.

I am fortunate to have worked with several of my colleagues in the Exeter Office of English Heritage for many years and I would like to thank them for sharing their experience of field archaeology in southwest England with me. Martin Fletcher helped with some of the field survey; Phil Newman surveyed the Trendle Ring and the copper mines at Dodington; Ben Moore worked at Kenley Copse, Nether Stowey Castle and Marsh Mills, and undertook research on limekilns for the project. John Winterburn considered some of the relict field systems on the Quantock Hills as part of his dissertation topic. Helen Winton made John's work possible, as she carried out the mammoth task of mapping the whole of the Quantock Hills from air photographs. Louise Martin commissioned the geophysical survey at Over Stowey and Martin Papworth of the National Trust carried out geophysical work at the Trendle Ring for the project.

I am indebted to Barry Jones for his hard work looking at the buildings in the Quantock Hills and for the many hours of discussion about those buildings in relation to the archaeology surrounding them. Barry undertook major pieces of work at Kilve and Court House and was always ready to answer questions ranging from 'what date is that farm building?' to 'how old is this fragment of worked stone?' Mike Williams and Sheila Ely investigated several of the industrial buildings which are tucked away in some surprising corners of the Quantock Hills.

I remain humbled by the ability of Peter Williams, Damian Grady and Jane Brayne to turn my faltering ideas about the visualisation of the historic landscape into such stunning images. Peter undertook the record photography for the project, including collections of photographs at Court House and Cothelstone, as well as most of the photography for this book. Damian was the only member of the project team to experience the Quantock Hills landscape from the air but his photographs convey that experience to those of us who keep our feet on the ground. I asked with mixed feelings for Jane's contribution, due to several comments best summed up as: 'the best things in the Exmoor book were the reconstruction drawings'. However, I swallowed my pride and I hope that many more such comments will follow the publication of Jane's images based on the Quantock Hills landscape.

The project could not have happened without the co-operation of local landowners and their tenants. I would like to thank Lady Gass of the Fairfield Acland Estate for her help in getting the project started, for allowing access across the estate, for discussions about the estate and the history of copper mining on the Quantock Hills. The estate also provided a financial contribution towards the project, which is gratefully acknowledged here. Colonel Sir Walter Luttrell of the East Quantoxhead Estate allowed us to investigate not only the farms, fields and common lands of the estate but also the buildings at Court House and Kilve. He proved to be an inexhaustible source of both historical fact and anecdote and Elaine and myself would like to thank him and his wife for their kindness while we were working at Court House. I would also like to thank Anthony Trollope Bellow for discussions about, and access to, Crowcombe Park; Hugh and Jane Warmington whose knowledge of the Cothelstone Estates could fill another book and Mary White of Durborough Farm, without whom the lost farmstead of Hamme would have remained lost. Nigel Garnsworthy and Tim Beazley helped with access on the National Trust Quantock Hills Estate, and the National Trust contributed financially towards the project. Nick Salter facilitated access to Forestry Commission land. Many other landowners allowed us to walk over their fields and farmyards and kept us supplied with coffee.

The chapter on the 20th-century landscape would have been very short without the memories of several people who lived and worked on the Quantock Hills during the Second World War and the Cold War. Jack Ash and his sister, Jean, lived at West Kilton Farm when the American army commandeered part of it for a tank training range; Peter White was stationed at Crowcombe Court with 493 Battery of the 76th Searchlight Unit between 1941 and 1944; Mr R A Lawry was a member of the Royal Observer

Corps and manned the underground monitoring post at Yards during the Cold War. I am grateful to them for sharing their experiences with me. Mal Treharne and Dave Pusill kindly allowed me access to unpublished information about Invasion Committees on the Quantock Hills and the Prisoner of War Camp at Halswell House, Goathurst. Richard Cobb provided invaluable comment on 20th-century industrial processes as well as tea and sympathy. Mark Bowden, Bob Croft, Chris Edwards, Elaine Jamieson, Bob Croft, Josh Pollard, Rob Wilson-North and Helen Winton all commented on the draft text and I am grateful for their tact and forthrightness in their response to it.

Finally, I would like to acknowledge the contribution that Paul Everson has made to the story of the historic landscape of the Quantock Hills. Paul's commitment to landscape archaeology and analytical earthwork survey, and his enthusiasm for research into the historic landscape, have inspired not only my approach in terms of fieldwork to the Quantock landscape and its buildings, but also many of the thoughts and ideas that underpin the distillation of that fieldwork into this book.

Thanks also to Dr David Jones, to Diana Smith and to Mark Simmons for their carefull editing, proof reading, and layout and designing of this book.

Summary

The Quantock Hills, an isolated area of upland in west Somerset, are formed mostly of resistant rocks of Devonian age. The hills lie to the north of Taunton and run up to the coast of the Bristol Channel on their northern edge. To the west are the Brendon Hills and Exmoor; the Somerset Levels and Moors lie to the east. The hills rise to more than 300m to the north and west, where unenclosed heathland is dominant. A characteristic of the Quantock Hills, however, is the diverse quality of the landscape. The open heathland gives way to glorious oakwoods in the eastern combes, beloved of the Romantic poets Coleridge and Wordsworth. The southern hills are primarily an agricultural landscape. The Quantock Hills were the first such area in Britain to be designated an Area of Outstanding Natural Beauty (AONB) in 1956.

This book tells the story of the development of the historic landscape of the Quantock Hills using the landscape itself as the main source of evidence. Detailed fieldwork by English Heritage archaeological investigation staff, backed up by a full air photographic transcription of the area, has made it possible to assess the field evidence for the historic landscape of the Quantock Hills for the first time. The survey work has been complemented by architectural investigation of selected sites and the interpretation of the evidence has been greatly enhanced by new ground and air photographs, and by a series of reconstruction paintings, which aim to people those historic landscapes.

The earlier prehistoric landscape is characterised by burial monuments: barrows and cairns, mostly dating from the later part of the 3rd and earlier part of the 2nd millennia BC. There have been no recorded excavations of any of these sites on the Quantock Hills, but detailed survey work and comparison with other analogous monuments elsewhere, particularly in southwest England and Wales, has enabled the identification of several monument types, including platform cairns and ring cairns. The distribution of these monuments is analysed and discussed. Fragmentary traces of possible settlement remains and field systems of the 2nd millennium BC have been located on the heathland.

There is a wealth of evidence for the later prehistoric and Roman periods on the Quantock Hills. As well as a number of very well preserved earthwork hillforts and enclosures there are numerous cropmark enclosures that probably date from this period on the southern edge of the hills. Recent excavation and geophysical survey of a sample of these cropmark sites has highlighted their complexity and longevity. One had its origins in the earlier part of the 2nd millennium BC; a Roman villa was found close to another, and a cemetery of Dark Age date was discovered when a third was excavated.

The evidence for the medieval landscape of the Quantock Hills is rich and diverse. The wealth of the landowners is reflected in the surviving medieval fabric of churches, chapels and manor houses. Studies of historic maps and documents have enabled the medieval landscape to be the reconstructed, with evidence for deer parks, rabbit warrens and dovecotes. By this time the pattern of land use and settlement on the hills was one familiar to that of today: the upland heath was common land, with settlements located at the foot of the combes below the heath, giving access to a variety of land types: upland pasture, woodland, meadow and arable fields. By the 17th century the practice of outfield cultivation on the heath was becoming widespread. The physical remains of this cultivation can be seen across great tracts of heathland and these relict field systems have been used to date, roughly, aspects of the historic landscape.

The formal, ornamental landscape can also be identified in the post-medieval period, including formal gardens, landscape parks, tree ring enclosures and plantations. Contrasting with this, and the Romantic landscape of Coleridge and Wordsworth, are the remains of an industrial landscape: textile mills, tanneries and copper mines were once common features on and around the Quantock Hills in the later post-medieval period.

The story draws to a close in the 20th century. Brutal concrete structures, built quickly in response to the threat of invasion in the early stages of the Second World War, are the silent reminders of a time when the Quantock Hills became the temporary home to troops from North America as well as to hundreds of Italian and German Prisoners of War.

The historic landscape of the Quantock Hills is rich, diverse, surprising and beautiful. Its conservation and management, informed by an enhanced understanding, must be one of the priorities for the Quantock Hills in the 21st century.

Résumé

Les Quantocks, région reculée de hautes terres dans l'ouest du comté de Somerset, sont essentiellement formées de roches résistantes datant du Devonien. Ces collines se trouvent au nord de Taunton et se prolongent jusqu'à la côte de l'estuaire de Bristol à leur extrémité nord. À l'ouest se trouvent les collines de Brendon et Exmoor, les terres basses des Somerset Levels et la lande des Somerset Moors s'étendent à l'est. Ces collines s'élèvent à plus de 300 m. au nord et à l'est, là domine la lande non clôturée. Cependant une des caractéristiques des Quantocks est la riche diversité de leurs paysages. Cette lande ouverte cède la place, dans les combes à l'est, à de magnifiques forêts de chênes, chéries des poètes romantiques Coleridge et Wordsworth. Au sud, les collines constituent avant tout un paysage agricole. Les Quantocks furent la première zone de ce type à recevoir le titre de Zone de Beauté Naturelle Exceptionnelle (AONB) en 1956.

Ce livre raconte l'histoire de l'évolution du paysage historique des Quantocks en utilisant le paysage lui-même comme principale source de témoignages. Une prospection détaillée, effectuée par du personnel d'investigation archéologique d'English Heritage, secondée par une transcription complète des photographies aériennes de la région, a pour la première fois rendu possible l'évaluation des indices de terrain concernant le paysage historique des Quantocks. Aux travaux de propection est venue s'ajouter une investigation de l'architecture de sites sélectionnés et l'interprétation des témoignages a été grandement étayée par de nouvelles photographies, aériennes et au sol, et par une série de peintures reconstructives, dont le but était de peupler ces paysages historiques.

Le plus ancien paysage préhistorique se caractérise par des monuments associés à des inhumations: tertres et cairns, datant pour la plupart de la seconde partie du 3ème et de la première partie du 2ème millénaires avant J.-C.. Il n'existe de fouilles répertoriées pour aucun de ces sites des Quantocks, mais des travaux de prospection détaillés et une comparaison avec des monuments similaires ailleurs, particulièrement dans le sud-ouest de l'Angleterre et au Pays de Galles, ont permis d'identifier plusieurs types de monuments, y compris des cairns en plateformes et des cairns en anneaux. On analyse et discute la répartition de ces monuments. Des traces fragmentaires de vestiges d'éventuelles occupations et de systèmes de champs datant du 2ème millénaire avant J.-C. ont été localisées sur la lande.

Il existe, dans les Quantocks, une abondance de témoignages pour la seconde partie de la période préhistorique et pour la période romaine. En plus d'un nombre de forteresses et d'enclos avec fossé bien préservés, il existe de nombreux enclos, dont les traces se révèlent dans les cultures, qui datent probablement de cette période sur le flanc sud des collines. Des excavations et une prospection géophysique récentes d'un échantillon de ces sites identifiés grâce aux traces dans les cultures ont mis en lumière leur complexité et leur longévité. L'origine de l'un remontait à la première partie du 2ème millénaire avant J.-C. ; on a trouvé une villa romaine à proximité d'un autre et on a découvert un cimetière datant de l'Âge des Ténèbres au moment de l'excavation d'un troisième.

Les témoignages concernant le paysage médiéval des Quantocks sont riches et variés. La prospérité des propriétaires terriens se reflète dans ce qui a survécu des édifices médiévaux tels que des églises, chapelles et manoirs. L'étude de cartes et de documents historiques a permis la reconstruction du paysage médiéval avec des témoignages de l'existence de parcs à cerfs, de garennes et de pigeonniers. À cette époque, le modèle de l'utilisation des terres et de l'occupation des collines ressemblait à celui qui existe de nos jours: la lande sur les hauteurs constituait un terrain communal, les occupations se trouvaient au pied des combes en bas de la lande, permettant l'accès à divers types de terrains: pâtures sur les hauteurs, forêts, prairies et champs labourables. D'ici le 17ème siècle, la pratique de la culture hors des villages s'était répandue sur la lande. Les restes physiques de ces cultures se manifestent sur de grandes étendues de lande et ces survivances de systèmes de champs ont été utilisées pour dater (grossièrement) certains traits du paysage historique.

On peut également identifier le paysage formel et d'agrément à la période post- médiévale, y compris des jardins formels, des parcs paysagers, des plantations et cercles d'arbres. Par contraste avec ceux-ci, et le paysage romantique de Coleridge et Wordsworth, on trouve les restes d'un paysage industriel: filatures, tanneries et mines de cuivre étaient des caractéristiques familières sur et à proximité des Quantocks au cours de la seconde partie de la période post-médiévale.

Cette histoire trouve sa conclusion au 20ème siècle. De grossières structures de béton, construites rapidement en réaction à la menace d'invasion au cours des premiers moments de la Seconde Guerre Mondiale sont les témoins silencieux d'une époque où les Quantocks servaient de résidence temporaire à des troupes venues d'Amérique du Nord, ainsi qu'à des centaines de prisoniers de guerre allemands et italiens.

Le paysage des Quantocks est riche et varié, beau et surprenant. Sa préservation et sa gestion, éclairées par une meilleure compréhension, doivent être l'une des priorités des Quantocks au 21ème siècle.

Traduction: Annie Pritchard

Zusammenfassung

Die Hügel von Quantock (The Quantock Hills), sind ein isoliertes Hochlandgebiet im Westen von Somerset. Sie wurden von wiederständigem Gestein im Devonischem Zeitalter (Devonian Age) geformt. Die Hügel liegen im Norden von Taunton und verlaufen bis an die nördliche Küste des Bristol-Kanals. Zum Westen sind die Hügel von Brendon und Exmoor. Die Ebenen und Moore von Somerset liegen im Osten. Die Hügel steigen bis zu einer Höhe von 300m im Norden und Westen, wo offenes Heideland dominiert. Die Haupteigenschaft der Quantock Hills ist jedoch die diverse Qualität der Landschaft. Das offene Heideland gibt Weg zu wunderbaren Eichenwäldern in den östlichen Kämmen und wurde von den romantischen Dichtern Coleridge und Wordsworth geliebt. Die südlichen Hugel sind vorwiegend ein argrarwirtschaftliches Gebiet. Die Quantock Hills waren die erste Landschaft in Grossbritannien, welche in 1956 als Gebiet von Herausragender Naturschönheit (Area of Outstanding Natural Beauty oder AONB) designiert wurde.

Dieses Buch stellt die Entwicklungsgeschichte der historischen Landschaft von Quantock Hills dar und benutzt dafür hauptsächlich die eigentliche Landschaft als Beweisstück. Detaillierte Feldarbeit der Archäologischen Untersuchungsabteilung von English Heritage, ergänzt durch eine volle flugfotografische Aufzeichnung des Gebietes, haben zum ersten Mal die Beurteilung der Feldmerkmale für die historische Landschaft von Quantock Hills ermöglicht. Die Untersuchungsarbeiten wurden von architektonischen Beurteilungen von ausgesuchten Standorten komplimentiert. Die Auswertung der gefundenen Beweise wurde erheblich durch neue Boden- und Luftaufnahmen, sowie durch eine Reihe von Rekonstruktionszeichnungen verbessert, mit dem Ziel die historische Landschaft darzustellen.

Die frühe prähistorische Landschaft is durch Begrabungstätten, wie Gruben und Steinhügel charaktesiert, welche auf das späte 3. und das frühe 2. Jahrtausend v.C. datieren. Es gibt keine bekannten Ausgrabungen dieser Standorte in den Quantock Hills, aber detaillierte Vermessungsarbeiten und Vergleiche mit anlogen Monumenten woanders, im speziellen Südwest-England und Wales, haben die Indentifikation verschiedener Typen von Begrabungstätten, wie Plattform- und Ringgrabhügel ermöglicht. Die Verteilung dieser Monumente wird analysiert und diskutiert. Fragmentierte Überreste von möglichen Niederlassungen und Feldsystemen aus dem 2. Jahrtausend v.C. wurden im Heideland gefunden.

Für die späteren prähistorischen und die römischen Perioden der Quantock Hills gibt eine Fülle von Beweisen. Neben einer Anzahl von sehr gut erhaltenen Erdhügelfestungen und Erdbegrenzungen gibt es verschiedene Getreidemarkierungen (Cropmarks), welche wahrscheinlich aus dieser Periode an der südlichen Seite der Hügel stammen. Ausgrabungen und geophysische Vermessungen der Getreidemarkierungen in den letzten Jahren weisen auf die vielfaltige Nutzung und die Langlebigkeit dieser Standorte hin. Eine dieser Markierungen stammt aus der frühen Hälfte des 2. Jahrunderts, eine römische Villa wurde neben einer anderen gefunden, und ein Friedhof des Finsteren Mittelalters wurde bei der Ausgrabung eines dritten Standortes gefunden.

Es gibt vielfältige und reiche Nachweise für die mittelalterliche Landschaft der Quantock Hills. Die Wohlständigkeit der Landbesitzer ist and Hand der erhaltenen Verwebung von Kirchen, Kapellen und Landhäusern erkennbar. Studien von historischen Landkarten und Dokumenten ermöglichten die Rekonstruktion von der mittelalterlichen Landschaft, mit Wildgehegen, Hasen-und Taubenschlägen. In dieser Periode war die Nutzung der Landschaft vergleichbar mit der heutigen Zeit. Die hochgelegene Heide war gemeines Land, mit Ansiedlungen und den Füssen der Kämme unterhalb der Heide, welche Zugang zu einer Vielfalt von Landtypen, wie Hochlandheiden, Waldgebiete, Weiden und bewirtschaftbare Felder gaben. Bei dem 17. Jahrhundert war die Anwendung von Aussenfeldbewirtschaftung mittlerweile sehr ausgeweitet. Die physichen Überreste dieser Kultivierungen wurden ihrer Zeit entsprechend über weite Striche des Heidelands, und die relikten Feldsysteme in der historischen Landschaft genutzt.

Die formelle dekorative Landschaft ist seit postmittelalterlichen Zeiten erkennbar. Sie beinhaltet formelle Gärten, Parkanlagen, Baumringgehege und Plantagen. Im Kontrast zu dieser und der romantischen Landschaft von Coleridge und Wordsworth sind die Überreste der industriellen Vergangenheit mit ihren Textilmühlen, Gerbereien und Kupferminen, welche in der postmittelalterlichen Zeit alltägliche Merkmale auf den und in der Umgebung der Quantock Hills waren.

Die Geschichte endet im 20. Jahrhundert. Brutale Betonstrukturen, schnell als Antwort zu der Gefahr einer Invasion in der frühen Phase des ZweitenWeltkrieges gebaut, dienen als stille Erinnerung für die Zeit als diese Gegend ein temporäres Zuhause für nordamerikanische Truppen und Hunderte von italienischen und deutschen Kriegsgefangenen war.

Die historsche Landschaft der Quantock Hills ist reich, divers, erstaunlich und schön. Die Konservierung und das Management dieser Landschaft muß, informiert durch ein verbessertes Verständnis, eine der Prioritäten für die Quantock Hills im 21. Jahrhundert sein.
Übersetzung: Norman Behrend

Introduction

In the early autumn of 1994 I met Chris Edwards and Tim Russell of the Quantock Hills AONB and Bob Croft, the Somerset County Archaeologist, on Steep Holm. We were sitting in the barrack block built in 1867, which housed the garrison stationed on Steep Holm to defend the Severn against a French invasion, eating a picnic lunch. We had a conversation along the lines of 'When are you coming to do an archaeological survey of the Quantock Hills?' 'When we have finished our survey work on Exmoor.' Well, we did finish our survey work on Exmoor, and this book is partly the result of that conversation. In the years between that first meeting with Chris and Tim, the Royal Commission on the Historical Monuments of England, which carried out the archaeological survey of Exmoor National Park, joined forces with English Heritage. The field work on Exmoor was followed by the publication of the survey work in *The Field Archaeology of Exmoor* (Riley and Wilson-North 2001), Foot and Mouth Disease and its restrictions on access to the countryside came and went, and finally, in the early autumn of 2002, we began work on a large scale earthwork survey of Dowsborough Camp. The fieldwork finished in the early summer of 2004 at Higher Castles, an Iron Age enclosure, nearly ten years after that initial request. I hope that the results were worth waiting for.

Those people who do not have the good fortune to be intimately acquainted with the Quantock Hills tend to see them as an extension of Exmoor and the Brendon Hills. How wrong they are. The Quantock Hills are 'in a more civilized part of the world' than Exmoor (Acland and Sturge 1851, 33). The climate is milder, the moorland is heathland, the barrow groups are more distinctive, the linear earthworks are longer, the Iron Age enclosures are bigger, the deer parks and landscape parks more numerous. I could go on. Suffice to say that the time I have spent becoming intimately acquainted with the Quantock Hills landscape and with its 'enchanting musty records of antiquity which have peacefully slept for ages' (Rack 1782–1786) has been a time of recapturing the excitement of the discovery of new sites and of new ways of perceiving well known sites.

I make no apologies for once again quoting Edmund Rack, writing to his friend John Collinson about his survey work in Somerset: 'I have passed through a variety of scenes and perils in my tour, being taken once for an American spy. In short I have been suspected to be almost everything but a Bishop and a Highwayman' (Rack 1784–1786). During the course of our survey work we were never suspected of either ecclesiastical or criminal intent, but suspicion was certainly aroused when the Global Positioning System (GPS) survey equipment was set up in some of the more remote parts of the heath, or when we were surveying charcoal-burning platforms in Hodder's Combe with a theodolite. I like to think that we experienced some of the excitement that those 17th- and 18th-century surveyors of Somerset felt when they encountered uncharted territory. Although some of the large barrows on the Quantock Commons are well known, we found many unrecorded examples, and added to the total number of burial mounds by nearly one quarter. The technique of peeling back the layers written onto the landscape led to the realisation that a rather scruffy-looking bank and ditch on the summit of Cothelstone Hill

had to have been constructed at least several centuries ago, and was most likely to be prehistoric in date. In one snowy week in February we encountered three new deserted medieval farmsteads, while days spent ascending and descending the precipitous fields of Terhill Park during the heat wave of 2003 were rewarded by the discovery of a carved stone head of Neptune set into a bridge.

This book is designed to be either read as a single narrative, which will tell the story, albeit an incomplete one, of the evolution of the landscape of the Quantock Hills, or to be sampled by topic or place. Whatever method is employed, the reader unfamiliar with archaeology may be reassured to know that a brief explanation of the terms used by landscape archaeologists and historians is set out below (Fig i.1). Dates are all given in calibrated radiocarbon years (BC and AD). Whether one's interest lies in the peculiar funerary habits of our Bronze Age ancestors or in the Ground Force like determination of the 18th-century gentleman for changing his landscape, there is something for everyone in the singularly special landscape of the Quantock Hills.

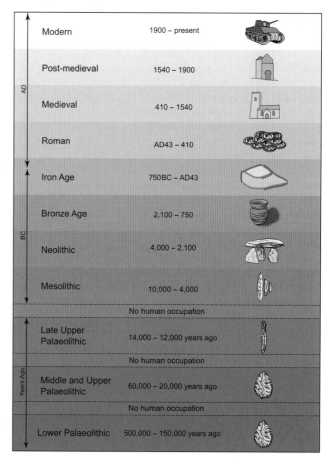

Period	Date	
Modern	1900 – present	
Post-medieval	1540 – 1900	
Medieval	410 – 1540	
Roman	AD43 – 410	
Iron Age	750BC – AD43	
Bronze Age	2,100 – 750	
Neolithic	4,000 – 2,100	
Mesolithic	10,000 – 4,000	
No human occupation		
Late Upper Palaeolithic	14,000 – 12,000 years ago	
No human occupation		
Middle and Upper Palaeolithic	60,000 – 20,000 years ago	
No human occupation		
Lower Palaeolithic	500,000 – 150,000 years ago	

Fig i.1
Major archaeological time periods.

1
A special place? The landscape of the Quantock Hills

Cheerful beauty: the natural landscape

The Quantock Hills are well known as a source of inspiration for Coleridge and Wordsworth and as the home of the democrat and tanner Tom Poole. The hills were also home to the Whig wit Sydney Smith, rector of Combe Florey, a village in the southwest shadow of the Quantock Hills. He lamented that his previous living, a remote Yorkshire parish, was 'twelve miles from a lemon', a description that also applied to Combe Florey. The theme of the remoteness of the hills is at odds with their proximity to the towns of Taunton and Bridgwater. The Rev William Nichols, who lived at Woodlands near Holford, described the chief characteristic of the Quantock scenery as 'cheerful beauty' (Nichols 1891,1). The landscape itself is one of contrasts: at Bicknoller Post deep combes suddenly open onto grand vistas; on Hare Knap heath gives way to woodland, at Cothelstone ornamental parkland and working farm lie side by side (Fig 1.1). The views out from the hills have given rise to an old chestnut, courtesy of Latin scholars, which can be forgiven for its inventiveness. Julius Caesar, on climbing to Dowsborough Camp, declaimed 'Quantum ab hoc!' (How much can be seen from here!) (Lawrence 1952). The name Quantock is probably of Celtic origin and means 'hill country', although a certain amount of gentle debate around this subject has given several alternative meanings: the land of openings or combes, little headlands, the water-headlands or the land of St Carantacus (Robinson 1992; Nichols 1891; Greswell 1900).

Location and topography

The Quantock Hills lie in Somerset, north of Taunton and south of the Bristol Channel (Fig 1.2). The area was designated an Area of Outstanding Natural Beauty (AONB) in 1956, the first such designation in England. The hills are formed of a narrow plateau of mainly Devonian rocks, which trend roughly northwest to southeast for some 19km. The overall width of the hills is 6km, and the AONB occupies an area of roughly 99 sq km. The Quantock Hills rise from just above sea level at the coast to a height of more than 380m at Wills Neck on the western escarpment. This western scarp rises sharply from the wide plain that separates the Quantock Hills from the Brendon Hills and Exmoor, and viewed from the west the Quantock ridge dominates the landscape. The eastern side of the ridge presents a gentler face, and several deep, narrow valleys, known locally as combes, reach far into the heart of the hills. The rolling hill country of the southern fringes rises to about 300m on Cothelstone Hill and Broomfield Hill (Fig 1.1).

The combes are drained by fast-flowing streams. Those that flow down Vinny Combe, Perry Combe, Smith's Combe, Dens Combe, Hodder's Combe and Holford Combe run into the sea where the coastal strip is punctuated by a series of

Fig 1.1
The Quantock Hills looking north from the Vale of Taunton. (NMR 21958/16) (© English Heritage. NMR)

Fig 1.2
The Quantock Hills:
location map. (Based
on an Ordnance Survey
map, with permission.
© Crown copyright.
All rights reserved)

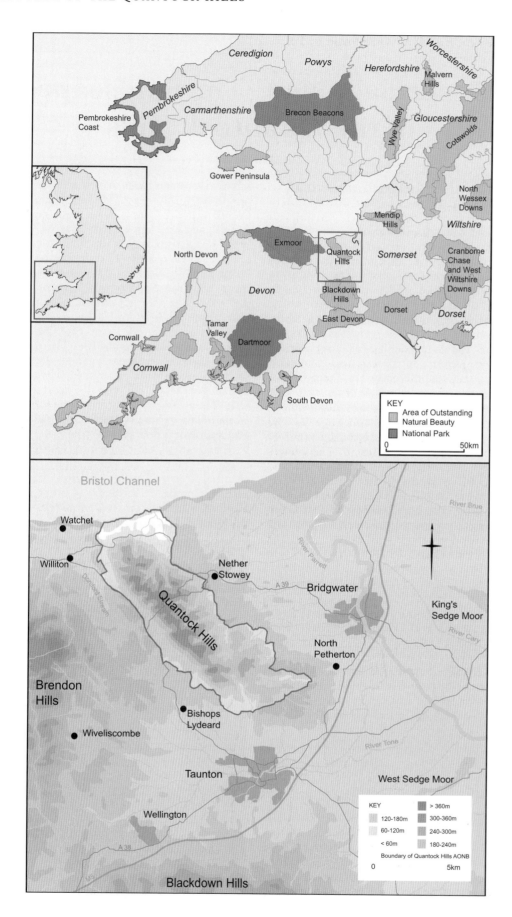

Fig 1.3 (opp top)
The Quantock Hills:
topography and relief.
(Based on an Ordnance
Survey map, with
permission. © Crown
copyright. All rights
reserved)

Fig 1.4 (opp bottom)
Geological map of the
Quantock Hills.
(Reproduced by permission
of the British Geological
Survey. © NERC.
All rights reserved.
IPR/71–02C)

gentle valleys at West Quantoxhead, Perry, East Quantoxhead and Kilve. The streams that drain the long combes of the east side of the hills – Rams Combe, Quantock Combe, Cockercombe – reach the River Parrett via a series of tributary streams that wander across the levels before being marshalled into the drainage ditches of the Somerset moors and levels. South of Triscombe, the streams flow into the River Tone, north of Triscombe the streams of Crowcombe, Halsway, Bicknoller and Weacombe flow into the Doniford Stream and reach the sea at Doniford (Fig 1.3).

The villages and farms of the Quantocks sit at the foot of the hills, where the sides of the combes widen and there is flatter ground for building. The villages along the western scarp illustrate this: Bicknoller, Crowcombe, Triscombe, West Bagborough and Cothelstone lie at the foot of the hill by the major combes, while farms and hamlets occupy similar positions in between the main villages. Likewise on the eastern scarp, Holford, Nether Stowey and Over Stowey lie at the foot of the hills, with the hamlets of Aley, Plainsfield, Aisholt and Merridge to the south. Exceptions to this pattern are where the topography is less extreme. The villages of West and East Quantoxhead, Kilve and Kilton all lie on the fertile coastal plain; in the southern hill country farms and hamlets straggle up the combes. North Petherton, Kingston St Mary and Bishops Lydeard are all important settlements on the southern fringe of the Quantock Hills (Fig 1.3).

Geology, soils and vegetation

The most profound factor in the natural landscape of the hills is their underlying rock and its history – a story told in millions and hundreds of millions of years. The underlying geology influences the natural landscape in a number of ways. It forms the bare bones of the landscape – the landforms on which the story of the occupation and exploitation of the land is told. Geology governs topography, altitude and soil type, which, together with climate, influence settlement and agricultural regimes. Certain geological deposits have an economic benefit, for mineral extraction, for stone and for water.

The Quantock Hills are composed mostly of rocks from the Devonian Period (Fig 1.4). These are sedimentary rocks, laid down under a shallow sea, compressed into hard rock, folded into a ridge and subject to hundreds of millions of years of erosion,

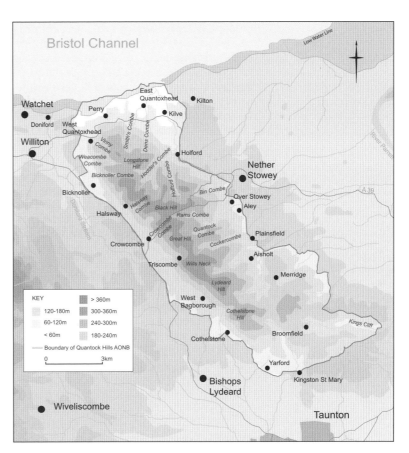

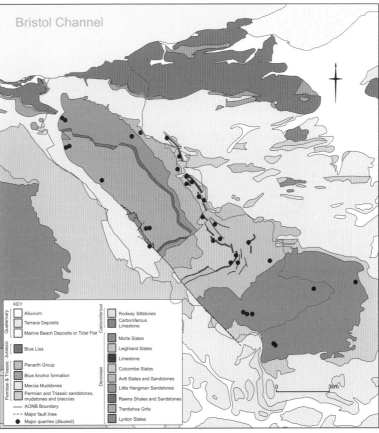

inundation and deposition. Geologically these rocks are the same as those that underlie the upland areas of Exmoor, but the Quantock Hills are separated from that land mass by a large fault, which is responsible for the steep western Quantock escarpment. The very oldest rocks on the hills are to be found in a narrow band at the foot of the hills between Crowcombe and Bagborough Hill. This is an outcrop of Lynton Slates of the Lower and Middle Devonian periods, rubbly green and brown slates, about 400 million years old. These rocks were used to build Combe Farm, whose ruins lie halfway up a small valley where the slate has been quarried from the valley side. Slightly younger than these slates are the Hangman Grits of the Middle Devonian Period. The rocks of this series underlie much of the heathland of the northern plateau and the area now occupied by Great Wood. The oldest of these rocks, the Trentishoe Grits, have been quarried for hundreds of years, for both roadstone and building stone, as evidenced by the abandoned stone quarries in Bicknoller Combe, and by numerous smaller roadside quarries and quarry pits. Triscombe Quarry has been worked for at least 200 years and was quarried for roadstone until its closure in the late 1990s. The Little Hangman series of sandstones have also been quarried, with good examples of remains above West Quantoxhead and at the foot of Smith's Combe.

The Hangman Grits are overlain by beds of Ilfracombe Slates to the east and south. These rocks include a mix of slates, silt-

stones and sandstones, together with bands of Roadwater Limestone. The Avill Slates and Sandstones contain small deposits of volcanic tuff. This rock, the Cockercombe Tuff, was formed as the result of submarine volcanic eruptions, and is only found at Cockercombe and in Holford Glen. The rock's greenish-grey colour gives Quantock Lodge and its gatehouse their distinctive appearance. Roadwater Limestone, with its associated quarries and kilns, occurs in intermittent narrow bands, running first southwest/northeast from Cothelstone to Merridge, then southeast/northwest from Merridge to Bincombe. On the southern edge of the hills, south of Cothelstone, Morte Slates overlie the Ilfracombe Beds. These rocks underlie the rolling hill country around Broomfield and Kingston St Mary, with its mix of arable and pastoral fields, and have been quarried for roof tiles at Rooks Castle. The distinctive red soil seen in the early winter in the arable fields around Crowcombe, Bicknoller and along the coast is formed on the younger Permo-Triassic rocks, only about 250 million years old, derived from material eroded from the Devonian rocks of the hills.

The evidence for the presence of metal-bearing rocks in the Quantock Hills comes mainly from accounts of the 18th- and 19th-century prospectors and miners (Hamilton and Lawrence 1970). There are accounts of copper ore, with a little iron, lead and silver. This suite of minerals suggests a moderate or low temperature origin: the Quantock Hills are a great distance from the intrusion of granite, which caused the mineralization around Dartmoor and in Cornwall. The most likely cause of the mineral formation in the Quantock Hills is the mobilisation and concentration of metals during a time of folding and faulting, causing minerals to form in the Devonian slates and sandstones and the Roadwater Limestones. The minerals reported from the younger Permo-Triassic rocks are probably derived from deposits in the underlying Devonian rocks (Edmonds and Williams 1985, 65).

The grey farm buildings, cottages and the great manor houses of East Quantoxhead and Kilve on the coastal strip contrast with the rusty red sandstone buildings found elsewhere on the hills (Figs 1.5 and 1.6). The buildings on the coast are constructed from the rocks that outcrop in a dazzling array of contrasting stripes of colour on the beach between Kilve and West Quantoxhead. These are alternating beds of

Fig 1.5
Devonian sandstone used in cottages, Over Stowey. (AA053365) (© English Heritage. NMR)

shale and limestone, the Lias formation of the Jurassic Period, the youngest rocks in the area and part of the Blue Anchor to Lilstock Site of Special Scientific Interest (SSSI) (Fig 1.7). During the last Ice Age, about two million years ago, the Quantock Hills, like the rest of southwest England, were not covered with extensive ice sheets, but they were permafrosted. The freezing and thawing in this extreme climate caused large areas of the hills to be covered with a deposit of rock and soil, known as Head. The impermeable Head deposits, together with the freezing temperatures, resulted in a form of surface drainage that created the sharply cut combes and valleys.

The soils that develop on the older, Devonian rocks are reasonably free draining and quite fertile. However, the influences of climate and human interference over time has caused the creation of poorly draining, thin peaty podzols of the Larkbarrow Association on the highest areas of the northern part of the Quantock Hills. Here there is acid grassland, heathland and bracken, extensively grazed by sheep, horses and some cattle. On the lower slopes of the southern hill country brown earths of the Milford Association have formed on the Morte Slates and Ilfracombe Beds, and stock farms are the norm. The mixed farms of the north and

west flanks of the hills use the fertile clayey loam formed on the Permo-Triassic rocks (Countryside Agency 2003).

The main area of heathland and the eastern combes form a large SSSI, covering an area of some 2,400ha. The Quantocks SSSI contains a wide variety of habitats: a mix of heathland, acidic flushes, semi natural broadleaved woodland and dense scrub (Fig 1.8). The western oak woodland of the

Fig 1.6
Lias stone from the beach used in the medieval manor house, Kilve. (AA048490) (© English Heritage. NMR)

Fig 1.7
The rocky foreshore at Kilve. (AA048486) (© English Heritage. NMR)

Fig 1.8
Heath gives way to oak woodland at Slaughterhouse Combe and Black Ball Hill. (NMR 21958/07) (© English Heritage. NMR)

eastern combes is additionally recognised as a Special Area of Conservation under the European Commission Habitats and Species Directive. The heathland is a mixture of upland heath, dominated by ling heather, and western heath, with dominant communities of bell heather and western gorse. Bracken is very common over much of the better drained lower slopes of the heathland areas. There are three main types of woodland, the western upland oak woods of the northwest hills, the ash-hazel woods to the south and southeast, and coniferous plantations. Great Wood is the most extensive of the latter, planted in the 1920s it now swathes a large portion of former enclosed and unenclosed land in the central part of the Quantock Hills. The proximity of woodland and heath creates the ideal habitat for a wide range of birds, invertebrates and mammals, including a large herd of red deer.

The man-made landscape

The historic landscape

The historic landscape *is* the man-made landscape. For thousands of years people have lived and worked on and around the Quantock hills and their actions have influenced the way the hills are now at the beginning of the 21st century. As such, the landscape is a document that can be deciphered. The earliest surviving monuments in that landscape are concerned with the funerary and ritual habits of Neolithic and Bronze Age people who used the hills between 6,000 and 3,000 years ago. The story of the hills during the next 3,000 years is one of success. The landscape fills up and is exploited in many ways. Earthwork enclosures that probably date from the 1st millennium BC can be seen on the heath and in the woods, while many more, now ploughed over in arable fields, are revealed on aerial photographs. Medieval buildings – farmhouses, barns, manor houses and churches – are still in use. Sheep, ponies and cattle still graze areas of common land, which are documented as such in the 14th and 15th centuries, but much of which was subject to periodic arable cultivation in the 16th and 17th centuries, and the remains of which can be seen over much of the heath. Great houses, formal gardens and landscape parks lie close to the remains of rural industries from the 18th and 19th centuries; concrete slabs mark the places where hundreds of troops were stationed in the run-up to D-Day. All of these features contribute to the character of the Quantock Hills landscape; some are of national and regional importance, but the historic landscape itself is a unique and priceless resource.

The Quantock Hills AONB

The National Parks Commission (now the Countryside Agency) designated the Quantock Hills an Area of Outstanding Natural Beauty (AONB) in 1956 – the first such protected area to be created in England. The Quantock Hills AONB is just one of a number of special landscapes in this part of southwest England. Standing on the highest point of the hills, close to the round barrow on the summit of Wills Neck, these protected areas are laid out before us: Exmoor National Park, the Blackdown Hills and East Devon AONBs, the Mendip Hills AONB and the Special Landscape Areas, the Environmentally Sensitive Areas and the SSSIs of the Somerset Levels and Moors. Across the Bristol Channel are the summits of the Brecon Beacons National Park, often glistening snow white in the winter. The Quantock Hills are at the centre of some of the most inspiring and special countryside in Britain.

The Quantock AONB Service is responsible both for the day to day management of the hills, and for protecting their longer-term future. Activities such as swaling (controlled burning) the heathlands and controlling bracken help with the location of prehistoric archaeology on the hills (Fig 1.9); sensitive management of both the heathland and the hill farming country around it help to maintain the traditional character of the Quantocks landscape, and successive management plans identified the need for the survey work that forms the core of this book (Edwards 1999; 2004).

The Quantock commons

The common land of the Quantock Hills has a long history. The owner of the common land was usually the lord of the manor, and villagers or tenants enjoyed certain rights in regards to this land. Tenants of the manor of Wick in Stogursey had rights to graze on the high ground in the north and northwest of Over Stowey parish in the late 13th century. Rights to graze and dig turf on East Quantoxhead common land existed in the 14th century, while unlicensed removal of furze, turf and stones was recorded in the 16th and 17th centuries. In the parish of Bicknoller, in the 16th century, there are complaints of unlicensed sheep grazing on the commons and in 1593, after a dispute with tenants, it was agreed to view, lay out and bound the Common Quantock. By the 18th century common rights were well established; for example, in East Quantoxhead a holding of two acres in the village had common for 20 sheep, one bullock or colt and two days cut of turf by one man (Dunning 1985, 15, 125; 1992, 165).

In the medieval period the area of common land was greater than that which remains today. The great commons of the manors of West and East Quantoxhead and Kilve occupied the northern plateau (Figs 1.10 and 1.11). Much of the land now occupied by Great Wood was common until the 17th century, when it was enclosed and allotted to local landowners in return for the surrender of common rights (Dunning 1992, 165). Until the early 17th century, then, a continuous block of common land stretched from West Hill and Pardlestone Hill in the north, down to Aisholt Common in the south. South of this again, common land was restricted to isolated areas on the edges of enclosed

Fig 1.9
Swaling on Quantock common. (Quantock Hills AONB Service)

7

Fig 1.10
The great commons of West and East Quantoxhead and Kilve. (NMR 21958/06) (© English Heritage. NMR)

farmland, including Merridge, Broomfield and Hawkridge Commons (Fig 1.11).

As well as the common land on the Quantock Hills, most of the parishes in and around the hills contained areas of low lying ground that were used as common land. These lowland commons were often the earliest to be enclosed and improved: land at Crowcombe Heathfield and Heddon in the headwaters of the Doniford Stream remained as common pasture for Crowcombe manor until enclosure in 1780, but by the early 15th century parts of these commons had been ploughed and rye was grown. Currill or Holford Common, on low lying ground to the east of Holford remained until the late 18th century. The lowland common to the southeast of Stringston, Stringston Heathfield, was being encroached upon by 1519, when two fields called 'ryecroft' are recorded, and was finally enclosed by 1807 (Dunning 1985, 54, 58; 1992, 172, 175).

The Quantock commons escaped the worst depredations of the private enclosure acts of the 18th century and 19th-century Parliamentary enclosure. In the mid- 20th century the main rights claimed by the commoners were rights of pasture, turbary and cutting fern. This tradition was recognised by the commoners in 1957. At the hearing of the Royal Commission on Common Land, it was stated that there were no cattle on the common, though there used to be some originally, and that the way to manage the common land was by the old traditional method. For many generations the owners of the soil controlled the water, mineral and sporting rights and took profits from the timber; all through these generations the commoners exercised the right of inter-commonage and co-operated together (Royal Commission on Common Land 1957, 1272–3). The Commons Registration Act of 1965 required the registration of all common land by 1970. The main area of

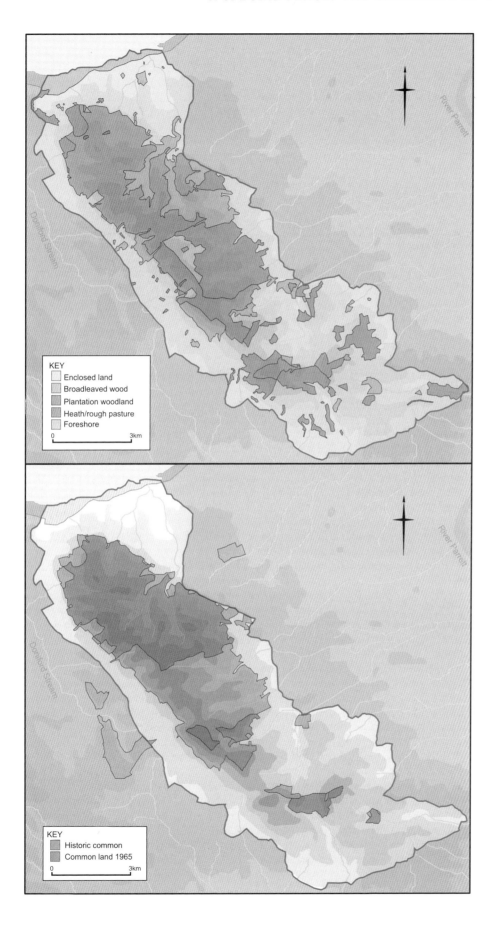

Fig 1.11
The Quantock Hills: land use and historic commons. (Based on an Ordnance Survey map, with permission. © Crown copyright. All rights reserved)

KEY
Enclosed land
Broadleaved wood
Plantation woodland
Heath/rough pasture
Foreshore
0   3km

KEY
Historic common
Common land 1965
0   3km

common land that survives today is the large block of heathland to the north, together with Wills Neck and Aisholt Common, an area of some 1,800ha (Fig 1.11). These areas are known as the Quantock Common and are managed by the Quantock Common Management Group (Harris 2000). These areas of common land form the most important resource in terms of the preservation of prehistoric sites and landscapes, as they have not been subject to centuries of enclosure and improvement.

Antiquarians, writers and artists discover the hills

The Quantock Hills were too far from the great centres of learning and civilisation to attract the attentions of any great antiquarians. Most of the cairns and barrows bear the signs of disturbance, but there are no accounts of any organised antiquarian activities. The Rev John Skinner looked across to the hills from the barrows on Mendip; Chanter and Worth stayed on Exmoor and Dartmoor, examining stone circles and hut circles; Bulleid and Gray only looked up to the hills while excavating the lake villages at Meare and Glastonbury on the Somerset Levels. What do survive, however, are a number of legends and tales, associating the barrows and hillforts of prehistory with dragons and giants. Dowsborough Camp and the enclosure at Norton Fitzwarren have their own dragon tales (*see* Chapter 3). The megalithic stones at Battlegore are said to be the result of a battle between the devil and a giant, and the ancient pond on Woodlands Hill above Holford has sinister connections with the devil's blacksmith (Wright 2002, 93–6; Grinsell 1969, 13; Cresswell 1904, 89).

Leland, tasked as he was in 1533 to search after 'England's antiquities, and peruse the libraries of all cathedrals, abbeys, priories, etc., and places where records, writings and secrets of antiquity were kept' (Bates 1887, 60), described the Quantock Hills thus: 'These Hilles renne in crestes from Quantok-Hedde toward Tauntoun, as from North to South Est' (Bates 1887, 94). This is one of the earliest descriptions of the hills, and is admirable for its brevity. Leland also left us a wealth of information about the landscape of the fringes of the Quantocks in the late medieval period, as he travelled from Athelney to Bridgwater and thence to Dunster in 1542. At Petherton Park, on the low lying ground close to the estuary of the River Parrett, the deer 'trip over the dikes, feed all about in the fens and resort to the park again'. At Bridgwater the castle, 'once a right fair and strong piece of work is now all going to mere ruin', and, although Stowey is 'a poor place, standing in a bottom among hills, it is redeemed by the goodly manor house' of Lord Audley with its famous double deer park for red and fallow deer (Bates 1887, 91–4).

Drayton's topographical poem *The Poly-Olbion*, written at the turn of the 16th century to celebrate the glory of the English countryside, captures the grandeur of the Quantock coast: 'where seaward Quantock stands as Neptune he contrld' (Buxton 1953). Thomas Gerard of Trent travelled in Somerset in the early 17th century, and his work, dated 1633, *The Particular Description of the County of Somerset* combined both topographic description and family history. His eye for the landscape is revealed in his observations, which link his visits to Alfoxton, Stringston and Stockland: 'Lett us now againe betake ourselves to Coast this Coast, and having recovered ye hills they yeild a pleasant prospect both by Sea and Land' (Bates 1900, 32). Robert Gay, parson of Nettlecombe between 1631 and 1672 described the barrows at Battlegore as: 'three huge moles or burrowes, each 120 yeards round the Basis, and so of a proportionall pyramidall height and forme' (Gray 1931, 10).

Thomas Carew (died 1766) of Crowcombe Court (Fig 1.12) was the first antiquarian proper to make observations about the archaeology of the Quantock Hills – he evidently knew the works of William Camden and John Leland. In the early part of the 18th century he began to collect material for a history of Somersetshire. This grand project was never completed, but the manuscript material survives and Carew's work laid the foundation for many of the later topographic and historical accounts of the county of Somerset. The importance of Thomas Carew to the history of the Quantock Hills is that he knew the area: the hills were the backdrop to his busy life. This is how he describes Crowcombe:

The parish is about 8 miles northwest from Taunton and contains within it about 3,500 acres of land, of which 1,200 are unenclosed, and for want of manuring the soil is very indifferent, the other, is enclosed for the most part, is good fertile land and has the benefit of being joined to the south side of Quantock, from whence water flows over great part of it and divides itself in the lower parts into several small rivulets, which at some minor distance erupt themselves into the sea near Watchet. *(Carew 1735–1750)*

Carew gives us some of the first written descriptions of archaeological monuments in the Quantock Hills, which are obviously based on first hand knowledge of the sites and his observations are echoed in subsequent 18th- and 19th-century accounts of the area. Dowsborough Camp and Nether Stowey Castle are described as:

two specimens of Antiquities viz. Dowseborough Castle and Castle Hill in both of which there yet remains footsteps of our Saxon ancestors the former of which is situated upon the Top of a steep hill and the avenues thereto are now through a wood. The ditch is now very deep and surrounds the plain part of the hill, which is about [ ] acre in circuit and from which you have a fine view of the Severn and Coast of Wales together with the Low lands over the greatest part of the County. Castle Hill is situate very near the town [Nether Stowey] the Fortification seems to be designed for its guard upon which was formerly some ancient buildings the remains of which are now dug up there. It is encompassed with a ditch that is now very visible....The town is not large but the streets are wide and the houses chiefly thatched.
(Carew 1735–1750)

John Collinson and Edmund Rack were collecting material for their *History and Antiquities of the County of Somerset* (Collinson 1791) during the 1780s. The work evidently drew on Thomas Carew's papers, but more archaeological sites were listed, and some original observations made. Thus, Dowsborough Camp consists of 'a double rampart, the fosse very deep and wide; the whole is thickly covered with an oak coppice wood' (Collinson 1791, I, 261). Collinson also notes that Bicknoller is, 'like many others [villages] in the vicinity of Quantock, of great antiquity. On the side of the hill above the church is an ancient fortification called Trendle-castle, the trench and entrance of which are still entire....There remains also a beacon upon a point of the same aspiring mountain' (Collinson 1791, III, 501).

Edmund Rack had the job of collecting material on the topography and natural history of Somerset. Much of his original observations on the landscape and agriculture of the areas he visited were not pub-

lished but survive in manuscript form. It is Edmund Rack's descriptions of some of the Quantock villages and parishes that really start to give us a feel for the area more than 220 years ago. Most of the 330 inhabitants of the parish of Broomfield lived in roughly-built, mud-walled stone cottages, with thatched roofs. The farms were small, with a mixture of meadow, pasture and arable land. The people were considered by Rack to be rather indifferent to their farm work, but he did praise their use of the hoe in the cultivation of considerable quantities of turnips, together with corn and flax, and the only manufacture was spinning. Broomfield might be considered careless in losing not one but two of its gentleman's seats. Andrew Crosse's mansion at Fyne Court was burnt down in 1894 and its landscape park is well documented. The second house is harder to track down. The Towill family had a fine house called Binfords near Rooks Castle. Edmund Rack tells us that this was 'a good house in a pretty romantic spot on the side of a narrow vale....the residence of John Jeane, who ornamented it with a small but very pretty elegant pleasure ground, skirted by a hill clothed with a noble wood' (Rack 1782–1786, f3/9).

Another antiquarian lived at the foot of the Quantock Hills. William Phelps was the vicar of Bicknoller between 1811 and 1854. He was the author of the *History of the Antiquities of Somerset* (Phelps 1836). Unfortunately his detailed observations and engravings by Philip Crocker are reserved for the eastern part of the county, but we get some tantalising glimpses of his eye for detail at the east entrance to Dowsborough Camp: 'Here are three pits or hollows formed of stone, fifteen feet in diameter,

Fig 1.12
Crowcombe Court, c 1860, home of Thomas Carew. (BB78/4697) (© James Parks)

and five deep; evidently sites of fire beacons; considerable heaps of stones on the same spot, indicate buildings to have stood there' (Phelps 1836, 113). The Rev J L W Page travelled across West Somerset in the latter years of the 19th century and left us rather romantic accounts of the hills and their villages. He visited the major prehistoric earthworks, however, and noted the condition of some of the main barrows and cairns, giving a snapshot of their appearance more than 100 years ago (Page 1890).

The remoteness of parts of southwest England, combined with the sense of rusticity, made it attractive to writers and artists in the 18th and 19th centuries. The paradox of the Quantock Hills was realised by Marshall: 'Their elevation, with respect to the adjoining lands, is considerable; though their positive height, above the tide, is not great. They are, however, too high and too mountainlike, in their general aspect, to be merely deemed upland; yet not of sufficient importance to be styled mountain' (Marshall 1796, 172). This essential dichotomy is a theme that is played out again and again and that underlies the landscape history of the Quantock Hills.

Much has been written about the short stay of Coleridge and Wordsworth at Nether Stowey and Alfoxden Manor in the final years of the 18th century (Sandford 1888; Nichols 1891; Lawrence 1970; Mayberry 2000). Their discovery of the Quantocks by walking and talking the length and breadth of them, and their delight in the landscape, is told in their poems, particularly those published in the *Lyrical Ballads* of 1798, and in the journals of Dorothy Wordsworth (Moorman 1971). The diary of William Holland, who was the rector of Over Stowey at this time, makes a contrasting read to Dorothy's journals. Holland grumbles about the weather, worries about his and his family's health, recounts the daily round and rails against Democrats, Methodists and Catholics (Ayres 1984). A few years later the faded grandeur of Halsway Manor was discovered by the artists John William North, G J Pinwell and Frederick Walker in the 1860s (Billingham 1977). The combination of the rather ruinous medieval manor house with the cheerful domesticity of the farming life pictured in several of Walker's paintings echoes the story of many of the grand medieval buildings of the Quantock Hills, which subsequently became tenanted farm houses and were allowed to decline gently (Fig 1.13).

The Rev William Greswell, vicar of Dodington in the early years of the 20th century, made an extensive study of medieval documentary sources for the Quantock Hills. He published several articles and books about the history and contemporary landscape of the Quantock Hills (Greswell 1900; 1903; 1922). Historical and descriptive accounts of the Quantock Hills by Cresswell (1904), Lawrence (1952) and Waite (1969) followed a similar narrative tradition. The Victoria County History has published its authoritative accounts for most of the parishes that make up the Quantock Hills (Dunning 1985; 1992), and a popular book is based on this work (Siraut *et al* 1992). Local historians have published detailed accounts of some of the Quantock villages, including Bishops Lydeard and Cothelstone, West Quantoxhead and Spaxton (Hinton 1999; Stafford forthcoming; Odlum 1974). A large collection of historic photographs of the Quantocks was collated by The Friends of Quantock, a society formed in 1949 to oppose the proposed afforestation of areas of the hills, and to promote their conservation and heritage. The society have published part of this collection, and the resulting book provides a rich seam of social history from the 19th and 20th centuries (Mead and Worthy 2001).

Archaeologists take to the hills

The 19th century saw the pursuit of antiquarianism metamorphose into the scientific discipline of archaeology. At the forefront of this change was General Pitt Rivers. Fortunately for the county of Somerset his right-hand man was one Harold St George Gray, who moved to Taunton following the General's death in 1900. Gray embarked on a tireless campaign of recording and excavation on sites of all periods across Somerset. His work in our area of interest included important excavations at Wick Barrow near Hinkley Point and at Battlegore in Williton (Gray 1908; 1931). His explorations at Ruborough Camp more than 100 years ago remained one of the few published accounts of an earthwork site on the Quantock Hills until very recently (Gray 1903). It was not until the latter part of the 20th century that any documented archaeological excavation or survey work was carried out on the Quantock Hills. Small excavations of a medieval enclosure and an Iron Age hill-slope enclosure were undertaken at Broomfield (Catling 1950; Pytches

Fig 1.13
'The Old Gate' by Frederick
Walker. (© Tate, London
2005)

1964). The importance of the fieldwork and research work of Leslie Grinsell should be emphasised here. Grinsell undertook a survey of the barrows and cairns of the Quantock Hills as part of his barrow surveys of southern England. The resulting published accounts and list of prehistoric barrows and cairns for west and south Somerset are based on this original fieldwork (Grinsell 1969). Grinsell also wrote the first account of the archaeology of the Quantock Hills, contained within his book *The Archaeology of Exmoor*, and published a list of prehistoric sites in the hills (Grinsell 1970; 1976).

Richard McDonnell transcribed the archaeological features from aerial photographs for the Quantock Hills AONB during the 1980s. This work, and subsequent fieldwork based on the transcriptions, has formed the framework for our knowledge of the historic environment of the Quantock

Hills (McDonnell 1990; Countryside Agency 2003; Edwards 2004). More recent survey work has included that initiated as a result of applications under the Countryside Stewardship scheme and prior to clear felling areas in Great Wood (Hollinrake and Hollinrake 1994; Nicholas Pearson Associates 1998; McDonnell 2003). A section was dug across Dead Woman's Ditch, one of the longest extant prehistoric earthworks in Somerset, as part of erosion control and monitoring within the English Heritage Monument Management Scheme (Grove 2002). An important project was begun in 2000 by King Alfred's College, Winchester. The Southern Quantocks Archaeological Survey was set up to investigate the cropmark sites that are so numerous between the south of the Quantock Hills and Taunton (Wilkinson and Thorpe nd). The sites have been recorded from aerial photographs and a sample of the cropmarks have been the subject of geophysical survey and excavation (Webster 2000; Thorpe 2002; Wilkinson *et al* 2003; Webster and Brunning 2004).

The English Heritage archaeological survey of the Quantock Hills AONB

The field survey work that forms the heart of this book was undertaken by the Archaeological Investigation team of English Heritage between 2002 and 2004. The project was set up in response to requests from Somerset County Council's Historic Environment Service and the Quantock Hills AONB Service, who realised the lack of current information about the historic environment of the hills as the AONB Service brought forward a management strategy for the 21st century (Edwards 1999). The Somerset Historic Environment Record (HER) and the National Monuments Record (NMR) provided the background information for the survey work. The work of the National Mapping Programme complemented the pro-

gramme of ground survey. This is a project carried out by the English Heritage Aerial Survey team, who are mapping the archaeology of England as seen from the air. More than 1,000 photographs were examined and the archaeology of the Quantock Hills AONB was transcribed at a scale of 1: 10 000. The results of this work provided the key to unlocking the story of land use and site survival on the Quantock commons.

The whole of the Quantock Hills AONB was considered as part of the programme of ground survey. All of the known or suggested prehistoric sites were investigated. A written record was produced for each site and the location was fixed using differential GPS (Fig 1.14). Representative examples of barrows and cairns and groups of these monuments were surveyed at scales of 1:200 and 1:500. All of the hillforts and hill-slope enclosures were surveyed at scales of 1:1000 or 1:500 depending on the size and complexity of the earthworks. The main sites discussed in the text are listed in Appendix 1. During the course of the survey, several sites and areas were the subject of large scale surveys, and a list of the reports written for these surveys forms Appendix 2. The Architectural Investigation team of English Heritage collaborated over several aspects of the project. Architectural investigation work was undertaken at Kilve, Court House, Cothelstone Manor and Marsh Mills. New aerial photographs of archaeological remains and landscapes were taken by the reconnaissance section of the Aerial Survey team and photographs of both buildings and archaeological features were taken by specialist English Heritage photographers. The basic records of the ground survey and the aerial photographic transcription are available for consultation in the NMR (the archive of EH at the National Monuments Record Centre, Swindon), as are the archive plans and drawings, photographs and site reports.

Fig 1.14
Surveying the Trendle Ring. (Hazel Riley)

2

A ritual landscape? The early prehistory of the Quantock Hills

Handaxes and early humans in the Lower Palaeolithic Period

The earliest evidence of human activity in the landscape is, of course, some of the most elusive, both to find and to interpret. Some 250,000 years ago archaic humans had discovered a fine source of raw material for their handaxes in the Axe Valley at Broom near Axminster in East Devon. The river gravels contained large amounts of orange and yellow chert nodules, washed down from the nearby Blackdown Hills. Here, on a wide valley floor, thousands of handaxes – the Swiss Army Knife of the Lower Palaeolithic Period – were made. These remarkable tools performed a variety of functions as butchery tools for skinning, boning and jointing carcasses. The tools have a long, sharp cutting edge and a variety of edge angles for scraping and slicing the skin and flesh. These people both hunted for food, killing wild horses and deer with sharpened wooden staves or spears, and scavenged the kills of other animals.

A L Wedlake found one of these handaxes, made from chert from the Blackdown Hills, on the foreshore between Doniford and West Quantoxhead in 1948 (Fig 2.1). This led to further fieldwork and research, resulting in the recording of 24 handaxes from the Doniford foreshore area, three handaxes from the Watchet and Williton areas, and a further one from Crowcombe Heathfield (Fig 2.2) (Wedlake and Wedlake 1963; Grinsell 1970, 14; Wessex Archaeology 1994, 90). The handaxes have a rather battered look, hardly surprising given their age, but also because they have been rolled and washed down into the river gravels before their discovery on the beach or where the gravels are exposed on the valley sides and cliffs (Fig 2.3). We do not know where these handaxes were originally used, but their presence in the Doniford area indicates the presence of archaic humans in west Somerset and east Devon well over 200,000 years ago.

In fact, the dating of the Axe Valley handaxes is still a matter for debate. The large numbers of tools shows that the chert deposits were used over a long period of time – hundreds or thousands of years. Also, our method of dating early Palaeolithic sites often relies on the interpretation of biological fossils and artefacts and their correlation with geological sequences. The Axe Valley handaxes may have been made more than 350,000 years ago, during a period of time known as the Hoxnian interglacial, or, as is more likely, some 250,000–200,000 years ago, during an early interstadial in the Wolstonian, a short lived period of warmer temperatures during a glacial phase (Straw 1999). A wonderful range of wild animals lived in the woods during these interglacial or interstadial periods. The hunters, part of a population whose number has been estimated at about 2,000 in southern England, could have tackled roe deer, wild pig, wild horse, aurochs (wild cattle) or scavenged on the carcasses of bear and rhinoceros (Wessex Archaeology 1994, 8; Barton 1997, 34). Of course, the handaxes found in the river gravels around Doniford and Watchet are not in their original context, but the people who made and used the tools lived and hunted in the area, using the resources from a large area that included the Blackdown Hills, the Brendon Hills and the Quantock Hills.

The ice was all around: climate change and the Middle and Upper Palaeolithic periods

There followed a period of perhaps 100,000 years when Britain was not occupied by humans. Between 150,000 and 60,000 years ago ice sheets in the north and cold tundra and open steppe in the south were followed by a warmer interglacial period, then climatic deterioration again. Seventy-five thousand years ago, ice once again covered northern Britain. It was the retreat of this ice from about 60,000 years ago that saw humans return to Britain. Between 60,000 and 25,000 years ago the dry grasslands of Britain supported the mammoth, woolly rhino, bear, giant deer, wild horse and

Fig 2.1
The valley of the Doniford
stream and the foreshore
between Doniford and West
Quantoxhead. (NMR
21902/36) (© English
Heritage. NMR)

Fig 2.2 (opposite)
The Quantock Hills: map of
Palaeolithic and Mesolithic
artefacts. (Based on an
Ordnance Survey map,
with permission. © Crown
copyright. All rights
reserved)

spotted hyena. The migration of these animals to Britain probably coincided with the arrival of Neanderthals, although none of their characteristic skeletons have been found in the country. However, handaxes from this Middle Palaeolithic Period (often known as the Mousterian of Acheulian Tradition) are often found with the remains of these animals at sites such as Uphill and Hyaena Den in the Mendip Hills and Coygan Cave in South Wales (Barton 1997, 36–7; 84). Teeth and tusks of extinct woolly mammoths have been found along the coast of the Quantock Hills. An inmate of Williton workhouse found a mammoth's molar tooth while digging gravel on the beach at Doniford in 1827, mammoth teeth have also been found on West Quantoxhead beach, Kilve and from the Doniford river gravels. Mammoth tusks were found during the Watchet harbour improvements in 1861, and from Kilve and the Doniford river gravels (Wedlake 1950; 1973, 4; Grinsell 1970, 14–15).

About 31,000 years ago anatomically modern humans appear in Britain, with a distinctive Upper Palaeolithic culture. The most famous of these is the Red Lady of

Paviland (actually a young man), buried with some ceremony in a cave on the Gower Peninsula, South Wales (Aldhouse-Green 2000). Some 20,000 years ago the British Isles were, once more, virtually covered with ice. During this period, the Last Glacial Maximum, ice sheets in Scotland were several kilometres thick and ice penetrated as far south as Glamorgan and Norfolk. Only the hardiest of plants and animals survived in the south of England – the landscape of the Quantock Hills was a polar landscape. Humans retreated to the south of France and Spain, and the extreme climatic conditions in the south of Britain led to erosion of upland areas and rapid deposition of material in the valley floors, and thus the disturbance of the deposits that contained the earliest records of human activity.

People returned as the ice retreated, groups of hunters exploiting animals such as wild horses, aurochs, saiga antelopes and red deer. Again, the Doniford river gravels have provided evidence that humans were living in the area during this period that is technically known as the Late Upper Palaeolithic. In 1972 two fine, large flint blades were discovered in the middle river

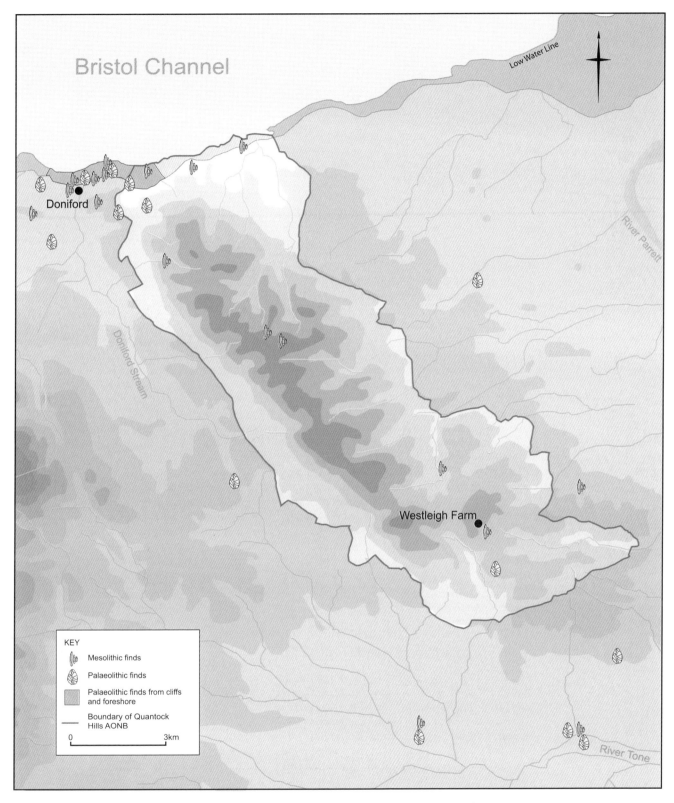

KEY

Mesolithic finds

Palaeolithic finds

Palaeolithic finds from cliffs and foreshore

Boundary of Quantock Hills AONB

0   3km

gravels in the cliffs at Doniford (Norman 1978). These sorts of flint knives and scrapers were part of a tool kit that was used for dealing with large prey animals such as red deer and wild horse. As well as meat, such animals provided hides for warm clothes, boots and tents, sewn together with needles and thread made from bones and sinew. The latter could also be used for snares, bowstrings and harpoon lines.

17

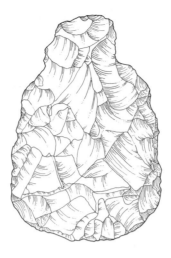

Fig 2.3
Palaeolithic handaxe from
Upper Cheddon, now in
Somerset County Museum.
(Scale 1:2)

Glue for hafting blades onto wooden handles could be made from the hooves.

No human remains have been found on the Quantock Hills from this time, but at Gough's Cave in Cheddar Gorge on the edge of the Mendip Hills the remains of at least three adults and two children have been identified. Their bones have been dated to about 14,000 years ago and examination of them revealed a large number of cut marks made by flint knives. The cut marks were in positions that showed that the bodies had been skinned and the joints dismembered, probably soon after death. Nick Barton suggests that the burial of the corpses at Gough's Cave was a two-stage process. First the body was dismembered, then the bones were scattered or collected in hide sacks and arranged against the cave walls (Barton 1997, 121–2). Britain was deserted once again during one final cold spell, before people returned to the country some 12,000 years ago – the beginning of the present postglacial period.

Hunters in the forest: the Mesolithic Period

In the early years of the 1920s a group of cavers, geologists and archaeologists explored the deposits at the mouth of a cave known as Aveline's Hole in Burrington Combe on the Mendip Hills. Earlier explorers had already disturbed some of the cave deposits but many pieces of human bones were found. These bones represent the remains of more than 70 people. Unfortunately, the circumstances of discovery means that we do not have a complete record for this, but two skeletons were found in 1924. They were tinged with red ochre and had grave goods, including orna-

ments of fossil ammonites, pig and red deer teeth (Davies 1924). Recent work on dating the skeletons has shown that burial activity in the cave took place during the course of a century or so, between *c* 8400 BC to 8200 BC (*English Heritage Research News* 2005, 1, 14–5). Aveline's Hole was the cemetery for several generations of people who perhaps had a claim to a territory or important resource in or around the Mendip Hills.

By this time the threat of advancing ice was long gone. Temperatures had risen rapidly from about 12,000 years ago, and were probably similar to those of today. The forests of birch and pine were already giving way to more open deciduous woods of oak and hazel; sea levels rose and by 8,500 years ago Britain became an island. Sea levels continued to rise for a further 2,000 years and if we stood on the summit of Beacon Hill 6,500 years ago we would have recognised the shoreline of the Bristol Channel. The people who lived on and around the Quantock Hills at this time adapted to this rapidly changing landscape. We know from the few flint tools of Mesolithic date that have been found on the Quantock Hills that small groups or bands of people were using the uplands of the Quantocks, but as yet no sites with evidence of occupation or settlement have been found or excavated on the hills themselves (Fig 2.2). The paucity of sites and the rather imprecise dating of the assemblages of flint tools that have been found means that the chronology of the Mesolithic Period in the area is not well understood. Work by Chris Norman has shown the presence of early Mesolithic material at several sites in west Somerset, while large quantities of later Mesolithic material has been identified from Chedzoy on the Somerset Levels (Norman 1975; 2001).

Greenway Farm, just south of North Petherton, and close to the M5, has produced more than 2,500 pieces of worked flint. The site lies on the south-eastern edge of the Quantock Hills, at an altitude of 50m OD, just above the floodplain of the River Parrett and the Somerset Levels and Moors. The flint was collected from the surface of a couple of arable fields during 1973, when construction work for the motorway was beginning. Most of the worked material was Greensand chert, originally from the Blackdown Hills, although chert nodules do occur in the local river gravels. The flint is grey or black, either from east Devon or the Wiltshire chalk. More than 50 cores were found, showing that flint knapping occurred at this site, and the set of tools includes microliths, burins (for piercing and engraving), blades, scrapers and knives, suggesting a range of bone, antler and hide working activities. The site has been dated to before 6800 BC by analogy with the flint assemblages from Thatcham and Greenham Dairy Farm in Berkshire, which have radiocarbon dates for this kind of Early Mesolithic or Maglemosian industry (Churchill 1962; Wymer 1962; Norman 1975). Eight kilometres to the west and easily accessible by the combes or by the ridge tops is Westleigh Farm, just outside the hamlet of Broomfield. A small number of cores and flint tools have been collected from an arable field, these include microliths, scrapers and burins, which are similar to those found in greater numbers at Greenway Farm. Several microliths, scrapers and burins have been found in the river gravels at Doniford, again mainly made from Greensand chert. A pebble mace head, often associated with this type of material, was picked up on the beach close to the Mesolithic site (Norman 1975). South of the Quantock Hills, at Fideoak Park on the floodplain of the river Tone, W A Seaby found more than 500 pieces of worked flint and chert during the construction of an electricity station (Seaby 1950; Norman 1975). Most of the material is of Greensand chert, with only a few microliths. Instead the assemblage contains tools suitable for the scraping of wood or bone, and a tranchet axe, used for wood working – felling trees to make clearings, making dugout canoes or paddles for skin boats.

This evidence suggests that the uplands were used as a hunting ground during the Mesolithic Period. The Quantock Hills were mostly wooded – oak with a dense hazel under storey – with some clearings kept open by browsing deer and wild horses. A complicated network of paths and trails led humans and animals from hilltop to clearing to muddy pool to sheltered combe and stream. The hunters, accompanied by their favourite dogs, stalked red deer, wild horse, elk, wild cattle and wild pigs. Off the hills, small camps close to rivers and streams were made; some of these became the home base for a group or band of hunters. At some of the camps tools for hunting, processing hide, antler and bone were made, at others fish, eels and wildfowl were caught, perhaps from dugout canoes or skin boats. By this time some of these bands of hunters had a

special place in the Mendip Hills – a cave on the edge of the hills used as a cemetery for about 100 years.

Landscapes of death and life in the Neolithic period

Evidence for the Neolithic landscape

Two little known but intriguing sites on the edge of the Quantock Hills show that the expanse of lower ground, west of the Quantocks and east of the Brendons, was important in the 4th and early 3rd millennia BC. The remains of a chambered tomb lie just outside Williton and the footprint of a timber circle west of Taunton can be seen on aerial photographs (Fig 2.4). These two sites span the period of time known as the Neolithic period, which radiocarbon dates place to between 4000 and 2100 BC. The beginning of this period of time is marked by people's first attempts at farming the land: growing crops and keeping domesticated animals as opposed to hunting wild animals and gathering food. This control over the landscape manifests itself in the first large-scale structures built by humans. The tradition of burying the dead under long mounds of earth and stone begins, and the individual bodies are treated in complex ways. Causewayed camps – roughly circular spaces or places enclosed by intermittent circuits of ditches and banks – become important features in the landscape. By the end of this period, stone circles and stone rows, henge monuments and the earliest round barrows and ring cairns mark the land.

At the beginning of the Neolithic Period the land was still mostly covered in deciduous woodland. Oak, elm, lime and ash were the main forest trees, with hazel and holly forming the under storey. The forest probably extended right up onto the hilltops and down into the valleys, where damper conditions favoured alder and willow. By the end of the 3rd millennium BC the hilltops were, in all probability, a mosaic of clearings in the forest, centred on the great barrow cemeteries of Wills Neck and Black Hill, linked by tracks and paths, marked by pollards and areas of coppice. On the lower slopes small fields of wheat and barley, isolated farmsteads, and the sanctuary areas at Battlegore and Norton Fitzwarren stood in clearings. Perhaps by this time the earliest agricultural clearings and plots had been abandoned and were now scrubbed over with birch, bracken and gorse. There have been no environmental studies carried out on the Quantock Hills, but layers of peat and the stumps of ancient forest trees are revealed at low tide along the west Somerset coast at Porlock, Minehead, Blue Anchor Bay, Stolford and Brean Down. These are the fossilised remains of the oak woodlands that once covered the area, killed off as the sea level rose

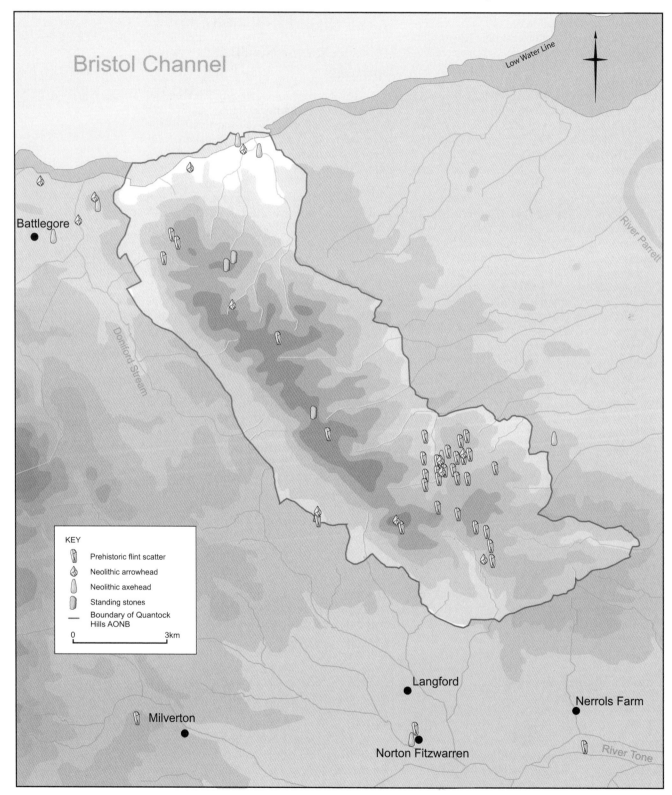

KEY

🪨 Prehistoric flint scatter

🪨 Neolithic arrowhead

🪨 Neolithic axehead

🪨 Standing stones

— Boundary of Quantock Hills AONB

0   3km

and preserved in acidic conditions. The oak trees at Stolford were growing about 4000 BC (Fulford *et al* 1997, 66–7). The woodland harboured a plentiful supply of protein: red and roe deer; wild horse, wild cattle and wild pig. Fish, shellfish and wildfowl from rivers, the coast and the wetlands of the Somerset Levels were all on the doorstep.

To the east of the Quantock Hills the peat that blankets much of the Levels and Moors conceals nuggets of information about past environments and the lives of our ancestors. Occasionally these are revealed by the activities of peat diggers and, latterly, archaeologists. The study of beetle fragments found in wood and peat more than 6,000 years old shows that winters were colder and summers were warmer than they are today, perhaps by as much as two or three degrees. The pollen grains preserved in the peat layers tell us that there was a lot of woodland on the fringes of the low lying areas; this was mixed forest – oak, elm, lime and ash, with hazel and holly as under wood and alder, willow and poplar on the wetter fringes. The lowest-lying areas were Phragmites reed swamp, rich in wildlife and plants. There were reeds, birch, willow and alder with pools of open water and a network of little streams. In winter, when the high tides met the sediment laden rivers and streams, a sheet of cold brown water covered the lowest ground. It was in this environment that a group of people, skilled in woodworking, built a sophisticated wooden track across the swamps. They also lost or, more likely, deposited on purpose, a very precious stone axe made of jadeite from the foothills of the Alps. This was found during the excavation of the Sweet Track, the earliest of a number of remarkable timber structures discovered during peat cutting operations (Coles and Coles 1986; Norman and Clements 1979; Norman 1980). These sorts of artefacts, preserved in special environments, remind us how little we know when we turn to the evidence for the use of the Quantock Hills by people in the 4th and the 3rd millennia BC.

Most of our knowledge of these people comes from chance finds of their tools, either the flint arrowheads that were lost during a hunting expedition, or the discarded flint and stone axes used for felling trees (Fig 2.4). The stone axes were prized possessions, as the raw material needed was hard, difficult to work and note widely available. The stone axe that was found by Robert Addison, a mole-catcher, at the foot of a hedge at Pilot's Helm, North Petherton, was made of rock from Mounts Bay, Cornwall. This axe is waisted for hafting onto a wooden handle (Fig 2.5) (Gray 1943). The raw material for the polished flint axes found at Kilve came from east Devon or Wessex. Finely-worked leaf-shaped arrowheads of the earlier Neolithic Period are occasionally found on and around the Quantock Hills, but a little known site to the west of the hills, near Milverton, has produced 98 of these arrowheads. Well in excess of 500 flint tools and implements were collected by C F Moysey in the first two decades of the 20th century. This amount of flint indicates a settlement of some size and importance in the area (Moysey 1918; Grinsell 1970, 23–4). Such sites are usually found on arable fields, where ploughing brings material to the surface, and their distribution often reflects two things: the incidence of arable land and the presence of a local collector. This is borne out on the Quantock Hills (Fig 2.4). The concentration of flint tools between Merridge and Broomfield is due to the work of S H Price who made extensive collections of worked flints from the ploughed fields in the area, showing the presence of people here in the 4th and 3rd millennia BC.

So far we have no evidence for the actual houses where Neolithic farmers lived in west Somerset, a situation repeated across much of Britain. The best examples come from sites in Wales, where rectangular houses at Llandegai, Caernarfonshire, and Gwernvale, Powys, date from the early 4th millennium BC (Houlder 1968; Britnell and Savory 1984).

In southwest England hilltops seem to be the focus for Neolithic activity. On the granite uplands of Dartmoor and Bodmin Moor the tors themselves have been used to form enclosures, which sometimes contain house platforms. In mid Devon a causewayed enclosure lies under an Iron Age enclosure at Raddon. In east Devon and south Somerset hilltop sites that are well known for their Iron Age earthworks were occupied in the Neolithic period. Hembury Castle and Membury Castle in east Devon, Ham Hill and South Cadbury in south Somerset are good examples (Oswald *et al* 2001). On the southern edge of the Quantock Hills a picture of the earlier Neolithic landscape is gradually beginning to emerge, as evidence from aerial photographs, field walking and excavation over the past 100 years is pieced together.

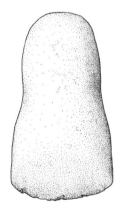

Fig 2.5
Neolithic stone axe from
North Petherton, now in
Somerset County Museum.
(Scale 1:2)

Fig 2.6
Norton Fitzwarren: the
hill has been a focus for
settlement for thousands of
years. (NMR 15859/35)
(© Crown copyright.
NMR)

At first sight the hill behind the village of Norton Fitzwarren is unremarkable: the summit is blurred by years of cultivation, garden plots and strips of woodland straggle up onto the hilltop (Fig 2.6). The hill, however, happens to command both the headwaters of the river Tone to the south and the valley of the Doniford stream to the north. The hill has been the focus for groups of people for more than 6,000 years, from Mesolithic times to the Roman period and beyond. Flint tools from the Mesolithic and earlier Neolithic periods were found when small sections of the earthworks that surround the hill were excavated in the 1970s. A long, curving ditch, interrupted by three causeways, to the north of the hill top, is visible on aerial photographs (Fig 2.9) (Ellis 1989). This ditch has not been sampled by excavation, but it may be related to the causewayed enclosure class of monuments, which date from the earlier Neolithic Period (Oswald *et al* 2001). A few miles to the west of Norton Fitzwarren, at the bottom of a valley that leads up into the southern slopes of the Quantock Hills, is Nerrols Farm, where excavations in advance of a proposed development uncovered part of a ditch containing earlier Neolithic pottery. As no definite evidence of occupation around this ditch was found, the excavator suggested that this site could be part of a cursus monument (Somerset HER 44791). These are parallel embanked linear ditches, marking or formalising ritual or symbolic boundaries, in use between 3600 and 3000 BC, and often found in association with henges and long mounds. Some of the best preserved examples are the Stonehenge Cursus and the Dorset Cursus on Cranborne Chase, which includes a massive long barrow at its southern end. The large numbers of flint tools collected around Milverton and the flint scatters that have been found on the southern part of the Quantock Hills show that this area was used and settled in the 4th millennium BC. The lower slopes of the Quantock Hills and the Brendon Hills would have been favoured areas for clearing woodland, building farms and laying out small plots of ground for cultivation. The hills themselves harboured deer, wild pig and wild cattle. The headwaters of the River Tone and the hilltop at Norton Fitzwarren were a focus for groups of people who lived in family groups in a sparsely populated landscape to come together at certain times of the year – for trade, for festivals and for celebrations of life and death.

The burial of the dead: Battlegore

Just outside Williton, in a small field, there are three large stones, partly hidden by a hedge. In the middle of the field is a large prehistoric burial mound and the remains of two further round burial mounds lie to the south (Fig 2.7). This is Battlegore or Grabburrowes, one of the most important prehistoric sites in west Somerset. There were several Danish raids on the west Somerset coast in the 10th century, with attacks on Porlock and Watchet. The tradition linking Battlegore with a great battle between the Anglo-Saxons and the Danes between Watchet and Williton is a strong one. Robert Gay, the parson of Nettlecombe in the 17th century, thought that the round burial mounds were thrown up over the bodies of the dead to mark a great triumph for the Anglo-Saxons. He records some important details about the site:

'For by the often digging, and often carrying away of much earth from these, to dress the ground adjoining, some times in one, and some times in another, have been found fragments of mens bones, and sometimes sepulchres composed each of three broad stones, like Tombe stones, two of them lying along on their edges, about two foot distance, and a third lying flat on the top, the both ends walled up closely, and the concavity containing pieces of mens bones'
(quoted in Gray 1931, 10).

Page visited the site in the late 19th century and recorded 'two enormous stones, the one lying on its side, the other leaning against the hedge, as well as a third and smaller block, nearly concealed by brambles' (Page 1890, 70). He suggested that they may be the remains of a cromlech – a megalithic

chambered tomb – and noted that in about 1850 the stone leaning against the hedge was upright. It was toppled against the hedge by some young men who were anxious to test the truth of the legend that it was immovable. In 1911 H St George Gray visited the site and observed 'a series of small earthworks, two tumuli (the third was hardly traceable) and the remains of what appeared to be a dolmen' (Gray 1931, 7–8). He left with the resolve to excavate the site and 20 years later he returned. Gray excavated an area some 10m by 4m around the stones. He found two stone holes, which indicated that the stones were roughly in their original location, and two of them had, at one time, stood upright (Fig 2.8). Gray noted a small ridge or mound of earth to the west and north of the stones, which he interpreted as probably of recent origin. However, he did find some flint tools in this material, including a flint arrowhead of later Neolithic type.

The stones are all that remains of a type of megalithic chambered tomb known as a portal dolmen. These tombs occur in west Wales and on the Gower peninsula, and stand in the landscape as exciting megalithic structures. Their form is very distinctive, with a tall, H-shaped portal fronting a single rectangular chamber covered by a massive, sloping capstone. The chamber is set in a relatively small cairn, which, as the tombs

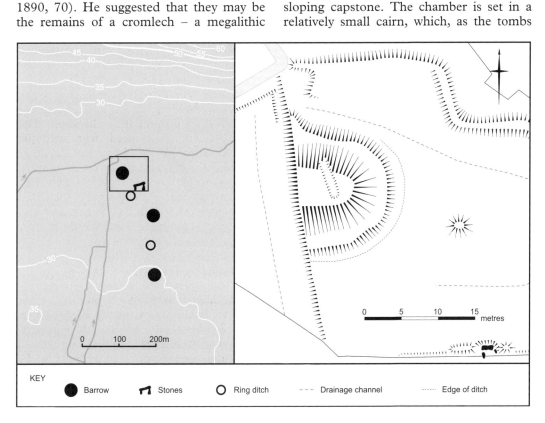

KEY ● Barrow   ⌐ Stones   ○ Ring ditch   --- Drainage channel   ······ Edge of ditch

Fig 2.7
Battlegore, Williton: plan of the barrow cemetery. (Based on an Ordnance Survey map, with permission. © Crown copyright. All rights reserved)

23

Fig 2.8
Battlegore, Williton:
reconstruction of the portal
dolmen.

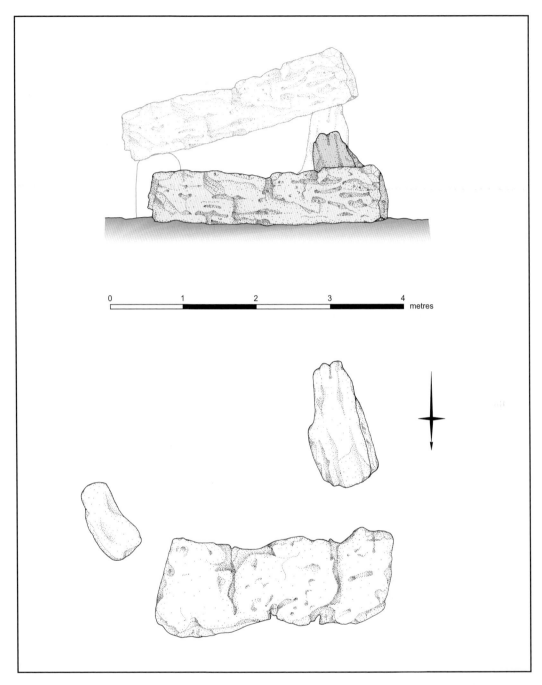

are often on lower slopes, on enclosed ground, rarely survive. Dyffryn Ardudwy, a complex portal dolmen in north Wales, had one of its chambers closed in the Early Neolithic Period, but these sorts of monuments were probably built and used during most of the 4th millennium BC (Lynch *et al* 2000, 70–3). A group of long barrows and chambered tombs on and around the Mendip Hills belongs to the same period. Farther west, four chambered tombs survive on the northeast corner of Dartmoor, but a journey to Wales or Cornwall is necessary to

see such sites in abundance (Daniel 1950).

The location of the tomb at Battlegore, near to the coast but enclosed in a shallow river basin, suggests that access to the site from the Quantock Hills, Exmoor, the Doniford valley and the sea was important. It was a communal tomb, serving several small, scattered communities. The presence of those round barrows, grouped around the portal dolmen, shows that this site was a special place for the people who lived in the shadow of the Quantock Hills for perhaps 1,000 years.

Timber circles and henge monuments

By about 2500 BC the construction of ceremonial circles of earth, stone and timber is well established in Britain. These are the evocative stone circles on Dartmoor and the Lake District, or the impressive earthwork banks and ditches of the henges at Stonehenge and Avebury. There are also many such sites that are now only visible from the air. Ploughing over hundreds of years causes the levelling of earthworks, with the erosion of banks and the infill of ditches. The footprints of such sites will show up on aerial photographs after a period of drought, when differential crop growth highlights ditches and pits. The excavations that took place at the hilltop enclosure at Norton Fitzwarren between 1968 and 1971 were published recently, and, while examining aerial photographs of that site, Peter Ellis noticed a curious circular shape on the aerial photographs taken by the RAF in 1947. Three concentric circles are visible (Fig 2.9). The outer circle is 60m in diameter and is defined by 13 sub-circular marks. The middle circle is 20m in diameter and is defined by 10 rather indistinct marks, and the inner circle, the only complete one, is 8m in diameter and is formed by 8 circular marks. This has been tentatively interpreted as a henge monument by its discoverer (Ellis 1986). Part of a ring ditch (the ploughed-over remains of a round barrow) lies outside the circle.

What do these circular marks mean? The Langford cropmark site appears to be the remains of a timber circle, although only excavation will reveal if the pits originally contained timber posts. About 40 of these sites have been identified in Britain and Ireland. They date from as early as *c* 3000 BC and decline in importance by *c* 1000 BC and are often associated with a distinctive type of pottery known as Grooved Ware (Gibson 2005). Most are simple, single circles, which range in diameter from *c* 7m to 30m. More complex examples, with multiple rings of posts, are large (often more than 20m in diameter) and some are associated with the large henge monuments at Durrington Walls, Stonehenge and Woodhenge. These sites have been interpreted as circles of posts. They may have been free-standing or linked by horizontal fencing, or tied together by lintels. The post holes have sometimes been interpreted as forming a roofed building, but the patterns

and numbers of the posts may have been the important features of the sites. What happened at these sites? The orientation of the entrances on mid-summer and mid-winter sunrise or sunset at some of the timber circles suggests one use for timing rites and rituals of annual regeneration. Although burials are often present they do not seem to have been the principal purpose of the monuments. There is often evidence for feasting as part of the ritual performance, as well as the deliberate placing of certain artefacts and food remains around the site. Some timber circles had a formal approach for processions to the monument, but the large timber uprights served to exclude visibility of the interior of the circle.

Fig 2.9

Langford, Taunton: aerial photograph transcription of pit circle, ring ditch and segmented ditch. (Based on an Ordnance Survey map, with permission.
© Crown copyright.
All rights reserved)

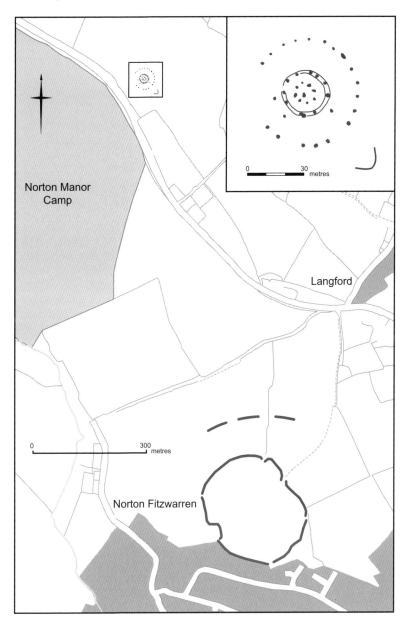

25

At Sarn-y-bryn-caled, near Welshpool, Powys, a complex of monuments includes a cursus, ring ditches, a henge and a pit circle. The pit circle was excavated and the evidence recovered suggested that a single ring of tall, wooden upright posts surrounded a smaller, central circle of posts. The outer ring was probably linked together with timber lintels. A cremation burial was found at the centre of the circle. The presence of four high-quality flint arrowheads in the body before it was cremated, together with the location of the burial at the centre of the timber circle (below), indicate a ritual killing rather than a murder victim, a battle casualty or death in a hunting accident (Gibson 1992, 91; 1994, 186–7).

Across to the east, the Mendip Hills were a particular centre of ritual monuments in the late Neolithic and Early Bronze Age and are unusual as many of the sanctuaries already referred to occur on flat land on the valley floor, at important points for moving through the landscape. The Priddy Circles – four large henge monuments – and the henge at Gorsey Bigbury are high on the western scarp of the Mendips, looking out over the Somerset Levels. At the henge of Gorsey Bigbury a man, woman and child were buried in a stone cist. The bodies were disinterred after their flesh had rotted. The man's skull was left in the cist, but the rest of his bones and the woman's were scattered in the earth around it. The skulls of the woman and the child were buried at the east of the entrance to the henge (ApSimon 1949–50). Farther to the east, and off the Mendip Hills, the complex at Stanton Drew, consisting of three stone circles, two stone avenues and a cove (a structure of three upright stones), compares in scope to that at Avebury (Grinsell 1994).

The Langford site may represent a large timber circle, some 60m in diameter. The upright posts may have been joined together by timber lintels, or they could have been freestanding. Either way, a ring of heavy oak posts would form an impressive setting for a central circular space, defined by two rings of posts, which may have formed a roofed or open wooden structure. The posts may have been elaborately carved or decorated with symbols or garlands of flowers. It was probably not enclosed by an earthwork, as traces of such a feature would be likely to show on aerial photographs along with the post holes. We can only guess as to what happened at such sites. Ritual enclosures create a real distinction between those who were allowed into the monument space and those who were not. Human sacrifice and burial seems to have played a part in some of the ritual activity carried out at stone and timber circles and henges, so does feasting and processions to and from the site. People came to such monuments at important times: for seasonal festivals or to celebrate birth and death. The shape of the monument – the circle – must have been important. As well as being easy to set out from a central point, circles can represent the sun and moon and the concept of continuity. A circle is also described as we look around and perceive our surroundings (Harding 2003, 43; Gibson 1994, 192).

Standing stones

Apart from the fallen stones at Battlegore, the only other surviving megalithic monuments on the Quantock Hills are three standing stones (Fig 2.4). There are no stone settings, like those on Exmoor, or paired stones, stone rows or stone circles, familiar monuments on Exmoor and the Mendip Hills. The underlying geology of the Quantocks is similar to that of Exmoor, so suitable material was available. Why is there no tradition of stone monuments on the Quantock Hills? The people who used the hills may not have built ceremonial monuments of stone, perhaps timber was their preferred material. Another reason is concerned with subsequent land use. As has already been discussed, much of the heath, where such monuments would be found, was common land. However, there is a long history of cultivation of the commons (see Chapter 4), and this process, of stone clearance and ploughing, obliterates monuments that consist of small stones, set upright, in rows or circles. The stone circle on Porlock Common was not discovered until the 1920s and many of the stone settings and stone rows on Exmoor were only found in the later part of the 20th century (Riley and Wilson-North 2001). Any small stone monuments on the Quantock Hills may have been destroyed, before they were known about, by the widespread cultivation of the commons. The standing stones that do survive are in areas that have not been subject to this process. The vegetation cover across large areas of the heath also makes the discovery of such monuments difficult.

The Long Stone lies on Longstone Hill, an elongated spur that runs from the heart of the hills at Bicknoller Post to their eastern edge at Holford. The standing stone lies at an altitude of 300m, below the summit of the hill but high enough to command spectacular views across the coast and the Severn Estuary to south Wales (Fig 2.10). There are few other archaeological remains in the area. A small area of relict field system lies just to the west of the stone itself, and further north is the Greenway barrow group. The stone had fallen down sometime after 1922, and was re-erected in 1964 or 1965 by the Friends of Quantock (Grinsell 1970, 49). As it stands now, the stone is only 0.8m high, but a photograph taken before its re-erection shows a fine monolith, tapering at one end, and at least 1.5m long. The Long Stone sits on the boundary between the parishes of Kilve and East

Fig 2.10
The Long Stone (top) and Triscombe Stone (bottom). The stones are both sited to command stunning views out from the hills.

27

Quantoxhead. Another stone marks the southwest corner of the parish of Kilve. This stone is much smaller than the Long Stone, only 0.2m high, and is similar to the small paired stones that are a feature of Exmoor's prehistoric landscape. The stone may be of prehistoric origin, or it may be a boundary marker set up in the historic period. Triscombe Stone lies on the boundary between the parishes of West Bagborough and Over Stowey and the old parish of Crowcombe. The stone also lies at the junction of two important routes across the hills, where the east-west road from Triscombe to Cockercombe crosses the north-south track along the western ridge, and commands views west to the Brendon Hills and Exmoor (Fig 2.10). The stone is not impressive, standing only 0.75m high, but it is certainly of considerable antiquity – a map of 1609 has the legend 'the way to triscombe stone' (SRO 1609) – and is very likely to be of prehistoric origin. This is reinforced by its location on the western scarp of the hills, close to the Great Hill and Wills Neck barrow groups.

The standing stones on the Quantock Hills date from the Late Neolithic and Early Bronze Age, a time when, as we have seen, timber monuments such as the post circles were in use alongside more durable monuments like stone rows and stone circles. The fact that we are looking at a skewed sample of the remains of prehistoric life must be kept in mind as we enter the Bronze Age.

The Bronze Age: funerary and mundane landscapes

Evidence for the Bronze Age landscape

The beginning of the Bronze Age marks the time of the introduction of metalworking technology to the British Isles. Traditionally, the Bronze Age was divided into three periods, largely on the basis of distinctive forms of metalwork. Radiocarbon dating has given an absolute chronology to these (slightly overlapping) periods of: Early Bronze Age 2300–1500 BC; Middle Bronze Age 1600–1000 BC and Late Bronze Age 1100–800 BC. The term harks back to a time when the European archaeological record was studied in terms of the development of stone and metal artefacts, as this was the key to chronology before the advent of radiocarbon dating. Changes in material

culture, such as the use of metal tools in favour of stone and flint were seen in Britain as marking the advent of new groups of people from the continent, bringing their innovative technology and artefacts and imposing this new culture on the indigenous people. During the past 30 or so years the information from excavations with radiocarbon dates has enabled archaeologists to rethink the processes of cultural change in British prehistory, and the establishment of a chronological framework has made it possible to consider the evidence without the need to invoke waves of invaders or immigrants from the continent. There has been more emphasis on the study of settlement and economy, and of the technology of mining and processing copper and tin ores and manufacturing metal objects.

As we have seen in the previous sections about timber circles and standing stones, there is actually little change in the types of settlement and burials that can be seen to mark the time of the introduction of metal into Britain. The first objects of metal arrived in Britain perhaps as early as the middle of the 3rd millennium BC, at a time when the landscape was dominated by funerary and ceremonial monuments, with only a few, if any, sedentary agricultural communities. People were free to move across the landscape, exploiting wild food as well as their own herds of livestock. It is not until the middle of the 2nd millennium BC that we see a more domestic or mundane landscape of farms and fields. The presence of houses, wooden and earthwork enclosures, field clearance cairns and field systems all indicate longer term and more permanent occupation.

A new technology: metalworking

The Bronze Age has recently been defined as a fairly arbitrary unit of time: 'the period when copper and copper alloys were used for the manufacture of the main forms of tools and weapons' (Barber 2003, 37). Copper and tin were used to make bronze objects – axes, spears, swords, jewellery – objects that were as much about prestige as they were about function. The people who knew how to find and process the copper and tin ores and how to make metal objects must have been powerful people. Several prehistoric copper mining sites have now been located in Britain (Timberlake 1992). At Great Ormes Head in north Wales there are extensive underground shafts and galleries of prehistoric origin and recent fieldwork has led to the discovery of several prehistoric copper mining sites in mid-Wales. The only English example comes from the Alderley Edge area in Cheshire. There is no evidence to suggest that the copper deposits in and around the Quantock Hills were exploited in prehistory, but tin came from Cornwall and Dartmoor (Timberlake 2001; Thorndycraft *et al* 2004).

Chemical analysis of metal objects and ore bodies has shown that ore from Ireland and Spain was used as well as British sources, suggesting a complex pattern of trade, exchange and travel of people, objects and ideas over wide areas of Europe, although the mechanism of the actual introduction of the first metal objects into Britain is not known. The new technology began to appear in this country during the 2nd half of the 3rd millennium BC. At the same time a distinctive form of pottery appears in the archaeological record, it is known as Beaker pottery as the most characteristic forms have been interpreted as drinking vessels. Beaker pottery is best known from funerary contexts, with inhumations in flat graves or under round barrows and cairns, but Beaker pottery is also found in other contexts and was used for both funerary and mundane or domestic tasks, in the period between 2500–1800 BC (Quinnell 2003). Much has been made of the association of the earliest metalworking in Britain with the users of Beaker pottery. This is because the earliest copper, bronze and gold objects in graves are often associated with Beaker pottery. However, most Beaker pottery is not associated with metalwork, and only a minority of excavated graves actually contain metalwork (Barber 2003, 169).

By the beginning of the 2nd millennium BC, the cremation of bodies becomes more common than burial in the archaeological record, with the cremated bones often placed inside pots before burial. These pots are known as urns (including Collared Urns, Biconical Urns and Trevisker Urns) and Food Vessels; Beaker pottery is rarely found with cremated remains. By about 2000–1700 BC urns and Food Vessels were the pots of choice in funerary rituals in southwest England (Owoc 2001, 196). There are a few good examples of earlier Bronze Age funerary pottery from on and around the Quantock Hills: a Beaker was excavated from Wick Barrow in 1908 (below) and an urn, now in Taunton

Fig 2.11
Bronze Age pottery: the urn from Westleigh Farm, Broomfield, now in Somerset County Museum. (Scale 1:4)

Museum, was found to the east of Westleigh Farm, Broomfield, when a field was ploughed (Fig 2.11). The empty pot had been placed, upside down, in a hole and no traces of a barrow mound were noticed (Somerset HER 10230). Studies of the actual fabric of Early Bronze Age pottery have led to some interesting observations about the relationships between pottery manufacture, the making of metal and the treatment of human remains. It has been suggested that the new technology has more in common with the processes of pottery making – finding a clay source, mixing the clay with temper, forming the pot and firing it – than with the manufacture of stone and flint tools by knapping, grinding and polishing (Barber 2003, 167). Old pots were ground up and used for tempering new pottery. This practice is common in Early Bronze Age funerary pottery and there may be links between the death of an old pot and its regeneration by its use in a new vessel and the growth of the dominance of cremation as the preferred funerary rite. The need for fire as the transforming agent in the birth of a new metal object may have influenced the growth in cremation as the preferred funerary rite.

Metalworking hoards and their meaning

Some of the most spectacular finds from Somerset are of Bronze Age metalwork, such as the great bronze shield from Cadbury Castle and the gold bracelets from Brean Down. However, the most numerous finds are finds of metalwork of Middle and Late Bronze Age date, with a particularly important concentration of Middle Bronze Age material from the Taunton area. In the 19th and 20th century hoards of metalwork were described as merchant's hoards, founder's hoards and personal hoards. In other words they were seen as the property of an itinerant metalworker, for example, concealed then never recovered by the original owner. Recent work, however, on the nature and context of these finds suggests that most were deposited deliberately, in a structured way and in a special place. Water was an important element in these special places where metalwork was deposited; rock outcrops and caves were also chosen.

Many hoards were discovered and reported in the 18th and 19th centuries and those found in and around the Quantock Hills are no exception. In 1794 a labourer was draining a marshy piece of ground on the south side of the Quantock Hills. He found two bronze torcs (neck collars), one placed within the other, a bronze palstave (a type of axe) was placed in each torc (Harford 1803, fig 2). The exact location of this find is not known, but it is thought to be somewhere on the Cothelstone estate. Of a similar date – Middle Bronze Age – is the hoard of eight bronze bracelets and two palstaves and an axe from Norton Fitzwarren, again the objects were deliberately ordered, with two groups of bracelets separated by a single bracelet placed perpendicularly to them. A large posthole by the entrance to the Late Bronze Age enclosure at Norton Fitzwarren contained 70 fragments of a mould used to cast a sword (Ellis 1989). Again, this represents more than just a rubbish pit – the deposit only contained mould fragments and was sited in a special place, close to the enclosure entrance. In the 19th century several pieces of Middle and Late Bronze Age metalwork were found when Lake's Meadow, close to Battlegore, was drained (Gray 1931). Metalwork was deposited in marshy or wet ground over hundreds of years, close to a long-lived funerary site, emphasising the importance of this place, which was used for more than 2,000 years. In 1870 a large hoard of Late Bronze Age metalwork was found in Wick Park, east of Stogursey (Hood 1873). This contained 147 pieces, including 28 socketed axes, two palstaves, two gouges, two daggers, 12 spearheads, 21 fragments of swords and a scabbard, copper cakes and casting jets. The exact location of the find is not known, but Wick Park is on the edge of an area of higher ground, close to what was most likely marsh or fen in the Bronze Age.

The hoard is described as 'discovered together in stiff clay in the space of a foot cube, two feet below the surface, while draining a field' (Hood 1870, 427), suggesting that the items may have originally been deposited in or very close to water. The swords were probably deliberately broken before their deposition, but the chape (metal tip protecting the scabbard), delicately made in fine metal, was complete (McNeil 1973). The symbolism of such complex deposits as the hoard from Wick Park may never be unravelled, but opposing themes such as fragmentation and wholeness; death and rebirth could be considered. The technology of working bronze was well understood and used in Somerset by the second half of the 2nd millennium BC, perhaps because it was in a special location with tin to the west and copper to the north.

The funerary landscape: Bronze Age burial monuments

Stand anywhere on the Quantock heath and you will never be very far from a barrow or cairn. These prehistoric burial monuments are the most visible and by far the most numerous archaeological sites on the Quantock Hills. The definition given by Phelps in his *History and Antiquities of Somersetshire* cannot be bettered: 'Barrows and tumuli vary much in their shape, size and construction; some are composed of stones piled up loosely together, and are called Caernedds, or cairns; others are formed of earth dug up on the spot, and are denominated barrows' (Phelps 1836, 123).

There are about 120 barrows and cairns on the Quantock Hills (Fig 2.12). They occur mostly on the unenclosed heath and commons, but some also survive in enclosed land – one of the largest cairns on the hills lies at the corner of an improved field on West Hill – and in woodland, for example in Bagborough Plantation and Muchcare Wood. The most striking feature of their distribution is the number of very large barrows and cairns that stud the steep western scarp of the Quantock Hills (Fig 2.22). From Cothelstone Hill in the south to Beacon Hill in the north 19 large barrows and cairns are sited in the most dramatic locations. This string of monuments forms the backbone to the distribution of these sites on the Quantock Hills. Most of these large barrows and cairns are not just isolated sites. They occur as part of a group of simi-

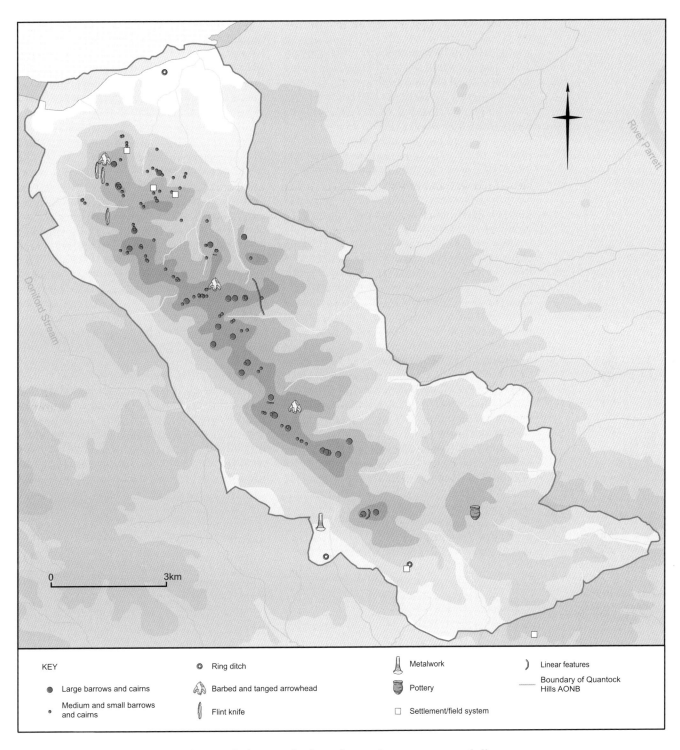

KEY

⊙ Ring ditch

● Large barrows and cairns

· Medium and small barrows and cairns

🜊 Barbed and tanged arrowhead

▮ Flint knife

⬗ Metalwork

⚱ Pottery

☐ Settlement/field system

) Linear features

— Boundary of Quantock Hills AONB

Fig 2.12
The Quantock Hills:
barrows and cairns. (Based
on an Ordnance Survey
map, with permission.
© Crown copyright.
All rights reserved)

lar sites, which include ring cairns and platform cairns, forming barrow cemeteries, such as those on Black Hill and Wills Neck.

Antiquarians

There is a long tradition of antiquarian interest in barrows and cairns. An enthusiast, often the local clergyman, would take a picnic and a workman or two and dig a central hole in the barrow to get at any treasure. Most of the larger barrows and cairns on the Quantocks show signs of this process – a depression in the centre of the mound – however there are no records of these excursions, nor are there any recorded archaeological excavations of any barrows or cairns on the Quantock Hills. We can, however,

31

date the monuments in general terms by referring to sites in southwest England and south Wales that have been radiocarbon dated. Large round barrows and cairns have their origins in the 3rd millennium BC, but the main period of use for the barrows and cairns was the first half of the 2nd millennium BC (Quinnell 1997; Lynch *et al* 2000). Some monuments were built or re-used in the later part of the 2nd millennium BC, and the morphology of some of the barrow groups strongly suggests that the monuments were constructed and used over many generations.

Close to the security fence that surrounds the nuclear power plant at Hinkley Point is a very large round barrow. Its position is unusual, on a low rocky knoll about 20m OD and close to the sea. Indeed, during the 2nd millennium BC Wick Moor would have been frequently flooded, giving the impression on misty winter mornings that this huge mound floated in the sea. In 1907 the Somerset Archaeological and Natural History Society and the Viking Club undertook a 'thoroughly scientific exploration' of Wick Barrow, resulting in the discovery of several burials, some Beaker pottery and flint tools. The barrow mound had a core of stone that contained the primary burial. Some 2,000 years after the mound had been constructed, someone dug

a hole right down into the centre of the mound and left a coin from the reign of the Roman Emperor Constantine the Great (AD 306–337) for the 20th-century excavators to find. Wick Barrow is also known as Pixies' Mound. The workmen who found the stone wall thought that it was actually the pixies' house and there are tales of pixies being caught threshing in the nearby barn and leaving a gift of hot cake to repay the mending of a broken wooden shovel (Gray 1908). Gray also excavated one of the round barrows at Battlegore, Williton, where a pot containing a cremation had a lid made of oak (Gray 1931). The only mention of finds from any of the barrows on the Quantock Hills comes from the late 19th century, when Page noted that Roman coins had been found in the 'cairns called Rowboroughs' (Page 1890, 265). These are the cairns on Lydeard Hill, most of which have been dug into at some time.

Beacons

The location of the large barrows meant that they have been used in historic times for beacon fires. Several hills attest to this: Beacon Hill and Fire Beacon Hill are both topped with large cairns and barrows; Hurley Beacon (Fig 2.13) was used as the site for a fire to celebrate the Queen's Golden

Fig 2.13
Hurley Beacon: a large cairn on the western edge of the hills. (Hazel Riley)

Jubilee in 2001. Grinsell notes that barrows were modified when used as the site of fire beacons by deepening the usual robbers' holes in the top of the mound to give some protection from the elements to the beacon fire, a process recorded in Devon in the 18th century (Grinsell 1970, 155). Possible examples of modification for a beacon fire can be seen on the barrows on Hurley Beacon, Wills Neck and Lydeard Hill, although these could equally be the result of unrecorded antiquarian excavations (Figs 2.14 and 2.21). An evocative account of Queen Victoria's Diamond Jubilee beacon fires is given in *The Times*, June 24th, 1897. A bonfire, built on the highest point of Wills Neck (on the barrow?), was 25ft high, took four or five wagonloads of wood and was crowned with two tar barrels.

Barrows and cairns

All of the known barrows and cairns on the Quantock Hills were recorded and surveyed, and selected examples were surveyed at large scale. The survey work showed that the monuments fell into three groups in terms of size (diameter): small (< 7m); medium (7–16m) and large (> 16m). Further divisions were possible in terms of height and (occasionally) structural features.

Round barrows

Round barrows are defined as circular mounds of stone and earth, which may be surrounded by a ditch. Ditches are rarely associated with barrows on the Quantock Hills; the best examples are those that surround the large, isolated barrow on Wills Neck and Thorncombe Barrow (Fig 2.14). Ditches, if they existed, may have become silted up with material that has weathered and slumped from the mound. The fearsome vegetation on parts of the hills can obscure slight earthworks and the later cultivation, which often encroaches on the mounds themselves, as on Beacon Hill, may have removed traces of any ditches that did exist; but it does seem that most of the large barrows were constructed from material

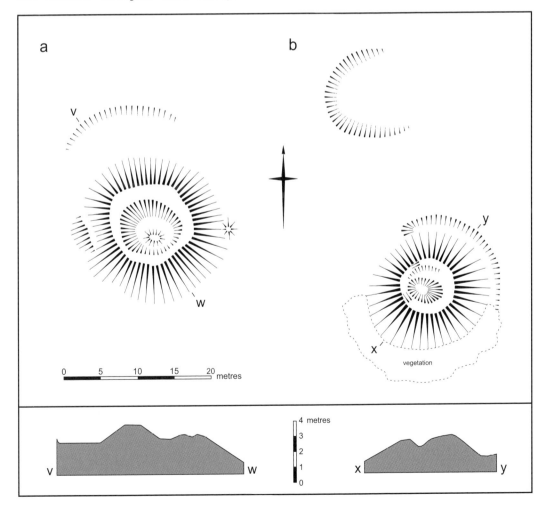

Fig 2.14
Barrows: Lydeard Hill (a) and Wills Neck (b).

derived from elsewhere. Indeed, the size of the ditches that surround the barrow on Wills Neck and Thorncombe Barrow suggest that this was the case and that the ditches may have performed a separate function such as defining the area before the burial was made and the mound constructed. On Exmoor several small quarries have been suggested as the site of barrow material for mounds on Cosgate Hill and Dunkery Hill (Jamieson 2002; Riley and Wilson-North 2001). A similar quarry lies on the western end of Cothelstone Hill, close to a large truncated barrow, and a slight depression to the northwest of the barrow on Wills Neck may have provided material for the barrow mound (Fig 2.14).

The barrows range in size from some 6m in diameter right up to more than 20m in diameter, like those on Beacon Hill and by Withyman's Pool (Figs 2.18 and 2.21). They show little in the way of structure. A kerb (or ring of upright stones marking the edge of a cairn or barrow mound) was recorded around the barrow on Wills Neck (Grinsell 1969, 40), but no stone is now visible.

Stone cairns

Some of the largest monuments on the Quantock Hills are the stone cairns of the western scarp. Those on Great Hill, West Hill and Fire Beacon Hill are the biggest, with diameters of 30m, 28m and 25m respectively (Fig 2.15). These cairns are part of a group of large platform cairns and barrows whose distribution hugs the ridge top between the Triscombe Stone and Crowcombe Gate (Fig 2.16). There is no vegetation cover on the Great Hill cairn, but many of the Quantock cairns have a partial covering of turf, gorse or heather. These large cairns are often located in areas where there are relict field systems, dating from the historic period (*see* Chapter 5). Stone clearance was an initial stage of cultivation, and many of the large cairns have probably been augmented in the historic period. Some of the smaller cairns that have been located within areas of relict field systems may be field clearance cairns, but this is unlikely due to the fact that they occur singly, not in groups, as is usual for field clearance cairns. Good examples of these small cairns preserved within areas of historic cultivation can be found on the Greenway spur and above Short Combe.

Satellite cairns

Some of the large barrows have one or two very small cairns, less than 5m in diameter, at the very edge of the mound. Good examples can be seen at the barrows on Lydeard Hill, Beacon Hill and by Withyman's Pool

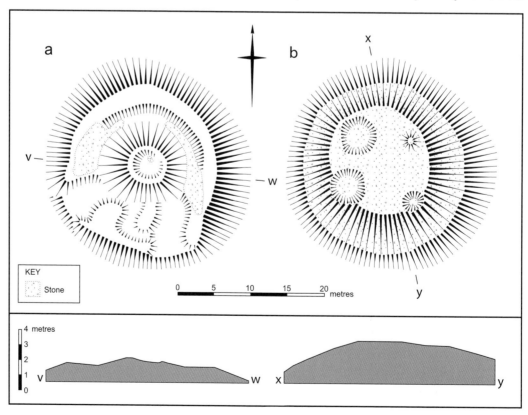

Fig 2.15
Cairns: West Hill (a) and Great Hill (b).

(Figs 2.14, 2.18 and 2.21). Sometimes the small cairns are not actually part of the large barrow, as at Hurley Beacon (Fig 2.21). A small, semi-circular cairn on the edge of the platform cairn in the Brenig Valley, north Wales, was excavated. Here, the semi-circular cairn was a later addition to the platform cairn and covered a pit that contained a small Collared Urn and some charcoal (Lynch 1993, fig 10.4; 110–1).

Platform cairns and truncated cairns or barrows

Many of the barrows and cairns on the Quantock Hills are not high barrows, with distinctive profiles, like those that cluster around Stonehenge or pepper the Dorset Ridgeway. They are, rather, low and flat-topped, and for this reason have been termed platform cairns. Many examples of these have been recorded on Bodmin Moor

(Johnson and Rose 1994, 18–9); similar monuments are the broad barrows of Wiltshire (McOmish *et al* 2002, 34).

The platform cairns are not impressive monuments, but they are carefully located so that they can be seen from both the surrounding hills and as they are approached up combes. The best examples of these are the group of cairns at the head of Bicknoller Combe (Fig 2.16) and the isolated barrows between Black Ball Hill and Halsway Post, which look east down Slaughterhouse Combe and Somerton Combe towards the Somerset Levels and Moors. Such sites on the Quantock Hills are often described as 'truncated'. This has sometimes been seen as the product of later robbing or disturbance. There is, in fact, evidence to suggest that the truncation was a deliberate feature, as in some instances later cultivation ridges can be seen to run right over the truncated

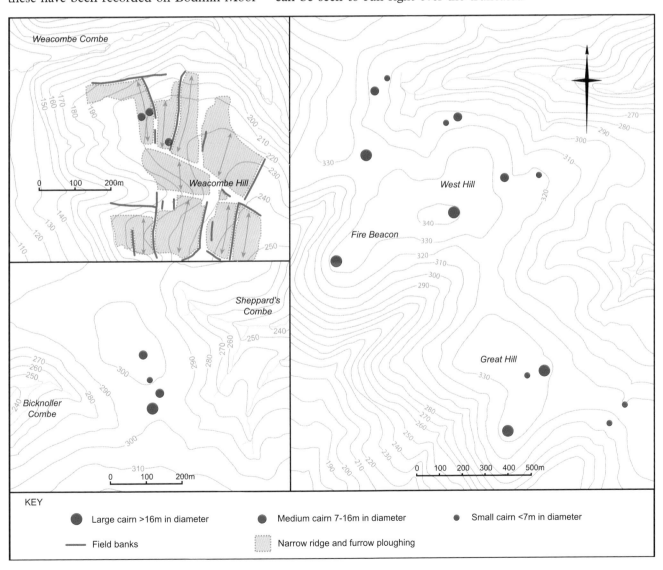

KEY
- Large cairn >16m in diameter
- Medium cairn 7-16m in diameter
- Small cairn <7m in diameter
- Field banks
- Narrow ridge and furrow ploughing

35

Fig 2.17
Platform cairns: Cothelstone Hill (a) and Crowcombe Gate (b).

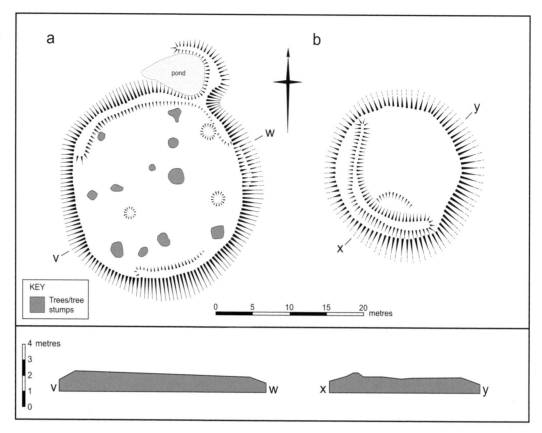

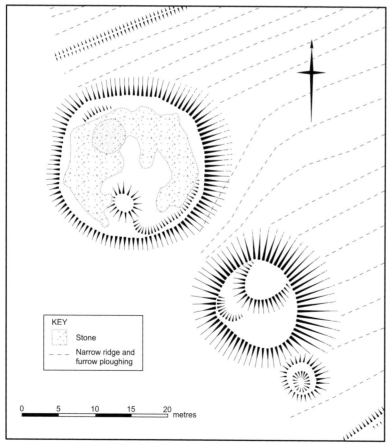

mound, showing that the truncation is earlier than the ploughing. This can be seen particularly clearly on the group of truncated barrows that lie on the north-west end of Weacombe Hill, above Round Plantation (Fig 2.16).

Several of the highest and largest barrows have flat tops. Although it is sometimes difficult to tell whether this is a result of modification of the mound for a beacon fire (*see above*), many of these barrows do seem to have been deliberately constructed with a flat top, such as the barrow on the southeast side of Lydeard Hill. This feature, both of lower platform cairns and flat topped barrows, could be interpreted as providing a platform from which one could reach the interface between the physical and spiritual world (Field 1998, 323). Intriguingly, some of the very large barrows (more than 3m high) in Wiltshire are flat topped, and these have been described as cone barrows. A massive cone barrow in the Sling Camp Group, nearly 6m in height, was excavated in the early 20th century. Its core was a huge pile of wood ash, showing that the barrow covered an enormous wooden structure (McOmish *et al* 2002, 34).

Two very large platform cairns were re-used in the 18th century as tree-ring enclosures (*see* Chapter 5). The conspicuous Seven Sisters beech clump on Cothelstone Hill appears to be planted on a platform cairn some 24m in diameter, and a similarly large platform cairn close to Crowcombe Gate (20m in diameter) has a low bank around its edge – the remains of a hedge bank that protected the young tree clump from browsing stock (Fig 2.17). On the Quantock Hills a feature of the distribution of platform cairns is their pairing with large barrows, as at Beacon Hill and Wills Neck (Figs 2.18 and 2.23).

Ring cairns and embanked platform cairns

Ring cairns are low, circular banks of stone, defining a central space. Sometimes there is a mound in the centre; often the central space is apparently empty. A variant of the platform cairn can, at first glance, be confused with a ring cairn. These are low, circular platforms of stone and earth, topped with a low bank, often with a central mound. There are nine ring cairns and embanked platform cairns on the Quantock Hills. Isolated examples occur on West Hill, at Knackers Hole and on the southeast side of Lydeard Hill in Muchcare Wood. The remainder, on Higher Hare Knap, Black Hill and Wills Neck are all part of larger groups or barrow cemeteries (*see below*). A feature of both the embanked platform cairns and the ring cairns is that the mounds are often placed off centre. Good examples of this can be seen at Wills Neck, east of Withyman's Pool and at Knackers Hole

(Fig 2.19). Most of the ring cairns and embanked platform cairns are turf covered and little can be seen of their underlying structure. However, a large ring cairn on the edge of Muchcare Wood was discovered by Anthony Locke in 1965, and 'rediscovered' in 2001 (Grinsell 1969, 27; Leach 2002). The cairn structure is revealed as the dense conifers have shaded out the ground flora, showing that the outer edge of the bank was defined by edge-set upright stones and that some of the stones were quartzite – material sometimes chosen by the builders of stone rows and barrows on Exmoor (Riley and Wilson-North 2001, 24, 37).

Excavations of ring cairns in Scotland, Wales and southwest England has shown that they were special monuments, sometimes directly associated with funerary activity, enclosing cremation burials, but often only containing charcoal filled pits (*see below*).

Barrow cemeteries

Black Hill

The most outstanding group of barrows and cairns on the Quantock Hills straddles the watershed of the hills. From Dead Woman's Ditch in the east to Hurley Beacon in the west 21 large barrows, ring cairns, embanked platform cairns and smaller cairns form a linear group some 2km long (Fig 2.20). At the heart of the group are those on Black Hill. Today they are a subtle group of sites, half hidden in thick gorse and heather, but the central ring cairn, platform cairn and

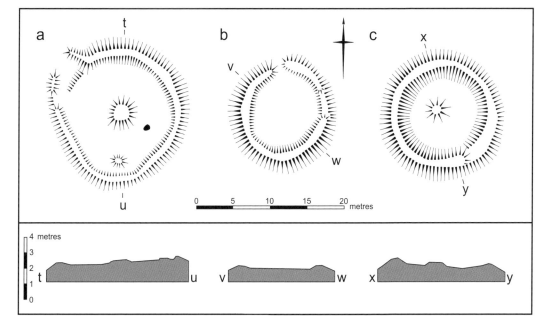

Fig 2.19
Ring cairns and embanked platform cairns: Wills Neck (a, b) and Withyman's Pool (c).

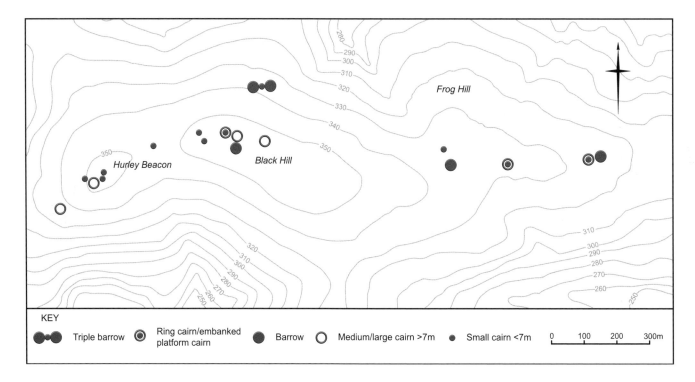

KEY

●■● Triple barrow   ◉ Ring cairn/embanked platform cairn   ● Barrow   ○ Medium/large cairn >7m   • Small cairn <7m

0   100   200   300m

barrow are fine examples of their type. A little to the north is an unusual grouping of three barrows, placed exactly at the head of Higher Hare Knap, and commanding both Frog Combe and Stert Combe. These three barrows are a fine example of Grinsell's triple barrow (Grinsell 1953, 20, fig 3), where a small barrow is placed in the gap between a pair of large barrows. To the west is the group of four cairns around Hurley Beacon, a good example of a clustering of small cairns around a larger monuments, and to the east are an important group of paired monuments: the embanked platform cairn and barrow by Withyman's Pool, and the ring cairn and barrow, discovered in the 1990s during swaling work by the AONB Rangers (Fig 2.21).

Wills Neck

Wills Neck is the highest point on the Quantock Hills. From the summit, at an altitude of more than 380m, the panorama of the hills and their surrounding landscape is laid out (Fig 2.22). A group of eight barrows and cairns occupy some of the most dramatic topography on the hills (Fig 2.23). A well preserved ring cairn lies right on the western edge of Wills Neck, with views across to the large cairns on Great Hill, Fire Beacon Hill and Hurley Beacon, with an embanked platform cairn below the summit on a spur above Triscombe (Fig 2.19). On the eastern end of the ridge a fine, ditched

Fig 2.21 (opposite)
Black Hill barrow cemetery:
Withyman's Pool (a),
triple barrow (b), east of
Withyman's Pool (c) and
Hurley Beacon (d).

barrow, which has been used as a beacon, is paired with a platform cairn. On the summit of Wills Neck a rather mutilated barrow, now surmounted with an Ordnance Survey triangulation point, lies close to one of the most intriguing prehistoric monuments on the hills. This is a circular bank with an external ditch, a mound to the western side of the interior, the whole being some 27m in diameter (Fig 2.24). This is 10m larger than the largest ring cairns on the Quantock Hills and a few metres larger than the largest ring cairns defined by Lynch (1993, 134). The enclosure on Wills Neck may have more in common with the two circular, ditched enclosures on Gittisham Hill and Farway Hill in East Devon described as Bronze Age ritual monuments (Simpson and Noble 1993, 16; 19). These are about 50m in diameter, have external ditches and are associated with a very large group of barrows – enough to be called a necropolis (Fox 1948). These large circular, ditched enclosures may have associations with the building of stone and timber circles and henges. Clearly, Wills Neck was a very special place in the 2nd millennium BC and was used over generations for burial and ceremony.

Ritual and burial

A group of cairns and barrows in the Brenig Valley, north Wales, were excavated in the early 1970s in advance of the construction

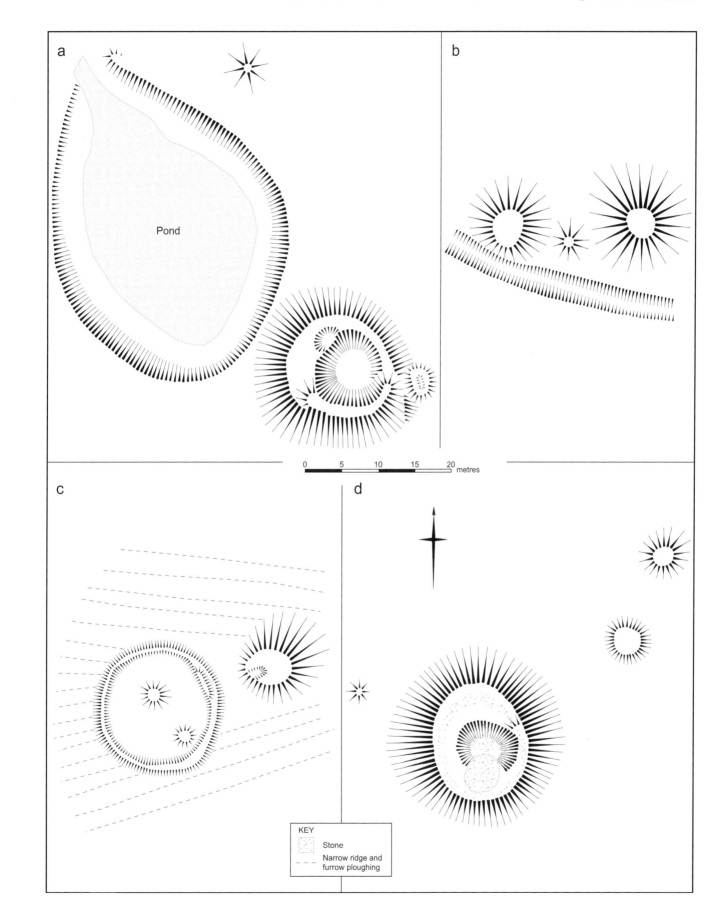

Fig 2.22
The western scarp of the
Quantock Hills, with Wills
Neck in the foreground.
(NMR 21958/09)
(© English Heritage. NMR)

of a reservoir. These sites give us some of the best information as to how barrows and cairns were constructed and what happened in the special areas around them. A platform cairn was built on an area that had been cleaned, stripped of turf and burnt. A burial took place and then a cairn was built with an open central area. A further cremation burial occurred and there was some form of ritual in the open, central area around an upright post (a totem pole?). The main cairn mound was completed, and some time later a small cairn was added to the edge of the main cairn. The interior of the Brenig

Valley ring cairn was used for burying charcoal in pits. Analysis of the charcoal suggests that it was not from the funeral pyres, which tended to be oak, but from other wood, perhaps from fires burnt specially to produce the charcoal, which was very clean at this site. The ground inside the cairn was scorched. Careful excavation at this site showed that the ring cairn was surrounded by a circle of wooden posts early on in its history. At another Welsh example a ring cairn was used for the re-burial of bones from elsewhere (Lynch 1993). On Farway Down, East Devon, some ring cairns enclosed burials and pits filled with charcoal. More than 100 pits, filled with clay, described as 'ritual pits' by the excavator, pre-dated the construction of two of the ring cairns (Pollard 1967; 1971).

The cairns and barrows on the Quantock Hills may have been used in similar ways. A significant feature is the pairing of monuments. On Beacon Hill and Wills Neck large barrows are paired with platform cairns. At Withyman's Pool and on Higher Hare Knap large ring cairns or embanked platform cairns are paired with barrows or cairns. The evidence from excavated ring cairns suggests that their primary function was not usually burial, but that they enclosed an important area where structured deposition of charcoal or other material, perhaps connected with the cremation of human remains, took place.

One interpretation of the paired monuments on the Quantock Hills is that a ritual connected with the cremation of the body was carried out in the course of its disposal and that the monuments reflect different stages of this activity. The body was burnt on a funeral pyre, after this event the cremated remains were placed in a pottery container and buried. The construction of the mound or cairn itself must have been equally as important as the cremation. Perhaps only certain people were entitled to see different parts of the ceremony, or it may have been a time for groups of people who spent long periods of time isolated from each other to come together. Some of the material associated with this ceremony, such as parts of the pyre or other wooden structures, may have been placed in pits inside ring cairns. The area around the barrows and cairns was as important as the monuments themselves and access to that space was probably restricted in some way.

It is difficult for us to understand exactly what happened at these sites, but we can attempt to reconstruct some elements of the ceremony (Fig 2.25). Clearly fire played an important part in the ceremony, as the careful burial of charcoal suggests. Homer's *Iliad* on the burial of Patroclus by his companion Achilles is more eloquent than any excavation report can be. Mules and men with axes and stout ropes are sent to fetch wood, which is stacked in a huge mound. A large procession of warriors, charioteers and horsemen forms and those closest to Patroclus carry his corpse, which is covered with locks of their hair. The corpse is laid on top of the pyre, then sheep and cattle are killed,

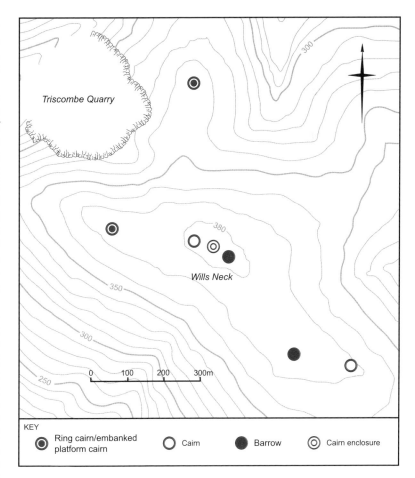

KEY

◉ Ring cairn/embanked platform cairn ○ Cairn ● Barrow ◎ Cairn enclosure

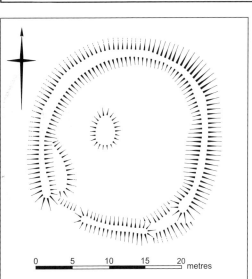

Fig 2.23
Wills Neck barrow cemetery.
(Based on an Ordnance
Survey map, with permission.
© Crown copyright.
All rights reserved)

Fig 2.24
Wills Neck: cairn enclosure.

their fat is used to cover the corpse and the animal carcasses are piled around the corpse. Jars of honey and oil are added, so are four horses, two of Patroclus' pet dogs and a dozen Trojans. Throughout the night, as the pyre burns, Achilles keeps a vigil, pouring out libations, weeping, and walking around the pyre. In the morning the fire is

extinguished with sparkling wine, then Patroclus' bones are collected and placed in a golden vase, which is sealed with fat. The barrow is designed by laying down a ring of stone revetments around the pyre and earth is piled up inside it. Finally, Achilles holds lavish games in celebration of his friend (Homer *The Iliad*, Book 23).

The mundane landscape: Bronze Age settlement

In contrast to the large body of evidence for burial and ritual in the earlier Bronze Age there is very little evidence for the more mundane side of life on and around the Quantock Hills from this time. We may, in fact, be looking at people who were not sedentary, but rather groups of pastoralists whose livestock ranged across large areas of upland grazing, the adjacent lowlands and the coastal plain. The traces of such people in the archaeological record are seen as burial monuments, not houses. The people moved across the landscape in a seasonal round of economic necessity and social obligation. Sometimes their seasonal sites became the permanent settlements of the Middle and Late Bronze Age: at Volis Hill on the southern edge of the Quantock Hills a pit containing Beaker pottery was found below the Middle Bronze Age enclosure (Thorpe 2002).

There is a small amount of evidence for settlement sites of the earlier Bronze Age to the northeast and south of the Quantock Hills. At Brean Down, a coastal site at the very tip of the Mendip Hills, excavations uncovered a substantial oval stone structure from the Early Bronze Age, which may have been a house, an animal shelter or for storage, and there was associated evidence for bone and leather working. The remains of two round houses of Middle Bronze Age date at Brean Down are structurally similar to the stone hut circles that survive on Dartmoor and Bodmin Moor (below). Careful excavation has provided a wealth of information about the people who lived here some 3,500 years ago. Around the fire, as well as cooking and food preparation, leather working, weaving and the final processes of salt preparation were carried out (Bell 1990, 62). At Norton Fitzwarren the excavations suggest a deliberately non-defensive, possible ceremonial site, originating in the Early or Middle Bronze Age (Ellis 1989, 66). To the south of Doniford, near the

Doniford Stream, a water pipeline cut through a series of Middle Bronze Age pits, containing Trevisker type pottery and giving a radiocarbon date of 1520–1290 BC (Hollinrake and Hollinrake 2003).

The uplands of southwest England are well known for their extensive Bronze Age settlements and field systems. On the more marginal areas of Exmoor, Bodmin Moor and Dartmoor, the traces of stone hut circles and field systems are highly visible, both on the ground and from the air. These remains are generally dated to the Middle Bronze Age (1600–1000 BC), but when such sites are excavated a more complex picture inevitably arises. It seems that the great land divisions of Dartmoor – the reave systems – were laid out in the Middle Bronze Age, but there is evidence from excavation that areas were in cultivation prior to this. Excavations have also shown that earlier and contemporary wooden structures lay around the stone huts that are so much part of the Dartmoor landscape today (Fleming 1988; Wainwright and Smith 1980).

These upland areas have had little cultivation in subsequent times, hence the prehistoric remains survive. On the Quantock Hills, however, large areas of relict field systems (*see* Chapter 5) show that the heath has been cultivated in the historic period. Finding traces of prehistoric settlement in more lowland areas, which have been subject to centuries of agricultural improvement, is difficult and relies on the use of aerial photographic evidence, on chance finds or on geophysical survey and excavation in advance of building work and road construction. In 1997 such work in advance of the A30 east of Exeter revealed enclosures of dates from the Middle Bronze Age to the Roman period (Fitzpatrick *et al* 1999).

Bronze Age hut circles and field systems on the Quantock Hills

There are no extensive Bronze Age field systems and settlements surviving on the Quantock heath. However, such areas must have been used during the 2nd millennium BC – we have seen how large areas of the hilltops were special places during the earlier part of the Bronze Age. Sometimes Beaker occupation is found underneath large barrows or ritual monuments, as under the platform cairn excavated in the Brenig valley, for example (Lynch 1993, 102–5). Certainly, there are enough barbed and tanged arrowheads recorded from the Quantock Hills to suggest that the hills were well used in the earlier Bronze Age. The earthwork remains of Bronze Age hut circles and field systems on Exmoor are, for the most part, slight and fragmentary (Riley and Wilson-North 2001, 44–6). Some hut sites are marked by platforms cut into the hillside – the level base for a wooden structure, while hut circles survive as low banks of earth and stone. As we have already seen, much of the Quantock heath has been cultivated at some time in the historic period, and this period of cultivation was probably enough to obliterate the traces of Bronze Age settlement and agriculture. Coupled with the challenging vegetation cover, even in the depths of winter, it is not surprising that there was no convincing evidence for Bronze Age settlement and field systems on the hills at the beginning of this project. Another factor that could influence the distribution of Bronze Age settlement is that access to the heath from the lower slopes, perhaps more favourable for settlement, is not difficult.

The hills may have been used in the Bronze Age for hunting, grazing and perhaps agriculture, but people may have lived on the lower slopes, as happened in historic times. On Exmoor, for example, there is evidence from palaeoenvironmental work of managed grassland in areas devoid of prehistoric settlement. On the Quantocks, some of the field evidence may have been removed by turf cutting. This practice is well documented on the Quantock Hills during the historic period (*see* Chapters 4 and 5) but leaves little in the way of physical remains, although a large mound north of the Long Stone may be the remains of a turf stack. We may also never be able to find the archaeology of wooden fences, hedged enclosures and wooden huts and houses on the hills without excavation.

West Hill and the Greenway

It soon became apparent that the only way to look for such evidence was to target areas that did not appear to have been subject to

Fig 2.26
Greenway: fragmentary remains of prehistoric enclosed settlement and cairns with associated field clearance banks.

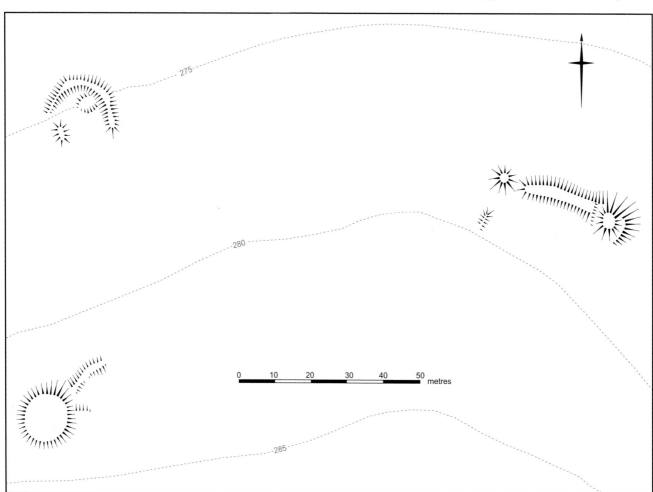

cultivation in the historic period and where the exuberant vegetation had been recently tamed by swaling. As a result of this process three areas were noted where the fragmentary remains of possible Bronze Age settlement or field systems survive.

The best evidence comes from the Greenway, that great spur of heath that reaches right down towards the coastal strip. Here there is a small enclosure, some 20m in diameter, with a stance for a hut (Fig 2.26). Some 80m to the south is a large burial cairn, and the linear mound on its north side is probably the result of clearing small plots of ground prior to cultivation – very different from the large scale field systems that characterise the historic cultivation on the heath. Such small linear mounds have been interpreted as Bronze Age field clearance on Exmoor (Riley and Wilson-North 2001, 43). A similar feature also occurs by a burial cairn to the east of the enclosure. Not far from this site, and overlooking the Greenway spur, are several similar small linear mounds. To the west of the Greenway spur, across Smith's Combe, is another great spur, West Hill, reaching down to the coast at East Quantoxhead. Here the evidence is rather equivocal (Fig 2.27). Two small platforms lie some 160m apart. These may well have been the sites for Bronze Age structures. There are several small, stony banks and seven small clearance cairns. Although there are the remains of historic cultivation close by, the size of the cairns and the presence of the platforms do suggest Bronze Age settlement and field system. A linear mound on the southern side of the embanked platform cairn to the south may also indicate clearance in the Bronze Age.

The spatial association of these features to ritual and burial monuments is significant (Fig 2.12). It cannot be demonstrated that they are contemporary but some fieldworkers in South Wales have drawn attention to the fact that clearance cairns and ritual and burial monuments do occur in close proximity in parts of the landscape, and have gone on to suggest that our separation of 'ritual' and 'economic' activities is false, and that ritual could have embraced economic concerns as well as funerary activity (Ward 1989, 15; Bradley 2005).

More familiar to us as a parallel is the Christian celebration of Harvest Festival. A find from Hillfarrance in the upper Tone Valley illustrates this. A watching brief revealed the ditches of a prehistoric field system. At the end of one of these ditches was a pit containing burnt stone, wooden artefacts and fragments of worked timber. The most exciting find was part of the representation of the lower torso of a human figure, made from a forked twig and found upside-down, pushed into the bottom of the pit. This was dated to 1410–1080 BC and is one of several such finds from the later Bronze Age and Iron Age in Britain and Ireland (Reed 2003).

So far we have looked at the evidence for Bronze Age settlement on the hilltops, in the form of hut platforms and field systems. In the latter part of the 2nd millennium BC the evidence for settlement and enclosure in the landscape of southwest England becomes more compelling. At its zenith, we see the massive banks and ditches of Iron Age hillforts in the earlier 1st millennium BC, but from about 1500 BC the domestic or agricultural enclosure becomes a distinctive part of the Bronze Age landscape. Evidence comes both from sites that survive as earthworks, and from those that have been ploughed over for many years and are only seen as marks on the ground when seen from the air (see Chapter 3). Excavations at Higher Holworthy, near Parracombe on the western side of Exmoor have shown that this small earthwork enclosure was in use by 1400 BC and abandoned by 1000 BC (Green 2004; R Wilson-North, pers comm). We have already encountered the hilltop enclosure at Norton Fitzwarren. Towards the end of the 2nd millennium BC the enclosure had a timber palisade and was associated with the manufacture of bronze swords. The SQAS excavations at Volis Farm and Ivyton Farm have demonstrated that cropmark enclosures on the southern edge of the Quantock Hills can have their origins in the second half of the 2nd millennium BC (Thorpe 2002; Roffey et al 2004). At Volis Farm a large enclosure, which was occupied in the 1st millennium BC, had a precursor of Middle Bronze Age date. A large complex of cropmarks occurs on south-facing slopes above Ivyton Farm on the very southwest edge of the Quantock Hills. These were sampled as part of the SQAS project, and a bronze sickle blade of mid-2nd millennium date was found in the ditch of a sub-circular enclosure, placing it in the Middle Bronze Age. Other enclosures in this complex dated from the earlier Bronze Age (ring ditches) and the Iron Age/Romano-British period (see Chapter 3).

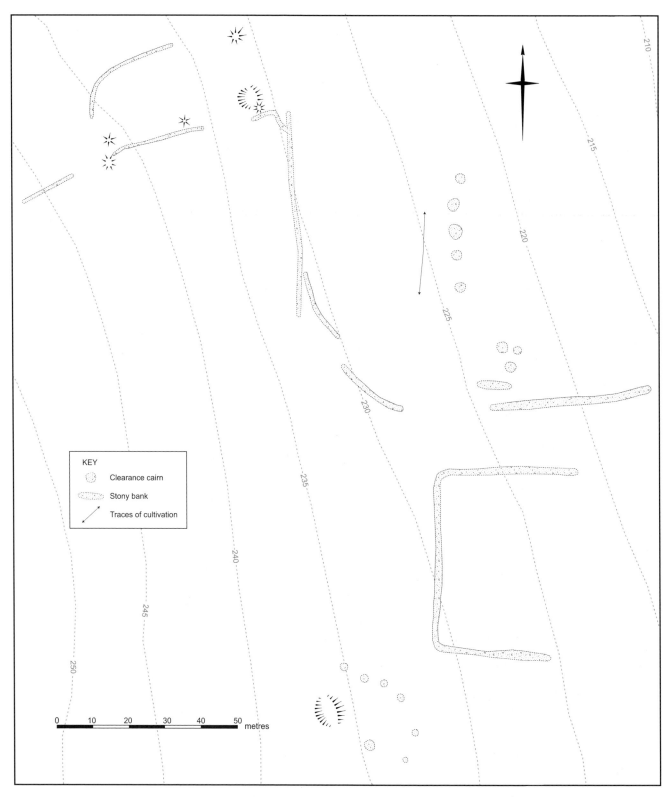

KEY

◌ Clearance cairn

▭ Stony bank

↕ Traces of cultivation

0 10 20 30 40 50 metres

Fig 2.27
*West Hill: prehistoric
settlement remains and
clearance cairns.*

Linear earthworks

Linear earthworks – banks and ditches – are a large class of monument ranging from the plantation and park boundaries of the historic period to systems of prehistoric land division. Those that can be assigned to the prehistoric period are generally dated to the later Bronze Age and Early Iron Age, although absolute dating evidence is often lacking. Some linear earthworks are many kilometres in length, such as the extensive linear ditch systems of Salisbury Plain. Others are shorter lengths of bank and ditch that cut off ridges or spurs (cross-ridge dykes or spur dykes), as found on the South Downs and the Dorset chalklands (Bradley *et al* 1994, 6–18). Some of the best preserved, and best studied, are those found on the chalk downland of Salisbury Plain. Here, the earliest of the linear earthworks date from 1200–1000 BC. Between 800 and 600 BC many of them are reworked and new ones are built. Reworking then continues throughout much of the remainder of the 1st millennium BC (McOmish *et al* 2002, 61). The linear earthworks of Salisbury Plain are rarely less than 500m in length, with the longest at more than 15km. A number of functions have been suggested, but their scale suggests that their primary function was a form of socially determined land division. On Salisbury Plain the frequent association between the linear earthworks and earlier barrow groups and settlements has been interpreted as a deliberate attempt by the monument builders to integrate their earthworks into a pre-existing monumental landscape. One of the largest and most impressive of these linear earthworks is a double linear that approaches the hilltop crowned by the hillfort of Sidbury. The linear pre-dates the hillfort but still channels one into the focus of activities on that hilltop.

The rolling hills of the North Yorkshire Moors contain a variety of linear earthworks. Those identified as prehistoric have been divided into two groups. A series of short linear earthworks, which cut off or demarcate spurs and promontories, are known as cross-ridge boundaries. These earthworks are very often associated with funerary monuments of the early 2nd millennium BC, and have been assigned to the later Neolithic and Early Bronze Age. The second group is an extensively distributed group of linear earthworks that are boundary systems of the 1st millennium BC or later (Vyner 1994; 1995).

The linear earthworks on the Quantock Hills

So how might the linear earthworks on the Quantock Hills fit into the archaeological record? There are four linear earthworks recorded on the Quantock Hills (Fig 2.12). Two others (Bicknoller Hill and Ruborough Camp) are directly associated with hillforts

and are discussed below (*see* Chapter 3). The longest, and best known, is Dead Woman's Ditch, a bank and ditch roughly one kilometre in length. It straddles Robin Upright's Hill, climbing the steep side of Rams Combe and descending to Lady's Fountain, a spring in Lady's Combe. The earthwork is substantial: the bank is 3m wide and 1m high, with a ditch, 3m wide and 2m deep, to the west. The name Dead Woman's Ditch appears on a map of 1782, seven years before the charcoal burner and locally notorious murderer John Walford was supposed to have hidden the body of his wife there. A section through the bank and ditch was excavated in 2001, where the earthwork crosses the top of Robin Upright's Hill (Grove 2002). This showed that the ditch was steep sided, there was a berm (level area) between the ditch and the bank, and that the bank had been revetted with large stones. Finds were confined to the uppermost layers and dated from the 19th and 20th centuries, and no material suitable for radiocarbon dating or paleoenvironmental analysis was recovered. Although there was no positive dating evidence from the excavation, the form and location of the earthwork, together with the way in which several deeply hollowed tracks and a woodland boundary of presumed medieval date cut through or cross the earthwork, strongly suggest a prehistoric date for the construction of Dead Woman's Ditch.

The other linear earthworks are not well known and of these only that on Higher Hare Knap had been previously surveyed (NMR ST 13 NW 27). This linear earthwork runs for some 95m, from the head of a small combe off Somerton Combe to the top of Higher Hare Knap (Fig 2.28). Here, the earthwork has been truncated by cultivation that occurred in the historic period, and there is no trace of the earthwork on the top of the spur or on its south side (which is cloaked in very thick gorse). The earthwork consists of a bank, 7m wide and 0.5m high, and a ditch on its south side, 3m wide and 1.8m deep. The form and size of the bank and ditch, its neat western terminal and the fact that the east end has been ploughed over in the historic period all combine to indicate that is of considerable age and probably prehistoric in origin.

A bank and ditch runs from the very head of Cockercombe across the spur to the north of the summit of Wills Neck to the edge of Triscombe Quarry – in fact the

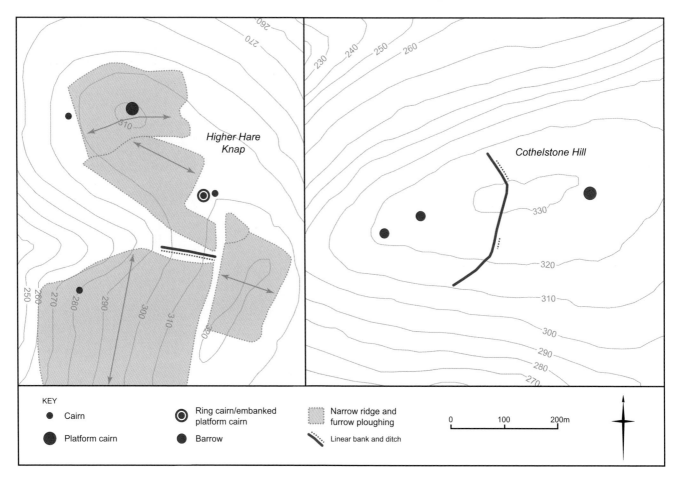

Fig 2.28
Linear earthworks on
Higher Hare Knap (left)
and Cothelstone Hill
(right). (Based on an
Ordnance Survey map,
with permission.
© Crown copyright.
All rights reserved)

quarry has taken away the western end of the earthwork. It is now 165m long and consists of a bank, 4m wide and 0.6m high with a ditch, 2m wide and 1m deep to the north. The earthwork lies on the edge of an area of relict field system and may have been utilised as part of it, but, as on Higher Hare Knap, this bank and ditch has been ploughed during in the historic period, again suggesting that is of considerable antiquity.

On Cothelstone Hill a linear earthwork 280m long runs across the western part of the hill from north to south (Fig 2.28). There are no direct dates for this earthwork, but its form and relationships with other archaeological features on the hill enables us to suggest that the earthwork is of prehistoric origin. The earthwork is neatly symmetrical with in-turned ends and is massive in form, being a bank 2.5m wide and 1.4m high, with an intermittent ditch 2m wide and 0.8m deep to the east – much larger than the field boundaries on the hill, which date from historic times. The remains of a tower that was built to ornament Cothelstone Hill in the 18th century lie on top of the earthwork, and a boundary that was constructed in the early post-medieval period cuts through the linear earthwork. Finally, the earthwork has been ploughed over in the historic period, just like those on Higher Hare Knap and Wills Neck.

A ritual landscape? The landscape defined

The linear earthworks of the Quantock Hills are not of a scale to be compared with the great systems of land division on Salisbury Plain, or with their counterparts in stone on Dartmoor. They do, however, compare to the smaller cross-ridge boundaries of the North Yorkshire Moors, which are associated, spatially, with barrow groups and funerary monuments. Looked at in isolation, each linear monument is associated with a barrow group. On Wills Neck the linear cuts off the high ridge of land that contains a group of barrows and ring cairns. The bank and ditch on Cothelstone Hill is an impressive monument that captures two large barrows. The linear on Higher Hare Knap bounds a spur that contains a

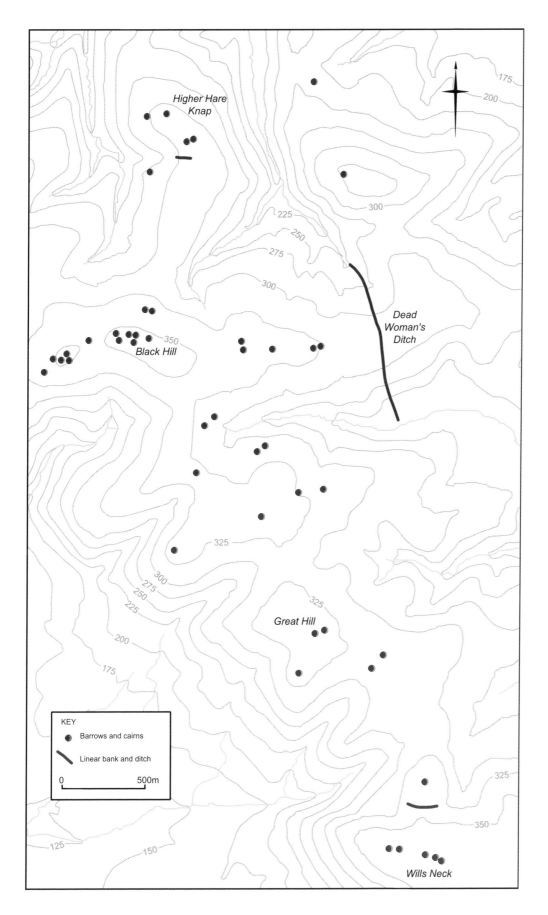

Fig 2.29
The landscape defined:
linear earthworks, barrows
and cairns. (Based on an
Ordnance Survey map,
with permission.
© Crown copyright.
All rights reserved)

group of a platform cairn, a ring cairn, cairn and a barrow. Dead Woman's Ditch provides an impressive barrier to the linear barrow cemeteries at Withyman's Pool and Black Hill. These two linear earthworks, although close to the hillfort of Dowsborough Camp, are not directly associated with it, but their location does serve to emphasise the isolation of Dowsborough Hill.

It is only when all of these linear earthworks are seen together with the distribution of the barrow cemeteries that the ritual landscape of the central part of the Quantock Hills is revealed in its true extent (Fig 2.29). The central part of the hills can indeed be considered a ritual landscape. We have already seen, with the proviso that historic land-use patterns may be skewing the evidence, that the evidence for settlement on the hills is confined to the northern spurs. The linear earthworks define a central part of the hills. Here are the largest barrows and cairns, the most elaborate types of ring cairns and platform cairns, and the best examples of barrow cemeteries.

It can certainly be argued that the central part of the Quantock Hills was, in the 2nd millennium BC, a ritual landscape, and that it was carefully defined as such by linear earthworks. These linear earthworks may, like those on the North Yorkshire Moors, have their origins as early as the late Neolithic/early Bronze Age, but it is perhaps more likely that they were built later on in the 2nd millennium BC to define and keep special the heart of the hills, which contained the remains of so many ancestors.

3

A defended landscape?
The Quantock Hills in Iron Age
and Roman Times

Beyond the pale of civilisation: the Iron Age

The Iron Age spans the period of time from the introduction of a new metalworking technology – the use of iron – in about 750 BC, to the Roman conquest of Britain in AD 43. Roman historians tell us a little about the tribes who occupied Britain towards the end of the Iron Age and their geographical location comes from studying the distribution of cultural material, particularly coins. Cornwall, Devon and part of west and south Somerset was occupied by a tribe called the Dumnonii, described as 'so far beyond the pale of civilisation that they minted no coins of their own' (Manning 1976, 16). South Somerset, the Polden Hills and much of Dorset was the territory of the Durotriges, while the Dobunni held north Somerset and parts of Wiltshire and Gloucestershire. The Quantock Hills were in an important strategic location at the end of the 1st millennium BC: on the edge of the Dumnonii territory and close to the Dobunni tribe to the northeast.

Evidence for the Iron Age landscape

The Quantock Hills contain the remains of several spectacular Iron Age sites: the Trendle Ring, perched high above Bicknoller (front cover); the hillforts at Dowsborough and Ruborough, now hidden in woodland but once statements of power and prestige. Little is known about these sites, and it is only now as new excavations of ploughed-over sites on the southern edge of the hills begin to yield new information that we can start to piece together the story of life in the Iron Age in the Quantock Hills.

Two remarkable sites on the edge of the Somerset Levels, where artefacts of wood and willow, as well as the more usual pottery, have been preserved in wet conditions, show the wealth of material culture that was available to the people of the Quantock Hills

before the Roman invasions. These are the 'Lake Villages' of Glastonbury and Meare. Both of these sites have been excavated at various times in the 19th and 20th centuries and seem to have been occupied from the 3rd century BC until the 1st century AD (Glastonbury) and probably later (Meare). At Glastonbury a large settlement, surrounded by a wooden palisade, was constructed on a structure of brushwood on the edge of a marshy area. At Meare the emphasis seems to have been on specialised craft production, including glass beads, and it may have been the site of an annual fair or meeting place for people from all around the region – perhaps from all of the three tribes described above (Coles and Coles 1986).

Most of the people, however, lived by agriculture, in farmsteads and small hamlets. The landscape was by now well populated, with productive arable fields, meadows and woodland, and large areas of upland pasture. Excavations show that such agricultural settlement sites may have had their origins in the 2nd millennium BC, and were occupied during the Iron Age and into the Roman period. Indeed they are often on the site of, or close to, the farms and villages that we read of in the *Domesday Book* (*see* Chapter 4). A good example of such an agricultural site is at Maidenbrook Farm, on the southern edge of the Quantock Hills, just north of Taunton. Here, a small enclosed farmstead probably began in the later Bronze Age and continued through the Iron Age and into the Roman period until the 4th century AD, possibly with a break in the early 3rd century AD (Ferris and Bevan 1993).

Hillforts

It is against this pastoral landscape of farmsteads and hamlets that the most visible and dramatic of earthwork sites in the archaeological record must be viewed. These are the great hillforts: enclosures, usually on hilltops, formed by one or more massive earthwork banks and ditches. Hillforts range in size from a few hectares, such as Cow Castle and Bats Castle on Exmoor, to the massive enclosure at Ham Hill (85ha) in south Somerset and the vast promontory fort of Wind Hill (35ha) on the north Devon coast. Hillforts are a common feature of the archaeological record in southwest England, and occur in large numbers in Somerset, where the Blackdown Hills and south Somerset, the Mendip Hills, Exmoor and the Brendon Hills are all fringed with massive Iron Age earthworks.

Hillforts are largely a phenomenon of the 1st millennium BC, with many having their origins in the later part of the 2nd millennium, and it is worth stating again that certain hilltops – Ham Hill, Cadbury Castle and Norton Fitzwarren for example – have been a focus for human activity and settlement from the Neolithic period onwards. Where we have the evidence from excavation, it seems that most hillforts were abandoned by about 100 BC, well before the arrival of the Romans. There is also evidence that many hilltop sites in Somerset were re-used in the early medieval period (*see* Chapter 4).

Traditionally hillforts have been interpreted as defended enclosures, and elaborate typologies were developed, based on the form and size of the earthworks, with corresponding waves of invaders from across the English Channel (Hawkes 1931). More recent work, however, has attributed a range of functions and socio-political meanings to them. Some see hillforts as the most important places in a settlement hierarchy, the central place, a place of refuge, ritual and a seat of power (for example, Cunliffe 2003). A study of the hillforts and other Iron Age settlements of Wessex has challenged this view. Here, hillforts are seen as liminal places, serving a community of rather independent groups of people who used them for communal rituals and festivals (Hill 1996).

Only a small sample of hillforts has been excavated using modern techniques and the results are diverse. Some hillforts were used for only a short period of time; some have evidence for hundreds of years of occupation. There is evidence for settlement: the remains of round houses, storage pits for grain, the manufacture of everyday objects such as pottery, metalwork and clothes. There is also evidence for ritual activity (Cunliffe 2005). Hillforts may also have functioned as meeting places for activities akin to our fairs, festivals and markets. Some hillforts were used as places of defence, but this seems to have been low level and local rather than out and out warfare. Finally, the physical location and appearance of the hillfort in the landscape has to be considered. The presence of these dramatic earthwork enclosures in the landscape gave messages of power, prestige, ownership and identity to those who saw them.

Cadbury Castle, northeast of Yeovil, is one of the few hillforts in the southwest that has been extensively excavated in recent years. The excavations showed that the hilltop was an important place for people from the Neolithic Period onwards. By about 300 BC the hilltop was encircled by a series of massive banks and ditches, and people lived in round houses built inside these earthworks, with the level of occupation declining before the 1st century AD. Late in the 1st century AD the hillfort was taken by the Roman military, who built their barracks inside the fort (Barrett *et al* 2000). During the Iron Age, Cadbury Castle may have been a tribal capital and a seat of power. The hillfort was also probably a social, ritual and religious centre, and, importantly, must have made up part of the identity of the people who were associated with it. The great earthworks that surround the hill are still visible from many miles away, when newly built they made a statement of power and prestige emanating from this tribal centre.

The hillforts of the Quantock Hills

The Quantock Hills contain three hillforts. These are Dowsborough Camp, situated in the very heart of the hills on one of the highest hilltops, Ruborough Camp, on a spur commanding the expanse of the Levels and Moors, and an incomplete enclosure on Bicknoller Hill (Fig 3.1). None of these sites have been paid much attention in the past. No recorded excavations or reliably provenanced finds are known from any of the sites, but Ruborough Camp has a string of legends attached to it. During the project, all of the hillforts were surveyed at a scale of 1:1000 (Appendix 2).

Ruborough Camp

Ruborough Camp is, like Dowsborough Camp, now cloaked in woodland. The site occupies a spur on the southeast edge of the Quantock Hills, high above two tributary

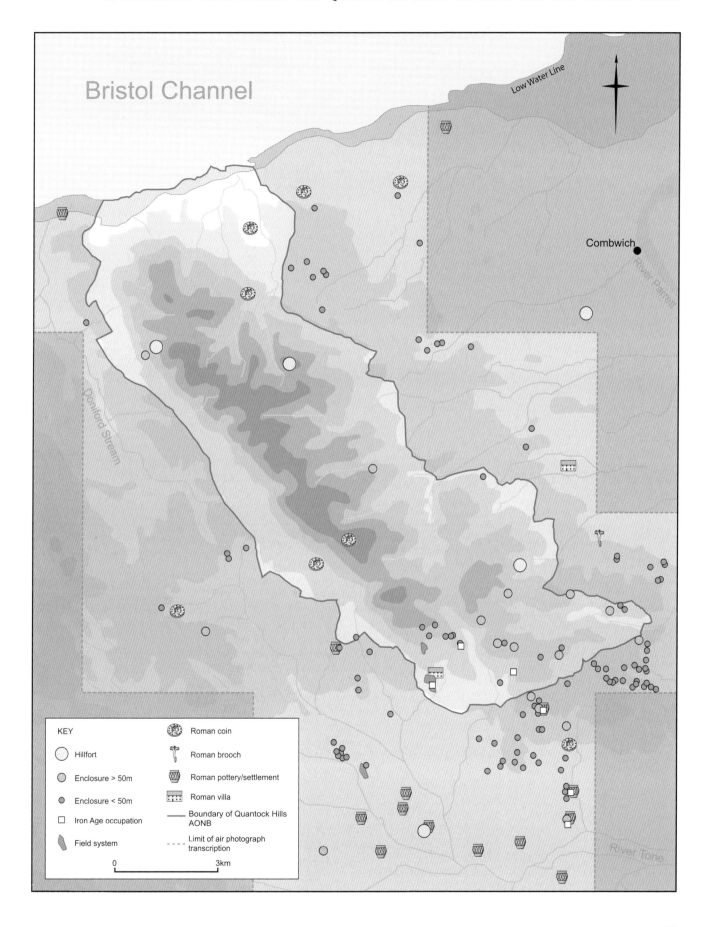

Bristol Channel

Low Water Line

Combwich

River Parrett

Doniford Stream

River Tone

KEY

Hillfort

Enclosure > 50m

Enclosure < 50m

Iron Age occupation

Field system

Roman coin

Roman brooch

Roman pottery/settlement

Roman villa

Boundary of Quantock Hills AONB

Limit of air photograph transcription

0   3km

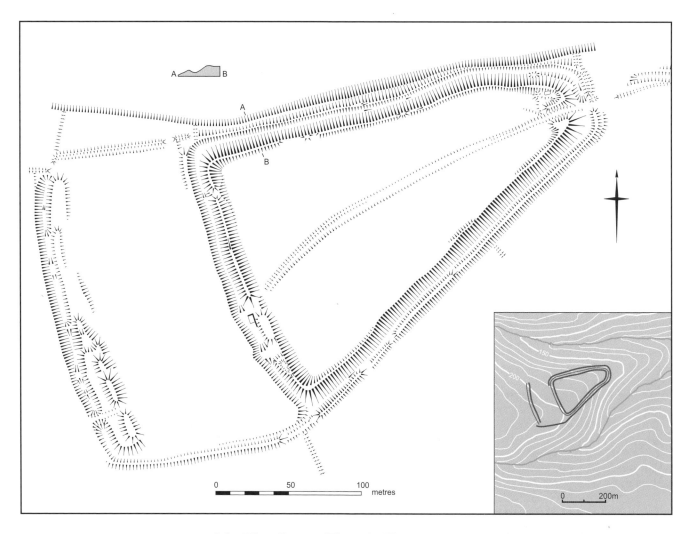

streams of the River Parrett (Fig 3.2). The ground slopes from west to east, from the outwork at 200m OD to the tip of the enclosure at 165m OD. The tree cover masks both its dramatic topographic location and the scale of the earthworks (Figs 3.2 and 3.3). An early account of Ruborough Camp gives some idea as to how remote and little visited this corner of the Quantock Hills was until quite recently. Page, writing in 1890, had to requisition a guide from some 'poor-looking cottages' near the Traveller's Rest for his excursion to the camp. The site was planted with young firs at the time of Page's visit. He mentions the name 'Money Field', given to the field in between the outwork and the main enclosure, a name still current locally. Page states that Roman coins have been found in the Money Field, and that querns were found either in that field or in the enclosure itself. He was also told of an old woman who found some cannon-balls, but he was unable to verify the story (Page 1890, 280–1).

In 1903 H St George Gray published one of the very few descriptions of an earthwork site on the Quantock Hills. Gray describes the earthworks and gathers together the accounts of finds and legends associated with the site. A turquoise and gold seal ring, solid gold bars and pieces of armour were apparently found before 1857. Gray also quotes a legend from local people, which was current by 1847. This is a tradition that underneath the enclosure of the camp is an iron castle full of gold and silver, guarded by gnomes and spirits. A visitor was told that there was more treasure under his feet than was contained in the palaces of all the kings in the world, but that there was an iron door, which could only be found at full moon. Various attempts to find this door by digging at the site during full moon have been aborted by mournful shrieks (Gray 1903).

Ruborough Camp contains three main earthwork elements (Fig 3.2). A large, triangular enclosure occupies much of the sloping spur of land. To the west of this is an outwork, possibly connected to the main enclosure. The earthworks of a well defined hollow-way (a deep track or lane) run up to the triangular enclosure. The massive earthworks that enclose the spur are formed of a bank (here of a scale to be called a rampart), a ditch and a counterscarp (outer) bank, overall 20m wide and 6m high. The earthworks are exceptionally well preserved, despite the later use of the site as an agricultural and woodland enclosure (Fig 3.3).

Access to the site was by an entrance at the top of the triangle, at the northeast end of the enclosure. Here the earthworks show the characteristics of an original Iron Age entrance. The counterscarp bank and ditch have well-formed, regular terminals; the main ramparts both turn sharply, forming a deep and impressive passage way into the enclosure. A hollow-way runs up the hill side to this entrance. The form of the earthworks shows that it is of some considerable age, and could even be the original way up to the site from the east. Similar features can be seen at the hillforts of Castle Ditches in south Wiltshire and Wooston Castle on the edge of Dartmoor.

A gap in the base of the triangle, at the west end of the enclosure, may also have been an Iron Age entrance, but it is now difficult to be certain as an out barn from Willoughby Farm – only 100m away as the crow flies, but a steep enough climb if you left your whetstone or lunchtime jug of cider on the kitchen table – now lies in the ditch at this point. A way into the main enclosure at this point would have been very useful, as some 90m to the west is an outwork, a massive earthwork formed by a bank and ditch, 30m wide and 3m high. Another bank links the outwork to the main enclosure on the south, with that bank, the outwork and the west side of the main enclosure forming a large, rectangular area. The northern side may have been enclosed by a wooden palisade or fence. This enclosure could have been used for all sorts of things, perhaps ritual, perhaps agricultural. It may have been a special field, for seed corn, herbs or medicinal plants. It may have been used for animals: horses, ponies, dogs, poultry and ducks, falcons, house cows, goats, milking ewes or a mixture of all of these. All sorts of craft activities may have been carried out here: the manufacture of pottery, textiles, wooden tubs and barrels.

Ruborough Camp has been described variously as a hill-slope fort (Grinsell 1970, 91), a univallate enclosure (Grinsell 1976, 19), a

Fig 3.3
Ruborough Camp:
southern rampart and
ditch. (Hazel Riley)

strongly defended hilltop enclosure (Burrow 1982, fig 9.2), a promontory fort (NMR ST 23 SW 1), and a large univallate hillfort (Somerset HER 10228). All of these descriptions and classifications have their strengths and weaknesses. In some ways, Ruborough Camp is the site that defies classification. A promontory fort generally suggests a spur of land cut off by an earthwork, not the case here. On the one hand, it is an enclosure on a hill slope, with an outwork upslope of it – very similar to the hill-slope enclosures of nearby Higher Castles or Myrtleberry Camp South on Exmoor (Riley and Wilson-North 2001, 65–73). On the other hand, the size of the enclosure and the scale of the earthworks suggest that we are looking at something different from the enclosed farmsteads suggested by the hill-slope enclosures recorded on Exmoor. Ruborough Camp is built on a hill slope, but its enclosure earthworks are of a scale generally associated with hillforts.

Ruborough Camp was constructed about the middle of the 1st millennium BC, probably between 600 and 300 BC. It may have functioned as an enclosed or defended settlement for a number of people or families, and the outer enclosure could also have been used for settlement or for other purposes such as a stock pound. Many other activities relating to everyday life may have been carried out at Ruborough, as well as trade, the practice of ritual and warfare. It could be that Ruborough Camp, situated right on the edge of what became the tribal area of the Dumnonii, was constructed in part to give a statement of ownership and identity to the people who occupied the land to the east of the River Parrett. We do not know when the site was abandoned, but the fact that a well-defined hollow-way leads up to the site suggests that the place was visited for many hundreds of years. In fact Ruborough is named in documents dating from the 9th and 10th centuries (Burrow 1981, 48).

At Cannington, some 7km to the north of Ruborough Camp, the hillfort and settlement to the south have produced Iron Age and Roman material, and a late Roman or early post-Roman shrine or mausoleum has been identified on the hilltop (Burrow 1981; Rahtz 1969; Rahtz *et al* 2000). A hint at post-Roman occupation at Ruborough Camp lies on the top of the rampart on the west side of the enclosure where the remains of a small building, 10m long and 4m wide, can be seen. It is difficult to be certain about the function of this building. A small ruinous building inside the hillfort of Mounsey Castle on Exmoor was interpreted as a charcoal burner's hut (Riley and Wilson-North 2001, 64). However, Ruborough Camp has been part of a farming landscape for more than 200 years, and the woodland here seems to be of relatively recent origin. The earthwork remains seem to be earlier than the plantation and the stone out barn in the ditch below. The building may relate to the use of the site for agriculture in the post-medieval period. It could equally be of some antiquity and could be an important survival from earlier in the historic period, when we do not know how Ruborough Camp was used.

Dowsborough Camp

Dowsborough Hill can be seen from most of the vantage points on the Quantock Hills: Black Hill, Wills Neck, Great Wood and Hare Knap all offer views of a wooded, slightly domed, isolated hill that rises to some 340m OD at its eastern end. The Iron Age hillfort, however, cannot be seen until you walk up through the woods and see the massive earthworks at close quarters, although when viewed from the air, before the oak trees are in full leaf, the earthworks come into focus (Fig 3.4).

During the earlier part of the Bronze Age a large round barrow was erected on the western end of the hill. Sometime in the 1st millennium BC a local tribe began the labour of digging the earthworks that now enclose the whole of the hilltop. These are a rampart, ditch and counterscarp bank, 20m wide and 5m high, which form an elongated egg-shaped enclosure of 1.6ha in area. The enclosure does not sit centrally on the summit of Dowsborough Hill, which is not completely enclosed by the earthworks (Fig 3.5). This was probably a deliberate choice by the hillfort builders, who made visitors to the site climb up the very steepest slopes to get to the only entrance. The interior of the site slopes away gently to the west to take in the Bronze Age barrow, which now sits very close to the hillfort ramparts (Fig 3.5). This, again, must have been a deliberate choice by the hillfort builders. They seem to have respected the barrow, as it still retains much

Fig 3.4
Dowsborough Camp: the hillfort lies in oak woodland but is still visible from the air. (NMR 21136/02) (© English Heritage. NMR)

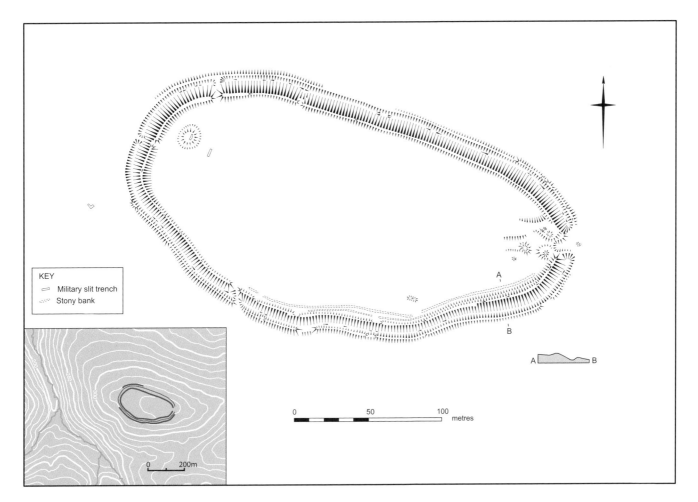

KEY
Military slit trench
Stony bank

0   50   100
                      metres

0   200m

A ▬ B

of its original form – the slit trenches on and around the monument date from the use of Dowsborough Hill as a military training ground in the 20th century (*see* Chapter 6). The barrow may even have been used as a marker when the hillfort was under construction. Its presence suggests that the hilltop was a favoured spot from the early 2nd millennium BC onwards and that the mounds of the dead were still known of and respected by the Iron Age tribes more than 1,500 years later.

Today, the easy path up to the hilltop is from the south, and a well-used track has forced a way through the earthworks on this side of the hillfort. The ascent from the east, however, is steepest and leads straight to the only Iron Age entrance on the rather pointed east end of the enclosure. The entrance has been disturbed and only the southern rampart and ditch terminals survive in their original form (Fig 3.5). The area immediately behind the entrance contains three large circular hollows, with several smaller hollows scattered around. Two of the larger hollows lie behind the rampart

terminals. These have been variously interpreted as a watch tower and fire beacon pits (Nichols 1891), fire hearths (Page 1890, 291) and circular guardhouses (Somerset HER 33306). Similar features occur at the eastern entrance to the hillfort of Cadbury Congresbury in north Somerset (Fowler *et al* 1970), where they have been interpreted as late Roman or post-Roman additions to the entrance (Burrow 1981, 68).

The examples here at Dowsborough have the appearance of quarry pits rather than of building remains, although the possibility exists that the hollows are collapsed structures that have subsequently been dug into. If this is correct, then by analogy with Cadbury Congresbury, there could have been late Roman or post-Roman occupation at Dowsborough Camp. The hollows may well be the remains of extraction pits or trial pits, here for copper ore – the copper mine at Dodington is only 2km to the northeast. Such trial pits in or around prehistoric earthworks are common on Exmoor, for example at the Iron Age enclosure of Myrtleberry North, where ironstone was

Fig 3.5
Dowsborough Camp:
location and earthwork
plan. (Based on an
Ordnance Survey map,
with permission.
© Crown copyright.
All rights reserved)

Fig 3.6
Crowcombe Church:
dragon bench end.
(AA053347) (© English
Heritage. NMR)

sought, and on the Mendip Hills, for example around the Priddy Circles, where lead ore was the prize. Ore prospectors or miners in the historic period looked for the earthwork remains of former mining and occasionally mistook prehistoric earthworks for old mining sites (*see* Chapter 5).

The whole of the hillfort is now clothed in sessile oak, coppiced up until the beginning of the 20th century (Fig 3.4). Woodland was certainly present on Dowsborough by 1620, when 80 acres of coppice were included in an area subject to common rights for sheep pasture, and by 1812 there was oak coppice on and inside the ramparts, with hill grazing outside (Dunning 1992, 172).

A dragon legend has strong associations with Dowsborough Camp. The dragon was the Great Worm of Shervage Wood, a huge, serpent-like creature who lived in the woods at Dowsborough Camp. The dragon was known to have eaten at least three men and most of the wild ponies in the area. One day a stranger (from Stogumber, three miles away) arrived in Crowcombe. He was persuaded to go up to Dowsborough to pick worts (bilberries) for an old lady in the village. The stranger sat on a log to eat his bread and cheese and felt the log move under him. He realised it was a dragon and slew the beast with his axe, cutting it in two. A fine carving from the early 16th century of the men of Crowcombe slaying a dragon still remains on a bench end in the parish church (Fig 3.6). Dragon legends are also associated with Norton Fitzwarren Camp, where the village church contains some remarkable carvings of the story (Wright 2002).

Bicknoller Hill

The summit of Bicknoller Hill is covered with the banks of relict field systems, which date from the historic period. A massive bank and ditch runs across the narrowest part of the spur, and the banks of the relict field system can be clearly seen running over this earthwork (Fig 3.7). A bank, ditch and counterscarp run for some 120m on the southwest edge of the spur. These two elements, combined with the very steep slopes to the north and south of the spur, form an enclosure on the top of the spur, enclosing an area of some 2.25ha (Fig 3.8). This sort of enclosure may never have been completed, it may have relied on the very steep slopes of the hill to define the north and south sides, or the rest of the enclosure may have been defined by fences or hedges. Incomplete or unfinished enclosures and hillforts are not uncommon in southwest England, for example Shoulsbury Castle on Exmoor and Elworthy Barrows on the east edge of the Brendon Hills (Silvester and Quinnell 1993).

Before the discovery of the rest of the enclosure, it was suggested that the linear

earthwork was in some way associated with the hill-slope enclosure known as the Trendle Ring. However, this explanation was never very satisfactory, as the Trendle Ring lies on a subsidiary spur to the south-west, and the linear earthwork does not define or defend this lower spur. Also, an explanation of the linear earthwork as

defining a Bronze Age ritual area is difficult, as there are no known funerary monuments on the spur end, although cultivation here in the historic period may have removed such evidence (*see* Chapters 4 and 5). The earthworks are best interpreted as a probable unfinished hilltop enclosure or hillfort.

Fig 3.7
Bicknoller Hill: the earthworks of an unfinished hilltop enclosure are overlain with narrow ridge and furrow ploughing. The Trendle Ring lies to the west (top). (NMR 21513/23) (© English Heritage. NMR)

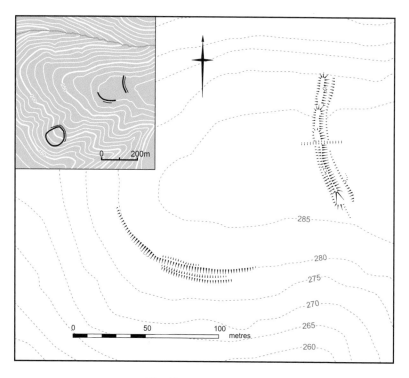

Fig 3.8
Bicknoller Hill: location
and earthwork plan.
(Based on an Ordnance
Survey map, with
permission. © Crown
copyright. All rights
reserved)

Enclosures

The term enclosure is a useful catch all term for a group of sites that range from small stock pounds, only tens of metres in size, to large settlements, enclosed by substantial earthworks. The need for enclosure in the landscape is a basic need: for keeping animals in or out of an area; for defining one's property or land holding and, as we have already seen (*see* Chapter 2), to define a special or sacred place. Some enclosures date to as far back as the Neolithic Period; some were made in the medieval period. In the landscape of southwest England enclosures are numerous and survive in the archaeological record either as upstanding stony banks or extant earthworks – banks and ditches – or as cropmarks. The stone and earthwork sites survive because they were built in the upland areas of southwest England, for example on Exmoor, Dartmoor and Bodmin Moor, where later land use has resulted in their survival.

Enclosures were not just built in these upland areas. A great deal of the lower ground has been cultivated for many hundreds, if not thousands, of years. When an earthwork bank and ditch falls into disuse the bank begins to erode into the ditch; cultivation of such a site will speed up this process, dragging the bank down into the ditch, until the bank is flattened and the ditch is level with the ground surface. The

deep fill of the ditch is rich in plant nutrients and is less prone to drought in periods of dry weather. Hence such sites can be seen from the air as cropmarks and it is the identification of such sites from aerial photographs that has transformed our ideas about the population density of parts of Britain in the later prehistoric and Roman periods during the past 30 or so years. In southwest England new sites have come to light around Dartmoor (Griffith 1994) and on the southern fringes of the Quantock Hills (Griffith and Horner 2000), where the cropmark sites have been studied by the SQAS project.

Most of the enclosures identified in the archaeological record are agricultural settlements, and sometimes the traces of field systems can also survive. Cropmark sites can often reveal a complicated pattern of enclosures cutting earlier features, and then themselves being overlain by yet more enclosures (Fig 3.9). Excavations at a number of sites across southwest England have shown that a substantial number of enclosures date from the 1st millennium BC, although there is a growing body of evidence that places their origins in the later part of the 2nd millennium BC (*see* Chapter 2). Some of these sites were occupied for hundreds of years, others for only a short time, or intermittently. It is also difficult to generalise about when these sites fell into disuse. In Cornwall many enclosures were occupied through the Iron Age and Roman periods and into the early medieval period. Somerset and east Devon were on the very edge of Romanised Britain, and it is here that we see instances of Iron Age settlement sites built over with high status Roman settlements – villas.

Hill-slope enclosures

Hill-slope enclosures are a common type of site in southwest England and south Wales. They are perfectly named, being enclosures located on hill slopes. The enclosures are formed of quite substantial earthwork banks and ditches and they vary greatly in size and shape. The Exmoor examples are generally under one hectare in area, while Clovelly Dykes in north Devon is more than 8ha in area. Owing to their location, the enclosures are not readily defensible, as they are overlooked from the upslope side, but the scale of the earthworks has invoked such an explanation in the past. On Exmoor several hill-slope

Fig 3.9
Cropmark complex at
Yarford. (DAP 6895/07)
(F M Griffith 1990.
© Devon County Council)

enclosures contain evidence for settlement inside them, often a single roundhouse towards the centre or at the upper end of the enclosure, for example at Bagley and Roborough (Riley and Wilson-North 2001, 65), and such sites may be interpreted as enclosed farmsteads, the home of a family group or extended family. Some of the larger enclosures, such as Clovelly Dykes and Milber Down in north Devon, have multiple enclosures and these have been interpreted as concerned with agriculture, specifically cattle management (Fox 1952). There is very little excavation evidence from these sites. Like the more general enclosures discussed above, they are common in the 1st millennium BC, but some had their origins in the 2nd millennium BC, and activity at such sites may well have continued into the Roman and post-Roman periods (below and Chapter 4).

The hill-slope enclosures of the Quantock Hills

There are four hill-slope enclosures surviving as earthworks on the Quantock Hills. These are the Trendle Ring, Plainsfield (or Cockercombe) Camp, Higher Castles (or Broomfield Camp) and Rooks Castle. As part of the project, all of these sites were surveyed at large scale (Appendix 2). Several other hill-slope enclosures, surviving only as cropmarks, have been identified from aerial photographs (Fig 3.1).

The Trendle Ring

The Trendle Ring is the best known of these sites. It is located in a very extreme topographic location, on a steeply sloping spur on the southwest edge of Bicknoller Hill, overlooking the village of Bicknoller. The sub-rectangular enclosure is defined by a bank and ditch on its north and east sides, and by a steep scarp on its west and south sides, giving an interior of 0.7ha. The interior was originally accessed through a gap in the east side, a way up to the enclosure from Bicknoller runs through the lower part of the enclosure from southeast to northwest. Two level areas, formed by cutting into the hill slope, can be seen just inside the bank on the northern side of the enclosure. The size and morphology of the earthworks suggest that the Trendle Ring was constructed in the later prehistoric period, but its function remains a matter for discussion.

The most striking things about the Trendle Ring are its location – perched above Bicknoller and clearly visible from the valley of the Doniford stream for several miles – and the fact that the area it encloses is so

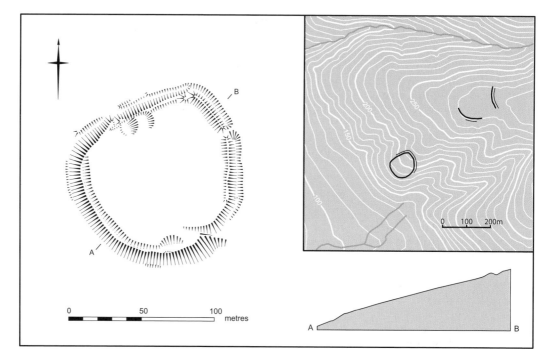

steep (Front cover and Fig 3.10). The ground height falls from 206m OD to 169m OD (37m in total) over a distance of 100m (Fig 3.10). This would make settlement inside the enclosure impractical, yet the two level platforms do look like building platforms. Furthermore, a geophysical survey of part of the interior has helped to suggest a date and function for the enclosure (Papworth 2004). This showed that the lower of the two areas probably contained a circular building, lending support

to their interpretation as stances for prehistoric round houses. The geophysical survey also showed two phases of cultivation, both later than the building platforms. The Trendle Ring is shown as an enclosure on a map of 1802, suggesting that it was in use, probably as a stock enclosure, until quite recently (OS 1802).

The earthwork and geophysical survey evidence do suggest that the enclosure contained buildings in the later prehistoric period. Perhaps the buildings were for

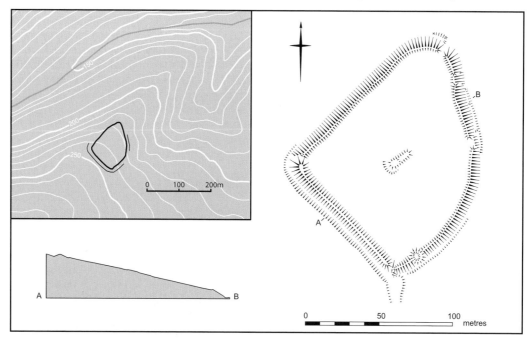

people who used the enclosure for livestock management, as it is difficult to envisage the site as an enclosed settlement or farmstead. The location of the Trendle Ring, overlooking the valley of the Doniford Stream and the approaches to Exmoor, and the fact that the site can be seen from these places, suggest that the enclosure earthworks functioned in both a symbolic and a practical way.

Plainsfield Camp

Plainsfield Camp lies on a spur on the south side of Cockercombe, at a height of 225m OD (Fig 3.11).The site now lies within Great Wood, but still commands spectacular views to the east, across the Levels and Moors to the Mendip Hills. The sub-rectangular enclosure of 1.2ha is formed by a massive bank and ditch, with an entrance at the northeast angle and a possible blocked entrance on the east side (Fig 3.11). Plainsfield Camp lies on a steep slope, but by no means as steep as the Trendle Ring. It is easier to believe that this enclosure functioned as a farmstead, although evidence for building platforms is not as clear as at the Trendle Ring, with a possible location close to the northwest rampart. This lack of remains in the interior is due to the fact that the enclosure has been used for various activities during the historic period. In the medieval period the enclosure lay with Plainsfield Park, and a pillow mound (artificial rabbit warren, Chapter 4) was constructed in its centre. In the post-medieval period cultivation of the interior occurred, and in the 19th and 20th centuries the enclosure was planted with trees.

Rooks Castle

Rooks Castle lies on the southwest edge of a small plateau at a height of 170m OD, overlooking a long valley formed by King's Cliff stream, a tributary of the River Parrett. The stream rises in the hill country around Broomfield, and the valley is some 3kms long. To the west a small combe leads down into the main valley, to the south the ground falls away steeply into the valley. The more level ground of the plateau top lies directly to the east and north (Fig 3.12). Despite its name, the site at Rooks Castle was only identified recently, when it was seen on aerial photographs by Anthony Locke before 1970 and described by Grinsell as 'a univallate hill-spur enclosure of about 2 acres, well preserved on the west and south sides, and normally under pasture. There is a possible outwork less than 100yd to the east' (Grinsell 1970, 91). In his later publication of prehistoric sites on the Quantock Hills, Grinsell is more cautious, omitting it from the distribution map and calling it a 'puzzling site....until a trial excavation has been done here it seems preferable to suspend judgement' (Grinsell 1976, 19). The site was investigated and surveyed by Ian Burrow, who identified two elements: 'the west and north sides of a hill-slope enclosure, and the remains of the documented medieval tile quarry' (1980, 124). The aerial photographs and the remains on the ground show two different sorts of earthwork enclosures, one much clearer than the other (Figs 3.12 and 3.13). The well defined, D-shaped enclosure to the west is medieval in date (see Chapter 4). The more blurred earthworks to the east are the ploughed-over remains of a sub-rectangular enclosure, with a large, oval enclosure joined onto its east side. The whole complex encloses an area of 1ha. Access to these enclosures was on the east side, seen on aerial photographs but not clear on the ground (compare the aerial photograph with the earthwork plan, Figs 3.12 and 3.13).

The complex is a good example of a small, later prehistoric agricultural settlement. The inner enclosure formed a safe, stockproof area for the farmhouse and outbuildings, here probably a large roundhouse of timber and thatch with timber structures for housing poultry, pigs and fowl, and raised wooden platforms for storing cereal

Fig 3.12
Rooks Castle: the slight earthworks of the prehistoric enclosure lie to the east (right) of a later enclosure. (RAF: CPE/UK/1944 FR.2034) (English Heritage (NMR) RAF photography)

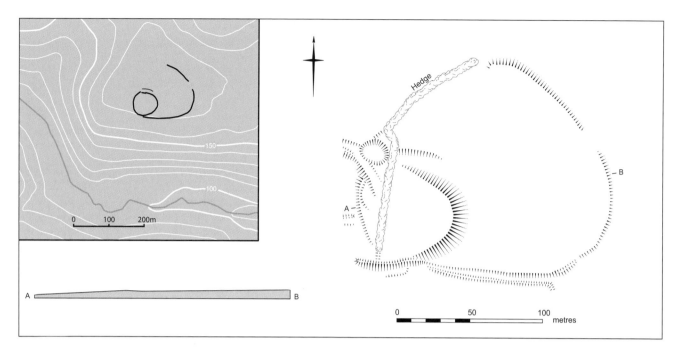

*Fig 3.13 (above)
Rooks Castle: location and
earthwork plan. (Based on
an Ordnance Survey map,
with permission.*

crops. As at Ruborough Camp, the outer enclosure could have been used for a number of activities. In this more domestic setting the enclosure probably had a role in managing the livestock – cattle, pigs, sheep, goats – or it may have been where the best grain was grown.

Higher Castles

Higher Castles lies on a small spur of land between two combes, at a height of 230m OD, with extensive views across the Vale of Taunton to the Brendon Hills and the Blackdown Hills. The ground falls away steeply to the south, with gentler slopes

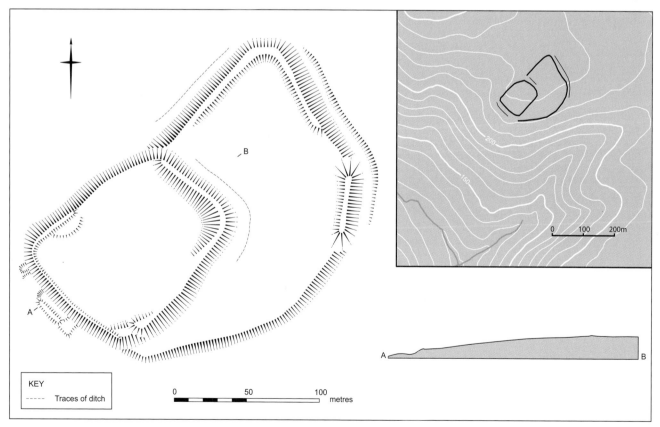

KEY
----- Traces of ditch

down to the combes on the western and eastern sides of the site. The land to the north rises very gradually (Fig 3.14). The tithe award for Broomfield parish (1838) gives the name 'Castles' for both of the fields occupied by the site. However, it was not until *c* 1950 that an archaeological site was recognised here, when Dr H W Catling identified a site from aerial photographs (Pytches 1964, 188).according to Grinsell, the site was also recognised by Anthony Locke at about the same time (Grinsell 1970, 91). An exploratory excavation was carried out by King's College, Taunton,

Archaeological Society on the 17th and 18th of May, 1964. A section 50ft long was dug close to the western angle of the enclosure. This revealed a U-shaped ditch more than 8ft deep and 12ft wide cut into the solid rock outside the bank. Part of the ditch fill was composed of loose rocks, which the excavators interpreted as a wall that originally stood on top of, or in front of, the bank. Two pieces of Iron Age pottery were found in the ditch; further unstratified finds of pottery and charcoal were also noted. The excavation was published as a short note in 1964, but no plans or sections were

Fig 3.14 (opp, bottom)
Higher Castles: location and earthwork plan. (Based on an Ordnance Survey map, with permission. © Crown copyright. All rights reserved)

Fig 3.15 (below)
Higher Castles: the prehistoric enclosure lies to the bottom left, the open summit of Cothelstone Hill is at the top. (NMR 21531/04)
(© English Heritage. NMR)

included in this publication (Pytches 1964). Ian Burrow located the original excavation plan and section at Taunton College, and these were subsequently redrawn and published by Dennison (1987).

Higher Castles is similar in form to the enclosures at Rooks Castle. An inner sub-rectangular enclosure has an outer, kidney-shaped enclosure joined onto its east side, with the whole complex covering an area of 2.2ha (Fig 3.14). Only the southwest side of the inner enclosure has escaped plough damage, but the earthworks are still substantial (Fig 3.15). The position of the entrance to the inner enclosure is difficult to discern on account of the ploughing, it may have been on its east or southeast side. An entrance can even be seen on the east side of the ploughed-over outer enclosure, this is probably the original entrance to the complex. Like Rooks Castle, Higher Castles is a good example of an enclosed, agricultural settlement, with an inner enclosure for the farmstead and an outer enclosure for other activities. There is evidence from Dartmoor and Exmoor that iron working was carried out at some of these sites. It may be that at the larger site of Higher Castles more specialised tasks were carried out by the groups of people who lived here: spinning and weaving, making tools of wood and iron, making pottery, baskets, jewellery, making buttons and toggles from bone and antler, making boots, belts, straps and cloaks from leather and trading these goods, as well as the busy daily round of self-sufficient farming (Fig 3.16).

The evidence from cropmark sites

When Grinsell compiled his list of prehistoric sites in the Quantock Hills in 1976, new earthwork sites, such as Higher Castles and Rooks Castle, were being discovered on aerial photographs. As land continues to be cultivated, and as the techniques of aerial photographic reconnaissance and interpretation advance, more sites are being discovered in the form of cropmarks. The cropmark sites described and discussed here were all transcribed by Helen Winton as part of the National Mapping Programme for the Quantock Hills AONB (see Chapter 1). The distribution of cropmark enclosures for the whole of the Quantock Hills is shown on Fig 3.1. Obviously, such cropmarks will only show on arable fields under suitable conditions, hence the concentration of sites on the fertile soils in the Vale of Taunton, between Taunton and Bishops Lydeard and the edge

of the hills. However, such cropmark enclosures do occur all around the hills, with the notable exception of the coastal strip. The underlying geology is the same (Fig 1.4); local climatic factors may affect the visibility of buried sites from the air, or it may be that this area would repay further aerial reconnaissance work. The gap in the record may be real, in which case we may be looking at the beginnings of the large coastal manors well before they are recorded in the historic period (see Chapter 4).

At the foot of the western scarp of the Quantock Hills are several sub-rectangular enclosures at Rich's Holford and around Lydeard St Lawrence; farther north is a complex at Lower Weacombe. East of the hills there are examples around Dyche near Holford and around Goathurst and Huntstile. The greatest concentration of cropmark sites, however, lies on the south and southeast slopes of the hills. There are four main groups of cropmark sites: around Bishops Lydeard; between Staplegrove and Upper Cheddon; between Clavelshay and Thurloxton, and between Hestercombe and Broomfield (Fig 3.1).

A complex of cropmark features lies on the very gentle, southwest-facing slopes of the River Tone at an altitude of 50–40m OD, between Bishops Lydeard and Norton Fitzwarren (Fig 3.17). The complex

Fig 3.16 (opposite) Reconstruction of life in the Iron Age at Higher Castles. (© Jane Brayne)

Fig 3.17 Settlements and field systems, Dene Cross. (Based on an Ordnance Survey map, with permission. © Crown copyright. All rights reserved)

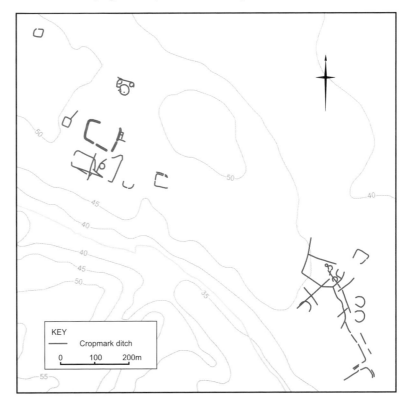

KEY

—— Cropmark ditch

0   100   200m

Fig 3.18
Settlements and field
systems, Upper Cheddon.
(Based on an Ordnance
Survey map, with
permission. © Crown
copyright. All rights
reserved)

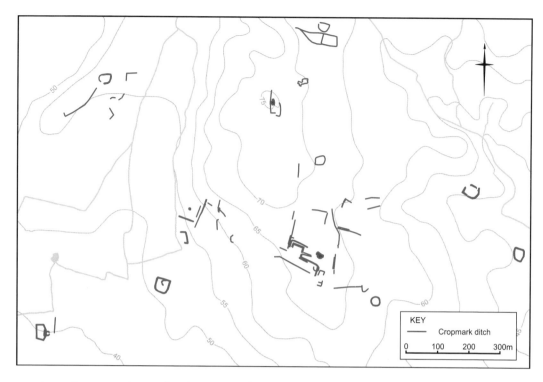

KEY

—— Cropmark ditch

0   100   200   300m

consists of rectangular and sub-rectangular enclosures, together with some linear features, and three small, regular, circular enclosures. The latter are probably ring ditches, the remains of ploughed-over barrows (*see* Chapter 2). The cropmarks can be divided into three main areas. North of Dene Cross is a sub-circular enclosure, 20m in diameter, associated with three smaller enclosures, linked by a ditch and approached by a track. These small enclosures are the remains of individual buildings, probably all round houses, and one is later than the larger enclosure (Fig 3.17). Four larger, more regular rectangular enclosures lie between Dene Cross and Dene Court. The largest is 100m by 50m and has an entrance gap on its south side. A circular enclosure may be a further ring ditch. Two smaller sub-rectangular enclosures may be enclosed settlements. Between The Firs and Longlands Farm is a small, regular, rectangular enclosure; to its south are a complex of linear features – the remains of a settlement and field system, approached by a double-ditched trackway.

Between Nailsbourne and Cheddon Fitzpaine, on gentle, south-facing slopes at *c* 50–65m OD are numerous small rectangular and sub-rectangular cropmark enclosures and fields. There are eight or nine sub-circular enclosures, mostly about 50m in diameter; one of these may be associated with a ring ditch. Towards the east of the complex is a far more regular rectangular enclosure, together with the remains of small fields and paddocks with tracks and paths linking fields and the rectangular enclosure (Fig 3.18).

To the north of these is a series of much larger hill-slope enclosures, mostly defined by cropmarks, one as extant earthworks (Fig 3.19). Nine of these large, sub-circular enclosures lie on the southern slopes of the Quantock Hills between Broomfield and Hestercombe. The enclosures differ from those described above in their size and morphology. The largest are ovoid or sub-rectangular in shape, and range in size from 0.4ha (Broomfield) to 1.3ha (Oggshole). The regular, ovoid enclosure at Hestercombe has two ditches. The sub-rectangular earthwork enclosure of Higher Castles has an annexe; and so does the probable cropmark enclosure north of Hazelmere Farm. Two slightly smaller, rectangular enclosures are included in this group: Volis Farm South has two ditches; Volis Farm North has two ditches and a complex of linear features around it. There are several small, rectangular enclosures around Upper Cheddon and Volis Farm and what appears to be a small settlement and field system west of Kingston Beacon. A small field system, and a paired rectangular enclosure and ring ditch lie to the west of Yalway Farm.

A complex of cropmark sites is grouped around Rooks Castle and Clavelshay, west of

Thurloxton (Fig 3.20). At Rooks Castle, a mixture of earthwork evidence and crop-marks shows two hill-slope enclosures (Rooks Castle and Kings Cliff Cottage) and two small sub-rectangular enclosures. South of this, between Clavelshay and Thurloxton, are 22 or 23 small rectangular and sub-rectangular enclosures. One has a complex entrance, comparable to the banjo enclosures on the Wessex chalk, where they are seen as high-status settlements. Others show detail indicating smaller enclosures joined to the main one or extra features associated with agricultural activity. There is also evidence for the phasing of enclosures and for trackways and field systems. Good examples of complex sites also occur away from the main concentration of cropmarks on the south edge of the Quantock Hills. South of Goathurst an enclosure is overlain by a later

KEY
— Cropmark ditch
— Earthwork

0   500m

Fig 3.19
Hillslope enclosures around Broomfield. (Based on an Ordnance Survey map, with permission.

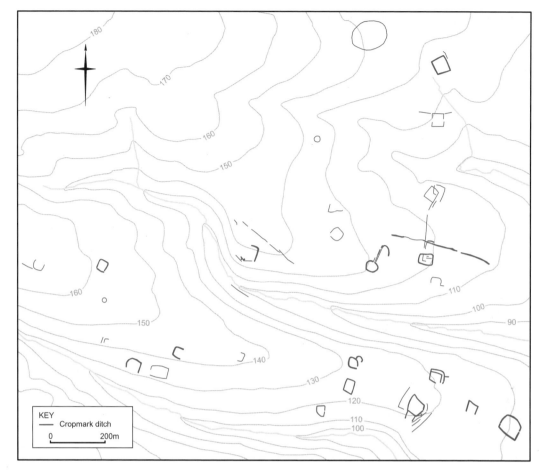

KEY
— Cropmark ditch
0   200m

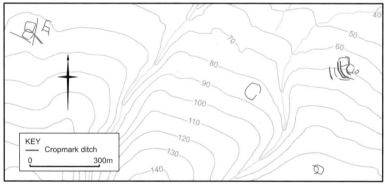

KEY
— Cropmark ditch
0   300m

enclosure and elements of trackways and fields can be seen (Fig 3.21). East of Huntstile are two double-ditched enclosures, one cut by a large linear feature. A much smaller, regular, rectangular enclosure lies close by. At Lower Weacombe a small oval enclosure is overlain by rectangular fields.

The evidence from excavation

Cropmark enclosures are difficult to date without additional information, such as finds recovered from fieldwalking or from excavations. Very few of the cropmark sites

in west Somerset had been excavated until recently. It was to look at the dates and functions of the cropmark enclosures on the southern edge of the Quantock Hills that the SQAS was instigated in 2000, by St Alfred's College, Winchester. Five areas of cropmarks between Cothelstone and Kingston St Mary have been investigated, resulting in several surprising discoveries.

Yarford

Excavations of a complex of field systems and enclosures (Fig 3.9) on a south-facing slope north of Yarford Farm showed that this area was used at different times for different activities for more than 1,000 years. In the early Iron Age, or perhaps even earlier than this, a series of regular, rectangular enclosures – fields – were laid out on this slope and these have been interpreted as for stock management. A few hundred years later, a funnel-shaped enclosure delineated a space used for ceremony or ritual. Large quantities of Middle or Late Iron Age pottery were found in the ditch of this enclosure. This was not simply a deposit of rubbish, as most of the pots were complete vessels and the deposit was sealed with red and grey clays that were not local to the area. At the very end of the Iron Age a sub-circular enclosure was constructed. This was an impressive feature, originally defined by two banks and two deep ditches, and the people who lived here used high-status pottery. This enclosure was deliberately back-filled, and in the 3rd century AD another high-status community lived here: a small Roman villa was built over the northeast corner of the enclosure (Wilkinson *et al* 2003) (*see below*).

Volis Hill

This enclosure is part of the remarkable series of sites that climb the lower slopes of the Quantock Hills from Kingston St Mary up to Broomfield. Three sub-rectangular enclosures lie within 500m of each other and part of the central enclosure was excavated in 2002 (Fig 3.22). Evidence for occupation at this site lasted for more than 2,000 years. The earliest use of the site was in the Bronze Age (above), and by the Middle to Late Iron Age a substantial ditched enclosure with an impressive entrance lay on the hillside.

The people who lived here were iron-workers. Three small hearths with roasted iron ore, charcoal and slag from smithing were found inside the enclosure. The enclosure ditch was backfilled in the Roman period, but before this a rectangular outer ditch was dug, probably in the latter part of the 1st century AD, and a gateway was constructed. A cremation burial in a pot was put into the ditch in the late 1st century AD and the site was abandoned at some time after this (Thorpe 2002).

Ivyton Farm

If the interpretation of this site is correct, it turns some of our ideas about the function of cropmark enclosures as farmsteads and small fields upside-down. At Ivyton Farm a large circular enclosure was examined. Excavation showed that it was not actually circular, but was rather formed from a series of straight ditch segments, and that it was of late Iron Age date. The most striking feature was a large hollow inside the enclosure, which either pre-dated or was contemporary with it. This has been interpreted as a hole formed from the roots of a large tree – the sacred tree or one of the trees from a sacred grove? Near by, but not associated with the Iron Age site, a large rectangular enclosure was associated with nearby Roman ironworking (Roffey *et al* 2004).

Fig 3.22
Excavation of the prehistoric and Romano-British enclosures, Volis Hill. (Hazel Riley)

Toulton and Stoneage Barton

Three rectangular enclosures lay on gentle, southwest-facing slopes at *c* 75m OD, to the south of Toulton. One contained at least one Iron Age roundhouse, one had no interior features but produced pottery from the 1st and 2nd centuries AD, one was dated to the 3rd and 4th centuries AD. Geophysical surveys showed that these enclosures were only part of a larger field system. Taken together, this indicates the site of a farmstead with occupation and activity throughout the later Iron Age and Roman periods. Rectangular enclosures at Stoneage Barton were dated to the 3rd or 4th century AD, with the biggest surprise here being the discovery of a 7th-century cemetery (Webster and Brunning 2004) (*see* Chapter 4).

The Iron Age landscape

The evidence from extant earthworks, aerial photographs and from excavations shows that the Quantock Hills were well used during the Iron Age, and part of a landscape of small farms and fields, woods, upland pasture and marshy river valleys. To the north, the hills were dominated by the hillfort of Dowsborough, and a similar site on Bicknoller Hill was never completed. Given our very limited knowledge of the chronology of the area, perhaps these hillforts were the communal centres for the people who lived in the rather scattered small, enclosed farmsteads in the Doniford valley to the west and between Kilton and Nether Stowey to the east.

On the south side of the hills, around Broomfield and Kingston St Mary, a series of enclosures, some with their origins in the

Middle Bronze Age, were used in the Middle and Late Iron Age. Here, the numbers of sites suggest that the landscape was well populated by this time. Perhaps the communal activities carried out at hillforts were no longer seen as important, as people were now living and working in close proximity to one another. There were organised settlements and field systems on the lower slopes of the hills but something more than a south-facing aspect drew people to this area. The clue to this is in the name 'Lodes Lane', a lane that leads north up the hillside from Kingston St Mary to Broomfield. Numerous trial pits and shafts were dug in this area in search of copper, iron, lead and silver in the 18th century (*see* Chapter 5). The mineral resources of the area were probably part of the reason why there were so many high-status sites in this area in the later part of the 1st millennium BC. The need to enclose or defend farms and larger settlements becomes increasingly important during this time – the landscape was filling up. Access to both mineral resources and to the resources of heath, pasture and wood on the higher hills were factors in the siting of the hillforts and some of the larger hill-slope enclosures.

It seems that, rather like today, the northern side of the Quantock Hills was used differently from the south. We can imagine a landscape perhaps similar to that of today, with much of the higher ground a mixture of heath, scrub and pasture, and wooded valleys providing fuel and building material. South of Wills Neck and Aisholt the more forgiving topography meant that small farms and fields could be established on the east and west of the hills, while a combination of good farming land and mineral resources encouraged the growth of a dense population around Broomfield and Kingston St Mary in the 1st millennium BC.

Business as usual?
The Roman occupation

The Roman conquest of southwest England

In the summer of AD 43 the Roman army landed in southern England, perhaps in the Solent, perhaps at Richborough in Kent (Manley 2002, 7). This was the beginning of the conquest that brought much of Britain under Roman control, although parts of southeast England were, to a greater or lesser degree, already 'pre-Romanised' during the century leading up to the invasion led by Claudius. Historical sources suggest that the invading troops met with some resistance and Vespasian is said to have conquered two strong tribes and taken more than 20 native townships. These have been assumed to be hillforts of the Durotrigian tribe in Dorset and Somerset, refortified against a Roman attack, although the interpretation of the archaeological evidence for this remains open to discussion (Manley 2002, 25, 66–7).

By AD 47 Somerset was under Roman control, and all of the Iron Age tribes had been conquered or had surrendered. There is little evidence for military campaigning in the Dumnonii tribal area, and they may well have made peace with Rome to prevent an invasion. By AD 55 a new legionary fortress was built at Exeter, and several other forts were built within Dumnonian territory at this time. At Wiveliscombe a fort looked over the Quantock Hills and the Brendon Hills, and there was probably a signal station near Stogumber (Fig 3.23). These forts oversaw the local population. Although the Roman conquest brought a new government, the system of agriculture and local politics remained; but the centre of power for the Dumnonii now lay to the south west at Exeter – Isca Dumnoniorum (Leach 2001a).

The Romans were quick to take advantage of the mineral resources of southwest England. On Exmoor the scale and nature of Roman iron mining and smelting is such as to suggest military organisation. On the Mendip Hills a fort was built close to the lead and silver mines at Charterhouse and by AD 49 the Roman military produced and exported lead and silver from the Mendip mines. Private individuals had taken over metal production by AD 69–79, reflecting the stability of southwest England by this time. The Second Legion were moved out of Exeter by AD 66 or 67, and most of the other forts in southwest England were vacated by the early years of the next decade (Elkington 1976).

The Romans on the Quantock Hills

Until recently there was little evidence for a Roman presence in west Somerset. During the past 30 years, however, a large number of new Roman settlement sites have been found. These have been located on aerial photographs and through geophysical survey and excavation when land is examined in advance of development. These sites show that business as usual was the favoured state for both Britons and Romans. There is evidence from excavations that some of the small, enclosed agricultural settlements were occupied during the Iron Age and Roman periods. At Maidenbrook Farm, south of the Quantock Hills and north of Taunton, an Iron Age settlement was succeeded by a rectangular ditched enclosure. By the 2nd century AD there were both circular and rectangular buildings within the enclosure, and occupation carried on into the 4th century AD (Ferris and Bevan 1993). At Holway, south of Taunton, rescue excavations in advance of the M5 in 1972 revealed an extensive settlement occupied from the 1st to 4th centuries AD, with evidence of Iron Age occupation before this (Dawson *et al* 2001, 46). About a kilometre to the northwest, an excavation at Hillyfields revealed small fields laid out along the hilltop in the Iron Age, farmed by a nearby community, with continuity into the Roman period. In the 3rd century the site was reorganised and there was a new arrangement of plots with small, regular enclosures for houses and other buildings, and larger paddocks and kitchen gardens. Wheat and barley were grown, for bread, animal feed and malting, and an iron anvil showed that smithing work was carried out on the site (Leach 2001b).

The Quantock Hills lie on the very edge of the *civitas* of the Dumnonii, closer to the large and prosperous villa based estates around Ilchester than to the *civitas* capital at Isca Dumnorium (Exeter) (Fig 3.23). It is not surprising, then, that the area in and around the hills has produced two of the most westerly Roman villas in Somerset and several hoards of Roman coins.

Spaxton Roman villa

The remains of a Roman villa lie on the southeast edge of the Quantock Hills, between Enmore and Charlynch, on a gentle east-facing slope, close to the Durleigh Brook. The site is at an altitude of 50m OD and looks out across the Levels and Moors. The site was found by the farmer in 1962 and excavated in 1963–4. The main building had a range of rooms aligned east-west, one with an elaborate mosaic with a floral motif. A further range of buildings running north–south was also suggested. The few finds included pottery that dated from the 3rd and 4th centuries AD, nails and roof and floor tiles (Somerset HER 10802).

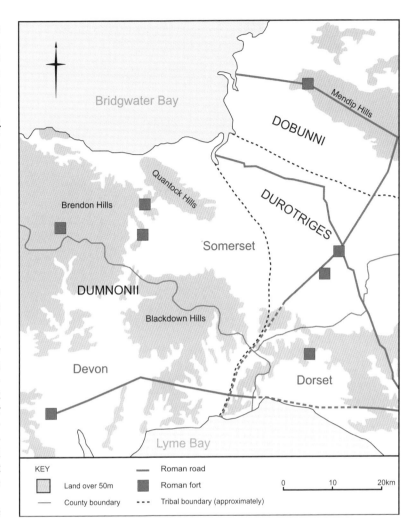

KEY
Land over 50m
County boundary
Roman road
Roman fort
Tribal boundary (approximately)
0 10 20km

Yarford Roman villa

Seven kilometres to the southwest, on a spur of gently sloping land above the hamlet of Yarford, is a complex of cropmarks (Fig 3.9). This was an area investigated by the SQAS in 2003. A detailed geophysical survey of the area showed a sub-circular, double-ditched enclosure, which, on excavation, proved to be of Iron Age date. The ditches of the enclosure were deliberately backfilled and contained Late Iron Age pottery. The remains of a stone building were found in the northeast corner of the enclosure. A platform was terraced into the hillside, built over part of the abandoned prehistoric enclosure and a substantial building constructed on this. The building proved to be a small Roman villa, of a type known as a corridor or portico villa (Fig 3.24). The main block of rooms was fronted by a portico and backed by a service block. A small outbuilding lay to the southwest and a badly robbed bath house lay to the southeast. The bath house was dismantled in the Roman period. The main room in

Fig 3.23
Roman forts, Roman roads and tribal areas at the end of the Iron Age. (After Leach 2001a, 8)

Fig 3.24
Excavation of the Roman
villa at Yarford. (The
University of Winchester)

room. An archway probably opened from this room onto the portico, with its stunning views over the Vale of Taunton beyond.

The mosaic floor was damaged at the very end of the Roman period or during the immediate post-Roman period. The wall plaster fell off and the walls were replastered, but the damaged mosaic was not repaired or replaced. The room was then used for different purposes: the floor shows evidence of burning and post holes were dug, suggesting a workshop or semi-industrial area with burnt antler and other debris. By the very late Roman period the villa was a mundane workshop. The coin sequence ends late in the 4th century AD, and it is not known if there was activity at the site into the 5th century (Wilkinson *et al* 2003; King 2004).

the villa, on its east end, contains a mosaic, making this site the westernmost Roman villa and mosaic in Somerset (Fig 3.24). The mosaic design is a grid of rectilinear panels containing large circular enclosures, with a cantharus (wine-mixing vessel) motif; this theme is normally associated with Bacchus and was appropriate for the dining room (Fig 3.25). The portico also had a mosaic floor. The Yarford mosaic dates from the 4th century AD, and was perhaps made by artisans from the workshops at Ilchester. This room was, then, very well appointed, with a mosaic and polychrome wall plaster, and must have been the main reception room or dining

Coin hoards

Just 5km to the northwest of the villa at Yarford another recent discovery of Roman material has been made. In 2001 a metal detectorist, scanning arable fields at West Bagborough, discovered a hoard of 4th-century Roman silver (Fig 3.26). The hoard contains 681 Roman silver coins and was buried *c* AD 365. Most of the coins were minted in the reigns of the emperors Constantius II and Julian and were manufactured in various places in the Roman Empire, including Arles, Lyon, Trier and

Fig 3.25
The central panel of the
mosaic at Yarford (10cm
scale). (The University of
Winchester)

Rome. The presence of unofficial copies struck from the same dies suggests that these were made locally. Found together with the coins were 73 pieces of hacksilver – scrap silver that has been melted down, poured out and cooled, then cut into pieces with a chisel and hammer. We do not know what the silver pieces were intended for, but the fact that each piece was a different weight suggests that they were intended for the manufacture of specific objects, perhaps pieces of jewellery. We also do not know why this hoard of silver was buried at West Bagborough. After the hoard was found, an archaeological excavation was undertaken at the findspot, but nothing was found to shed light on the mystery (information from Somerset County Museums Service website). The burial of one's savings as a coin hoard was a common practice in Roman Britain – there are some 2,000 recorded (Abdy 2002). The West Bagborough hoard may have been buried by a wealthy estate owner who failed, for some reason, to return and recover his or her savings.

Several large hoards of silver denarii were reported from the vicinity of the Quantock Hills in the 17th and 18th centuries. Two hoards were found in 1666. The description of the find records that 'Two large earthern pitchers, full of Roman medals, each 80 pounds Troy weight, were digged up by labourers with mattocks in ploughed fields' (quoted in Haverfield 1902, 343). The exact locations of these finds is now lost, but one was from Capton, south of Williton, the other from Lydeard St Lawrence. Two coin hoards are recorded from the northern end of the Quantock Hills, on the coastal strip. Again, their exact provenances are unknown; they may even be one and the same find.

A hoard of Roman coins, apparently from the mid-3rd century, was found near Kilton at the beginning of the 18th century and in the early 18th century a coin hoard of late 3rd-century date was found at Putsham (Collinson 1791). Page records Roman coins from the cairns on Lydeard Hill, but gives no further details (Page 1890, 265).

The Roman landscape

There is, then, plenty of evidence for the Roman landscape on and around the Quantock Hills (Fig 3.1). The Roman occupation of the area did not cause a massive disruption to the well-ordered and well-populated landscape at the end of the 1st millennium BC. There is evidence that many farmsteads and larger settlements carried on as before; centres of population grew up around the Roman garrisons, at Exeter and Ilchester, and along the roads that linked these towns to each other and to important resources. East of the Quantock Hills, towns became established at Combwich and Crandon Bridge on the River Parrett during the Roman period, but the dominant form of settlement was still the farmstead. We have

Fig 3.26
Part of the West Bagborough hoard of Roman silver.
(Somerset County Museums Service)

seen Roman agricultural sites near Taunton at Nerrols Farm, Maidenbrook Farm, Holway and Hillyfields, and to that list can be added several further sites discovered around North Petherton and Taunton as the M5 motorway was constructed (Dawson *et al* 2001). The excavation of samples of cropmarks has shown occupation throughout the Roman period on the south side of the Quantock Hills. Roman pottery, indicating the sites of such settlements, has been found in the fields around Norton Fitzwarren, and the hilltop site there was re-occupied during the 3rd and 4th centuries AD (Somerset HER 43397; 43398; 43402; 44483; Ellis 1989). Roman settlements have been identified on the coast at Hinkley Point and Doniford (Somerset HER 35283; 34176). At Hinkley Point a small farming settlement was occupied in the 3rd and 4th centuries AD, perhaps the same community who dug into Pixies Mound (*see* Chapter 2). At Doniford a Roman settlement was recorded as it eroded from the cliff edge. Near Williton, a field that contains several rectangular cropmark enclosures has produced Roman pottery (Somerset HER 34204).

The Quantock Hills lay on the very edge of Romanised Somerset. Around Ilchester and on the edge of the Polden Hills were the great villa based estates of south Somerset, but the south and southeast slopes of the Quantock Hills proved a successful place to live and work. As in preceding times, farms and fields occupied the area, but small-scale industry or craft manufacture was important, as shown by the evidence for ironworking at Norton Fitzwarren, Ivyton and Hillyfields. The area was close enough to Ilchester and Bath to be influenced by Roman culture: small towns and large villages grew up along roads and rivers to the east and south. In the 3rd century a wealthy person built a small but high status home overlooking the Vale of Taunton, on the site of a settlement that had been used some 300 years before. Parts of the landscape were, by now, filling up with people and their homes, with an ordered layout of arable and pasture land, woods and upland pastures to the north. By the 4th century the hilltops to the

east and south of the Quantocks were important as special places: temples have been excavated at Brean Down, Brent Knoll and Cadbury Castle. The laborious process of draining and reclaiming parts of the Somerset Levels and Moors began during the Roman period, but the Brue Valley was kept wet as salt production was undertaken there (Leach 2001a, 95–6).

There is evidence that the coastal strip was well used, with settlements at Hinkley Point and Doniford, but, surprisingly, no cropmark sites have been recorded so far from the arable fields of the area between Lilstock and West Quantoxhead. This may be a function of site visibility, or it may suggest that the origins of the medieval manors that occupied and shaped this coastal strip go back well beyond the historic period and this area could, conceivably, have functioned as a large estate that had access to good arable land, upland grazing and the sea.

The Quantock Hills are flanked by two hilltop sites that may have been used in the Roman period and later. To the east, close to the River Parrett and the Roman town at Combwich is the isolated knoll of limestone at Cannington. The hilltop has been visited and used for thousands of years. During the Iron Age a hillfort was constructed and a settlement established on the hillslope below. During the late Roman and post-Roman periods an important cemetery grew up below the hill, and there may have been some contemporary settlement on the hilltop (Rahtz *et al* 2000). On the coast at Daw's Castle, on the edge of Watchet, possible late Roman or post-Roman burials were recorded in the 19th century (Page 1890). Towards the end of the 4th century, the Roman Empire was no longer able to help Britain to maintain its security and independence in the face of invasion and rebellion.

By AD 410 Rome had severed its links with its former province, and the Romanised Britons were left to fend for themselves. In Somerset it was to be another 300 hundred years before the Anglo-Saxon kings established control of the area.

4

A managed landscape?
The Quantock Hills in the
medieval period

The migration and early medieval periods: Britons and Anglo-Saxons

The Dark Ages?
Evidence for the early medieval landscape AD 400–700

Traditionally known as the Dark Ages, this period of time between the end of Roman Britain and the establishment of Anglo-Saxon rule is one from which we have very little archaeological and historical evidence. Such evidence takes the form of early Christian (often called 'Celtic') church dedications, such as those to St Carantoc at Carhampton and to St Decuman at Watchet, and stones inscribed with pre-Saxon Christian symbols or memorial inscriptions, such as the Caratacus Stone on Exmoor. A type of fine pottery imported from North Africa and south Europe occurs in the archaeological record at this time. Dated to the 5th and 6th centuries AD, it is often associated with high-status, defended sites such as Tintagel in Cornwall. Hilltop sites were occasionally re-occupied in this period, and burial grounds or cemeteries, which have been identified as Christian, are found in western Britain. These cemeteries are characterised as Christian by their east–west grave orientation and by the lack of accompanying grave goods. Somerset has a particular concentration of such sites, and some are physically close to, or associated with, late Roman temples. At Carhampton, in between the Quantock Hills and Exmoor, excavations have uncovered an ironworking site associated with sherds of post-Roman imported pottery, probably of the 5th to 6th century AD (McCrone 1994). The Quantock Hills have, so far, only one site that can be definitely ascribed to this period, the post-Roman cemetery at Stoneage Barton (below).

It is hard to imagine the complete collapse of the thriving rural economy described above (*see* Chapter 3). However, it does seem that the withdrawal of Roman imperial administration caused an economic collapse, with ensuing political and social disruption. This is seen in the archaeological record at sites such as the Roman villa at Yarford, where the final use of the once grand, mosaic-floored dining room was as a workshop in the late Roman period, and at Maidenbrook Farm and Hinkley Point, where occupation of the farmsteads ended in the 4th century AD. It is worth pointing out, however, that very little pottery, such a good indicator of Roman rural settlement sites in the preceding centuries, is produced in this period in southwest England and that we do not know enough about the chronology of the cropmark enclosures, or, indeed, the earthwork enclosures (*see* Chapter 3) to make more than the broadest of generalisations.

In the 300 years between the end of the Roman period and the coming of the Anglo-Saxons, Somerset suffered a decline in population from the preceding centuries. The economy was organised around the estates of the leading men and women who managed to retain control of their land during this time of unrest, and some of these early estates have been tentatively identified, for example those centred at Congresbury, Brent Knoll and Cannington (Costen 1992, 61–5). Putting aside the myth and mystery of King Arthur, it does seem that, during this time, the threat of barbarian invaders across southern Britain led to warfare and the appearance of local rulers, one of whom set up a small state with its headquarters at Cadbury Castle. The common feature linking these sites is the presence of a hillfort. Several hilltop sites have been identified as probably used or occupied in the late Roman and post-Roman periods in Somerset (Burrow 1981), but those with unequivocal evidence from excavation are rather few in number. Imported pottery and glass from post-Roman features at Cadbury-Congresbury and Cadbury Castle suggest that important people lived at these particular centres.

There is no excavated material to indicate that any of the Iron Age hillforts and enclosures of the Quantock Hills were used in the post-Roman period. There is, however, a small amount of evidence to suggest that Dowsborough Camp and Ruborough Camp were used at this time. At Dowsborough, the earthwork evidence is equivocal but may hint at late Roman or post-Roman occupation in the east end of the hillfort (*see* Chapter 3). The names Rugan beorth and Ruwanbeorge from charters of 854 and 904 are names for Ruborough Camp, showing that the site was a recognised part of the 9th-century landscape (Burrow 1981, 48). The hollow-way leading to the east entrance suggests, at least, that the site was visited for many hundreds of years and a small building platform cut into the rampart could date from the early historic period (*see* Chapter 3).

West Somerset saw little trouble from the Anglo-Saxons until the later part of the 7th century. The traditional date of AD 658

for the defeat of the Britons at the battle of Penn (probably Penselwood near Wincanton) is in some doubt, but it does seem that by about AD 680 west Somerset was under Anglo-Saxon control and became part of the West Saxon kingdom (Costen 1992, 79–80).

The cemeteries at Stoneage Barton and Cannington

A sub-circular enclosure at Stoneage Barton, south of Cothelstone, was selected as one of the sites for the excavation of cropmark features as part of the SQAS project. Right at the end of this excavation a single, grave-shaped feature was noted, and its orientation, east–west, together with the presence of a stone lining suggested that it might be part of a post-Roman cemetery. Further excavations confirmed this.

In total, five graves were located (Webster and Brunning 2004). Grave 1 contained the degraded and fragmentary remains of a woman who was 35 to 50 years old. She was buried lying down, with her head to the west, in a stone-lined grave (Fig 4.1). Fragments of charcoal suggest the presence of a wooden coffin or grave lining. Grave 2, not excavated, lay immediately to the north; both were contained within a square, ditched enclosure with an entrance to the east. A few metres to the north of this enclosure was Grave 3, with post holes at three of its corners, a stone lining and evidence of a wooden coffin or grave lining. No bone was found and the grave lay within a square enclosure, very similar to that containing Graves 1 and 2. Grave 4 was only partially excavated and Grave 5 was a small stone-lined pit, which may have contained a child burial. The presence of further burials is suggested by a possible third enclosure at the southern edge of the excavated area. A bone from Grave 1 gave a radiocarbon date of AD 600–690.

Stone-lined graves have been found in many British post-Roman cemeteries, including Brean Down, where the stone-lined graves had stone markers (Bell 1990, 74–83) and Cannington where some graves had stone linings, a few had more substantial stone burial chambers (Rahtz *et al* 2000, 104–6). The presence of the square, ditched enclosures, however, makes the site at Stoneage Barton special, as only a few examples of post-Roman cemeteries with these enclosures are known. These sites are distributed over a wide area of Britain,

Fig 4.1
Part of the post-Roman cemetery at Stoneage Barton, Cothelstone. (After Webster and Brunning 2004, fig 2)

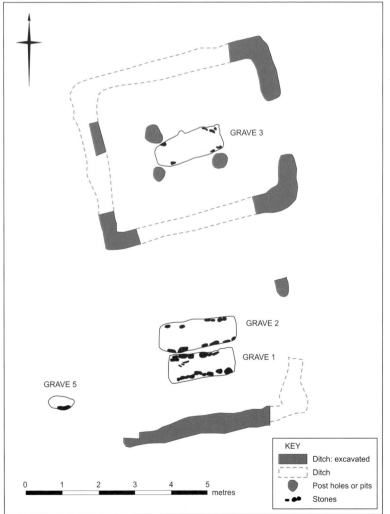

GRAVE 3

GRAVE 2

GRAVE 1

GRAVE 5

0 1 2 3 4 5 metres

KEY

Ditch: excavated

Ditch

Post holes or pits

Stones

across those areas that were outside Anglo-Saxon control before the 8th century. Within the cemeteries only a small number of graves had enclosures and it is suggested that the square-ditched burials were for high status individuals, copying the Roman practice of mausoleum burials (Webster and Brunning 2004, 73–9).

The burials from Stoneage Barton are an important piece of evidence to add to the small amount of information we have about the area at this time, suggesting that there was a high-status Dark Age settlement near by. The presence of the cemetery also hints that there may have been a late Roman shrine or temple site on the hills above: perhaps on Cothelstone Hill or Lydeard Hill, although the only evidence we have is a reference to Roman coins found in the cairns on Lydeard Hill (Page 1890). The holy well dedicated to St Agnes at Cothelstone shows the continued importance of the site in the medieval period.

The outlier of Carboniferous limestone at Cannington has been quarried for at least 150 years. During the quarrying operations large numbers of skeletons have been found, but it was not until the 1960s that systematic excavations of the remaining part of the site were carried out (Rahtz et al 2000). The excavator suggests that between 1,500 and 5,500 people were buried in a cemetery that may have begun as early as the late Roman period and was in use until about AD 700. These people may have lived in a single, nucleated community on and around the limestone hill, where the Iron Age hillfort provided a focus for activity. A more dispersed community could have included the hilltop together with small, scattered farmsteads and hamlets to the west and south of the River Parrett. In other words, these are the people who lived and worked on the large estate discussed above. Some of the people buried at Cannington had access to high-status goods such as glass and imported pottery, but none were buried within square enclosures like those at Stoneage Barton. The excavations uncovered artefacts and structures that showed that the cemetery was not just a place where the dead were buried. There was evidence of metalworking and the working of bone and antler. The antler was used to make the handles of iron-bladed knives and other tools, and given their presence in a cemetery, a place of continuous ritual practice, the possible association of antler with the pagan, horned god Cernunnos has been noted

(Leech 1980). One intriguing find was a stone mould for casting rings or parts of brooches (Rahtz et al 2000, fig 189). The stone, a silty shale, is probably from the Quantock Hills, perhaps from the Lower Devonian Lynton Series (see Chapter 1). This outcrops in a very limited area along the northwest edge of the hills, between Crowcombe and Bagborough Hill, close to the cemetery at Stoneage Barton.

The Anglo-Saxons: evidence for the early medieval landscape AD 700–1066

By the beginning of the 8th century AD west Somerset was firmly part of the West Saxon (Wessex) kingdom, a kingdom that was ruled from four counties: Hampshire, Wiltshire, Dorset and Somerset. There were important royal centres in Somerset at Glastonbury, Bath, Frome, Somerton and Cheddar. Excavations at Cheddar uncovered a royal palace, used by the kings of Wessex between 850 and 930. Here was a hall large enough to accommodate the king and his followers, lodgings, stables and barns (Rahtz 1979). There were no towns in Somerset in the 8th and 9th centuries, but manufacturing and trade took place in the royal centres: metalworking at Cheddar, for example. Towards the end of the 9th century King Alfred set up a system of burhs or fortified places to protect the whole of southern England against attacks from the Danes. Some burhs were simple refuges, others were planned as towns, showing the importance of trade by this time. We know from the survival of the document known as the Burghal Hidage – an administrative text that names the burhs and outlines the system set up for their maintenance and defence – that Watchet was one of the five burhs established in Somerset.

As well as the royal palaces at sites like Cheddar, it seems that several early royal centres or estates can be identified in Somerset and, in particular, the Quantock Hills are surrounded by a number of these sites (Fig 4.2). The very first Anglo-Saxon estates in Somerset were large and centralised, under the control of the king. This central authority was served by scattered hamlets and farmsteads whose people were subservient to it, both socially and economically. As time progressed, such large estates tended to become fragmented and smaller, but in Somerset the early pattern of large estates seemed to persist through the Anglo-

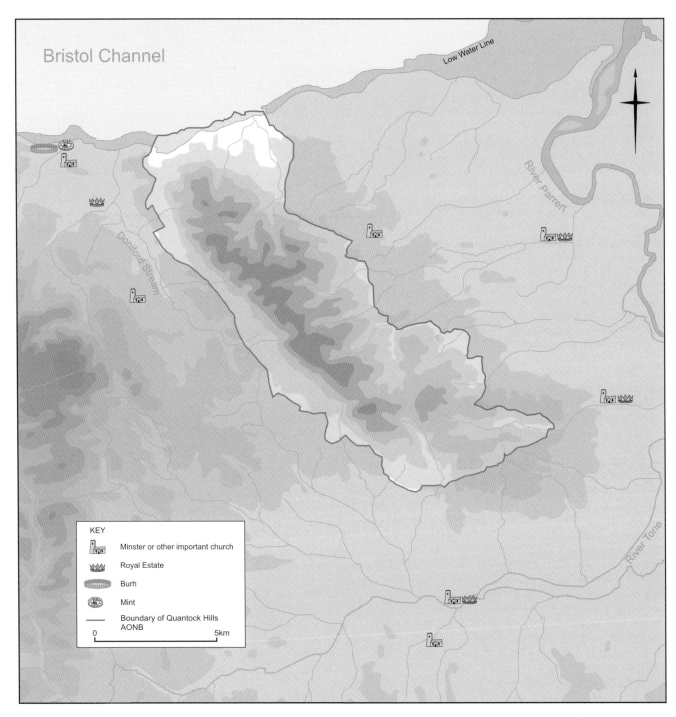

Bristol Channel

Low Water Line

River Parrett

Doniford Stream

River Tone

KEY

Minster or other important church

Royal Estate

Burh

Mint

Boundary of Quantock Hills AONB

0   5km

Fig 4.2
The Quantock Hills:
Anglo-Saxon sites. (Based
on an Ordnance Survey
map, with permission.
© Crown copyright.
All rights reserved)

Saxon period as much of the land remained in the possession of conservative landowners – the king and church. Four such large estates have been recognised around the Quantock Hills, centred at Williton, Taunton, North Petherton and Cannington. The latter may have had its origins back in the 5th or 6th centuries (*see above*) (Costen 1988; 1992). Excavations close to St Mary's Church, North Petherton, however, showed that the settlement was probably a new

foundation, with dating evidence from late Saxon pottery of the 10th or 11th centuries. The excavator did note that there may have been a pre- 10th-century aceramic (without pottery) phase of settlement (Leach 1977).

By the time of the Domesday survey (1086) these estates were still very large and owned by the king or by the church. Cannington was linked to Williton and Carhampton to form three units with 100 ploughlands between them; North

Petherton had 30 ploughlands. These royal centres, dating from the earliest phase of the Anglo-Saxon occupation of the area, perhaps originally consisted of a hall and service buildings surrounded by a bank or wooden palisade. We know that the king was in the habit of visiting the area in the early 10th century, when a document from 904 lists liabilities for a night's lodging for the king, for eight dogs and their keeper and the king's falconers and attendants, horses and carts when the king was travelling to 'Curig' (North Curry) or 'Willettun' (Page 1911, 550). But by this time the kings of Wessex were the kings of England. Somerset was still a popular place for royal hunting parties with its royal forests (*see below*), but the centre of power moved to the east and the smaller royal centres around the Quantock Hills, with the exception of Taunton, can be seen as supply centres – the hubs of large agricultural estates – rather than as administrative centres and places regularly visited by the king and his court.

The widespread adoption of Christianity in England went hand in hand with the rule of the Anglo-Saxon kings, although there is evidence that this religion, present in later Roman Britain, was also practised in post-Roman Britain. The king was responsible for building the church – the minster at the early royal centres. In and around the Quantock Hills there is scant evidence of any church fabric that can be dated to before the 11th century, but minster churches were probably built at the royal centres of Cannington, North Petherton and Taunton (Costen 1992, 153–7), and at Daw's Castle, Watchet (*see below*). Local parish churches came about as these great royal estates began to break up in the 10th century, towards the end of the Anglo-Saxon period. The new estate owners wanted to show their independence, wealth and social status – the building of a church next to their hall was a way of doing all these things, as well as bringing in income and extending the obligations of their workers.

Daw's Castle: an Anglo-Saxon burh

We have seen how ceremonial or burial places can remain special places in the landscape for many hundreds of years, at Battlegore for example, and on the ridge tops of the Quantock Hills (*see* Chapter 2). This tradition persists in the historic period. St Decuman's Church stands on a hill, away from the town of Watchet, which it now

Fig 4.3
St Decuman's Church and Watchet. (Hazel Riley)

serves (Fig 4.3). To the north, right on the cliff edge, is Daw's Castle, site of King Alfred's *burh* or fortified place. There has been a large amount of erosion on the cliff edge, but earthwork survey, documentary evidence and some small scale excavations at the site have combined to tell the story of the settlement and church. The earthwork survey carried out in 2004 records a curving bank some 300m long and cut by cliff erosion at its north end. A plan published in 1911 shows that the present bank was probably part of a continuous circuit, forming an elongated oval enclosure, some 170m long and 75m wide (Page 1911). The size correlates with that given in the Burghal Hidage of *c* AD 914 (McAvoy 1986, 57).

In 1982 a small-scale excavation was carried out, with the aim of establishing whether this was an Iron Age hillfort or King Alfred's *burh*. These excavations showed that the site was indeed an Anglo-Saxon enclosure. There were two phases of mortared stone wall; the latest of these was very substantial: 1.4m wide and perhaps 3.5m high. Behind it was a massive bank, nearly 8m wide, and in front of the wall was a ditch, separated from the bank by a broad berm (level area). The form of this wall, like those of other Wessex *burhs*, together with radiocarbon dates and pottery all show that the site is Anglo-Saxon in date (McAvoy 1986).

To the east of Daw's Castle is Old Minster Field, named on a map of Watchet from 1801 (SRO 1801). Churches were founded inside new *burhs* or very close to them, next to the gates or walls, so Old Minster Field

Fig 4.4
Anglo-Saxon and early
medieval coins from
Watchet mint: Aethelred II
(left), Cnut I (centre),
William I (right).
(Somerset County
Museums Service)

may well be the site of the original Saxon minster church. The burials recorded from Daw's Castle in the 19th century could be associated with this or they may relate to a post-Roman cemetery (Page 1890). The parish church of St Decuman's now stands 500m to the southeast of Old Minster Field, on the opposite side of the valley of the Washford River, above the town of Watchet, and is first referred to on this site in the 12th century (Dunning 1985, 166). It has been argued that this site was already a special, venerated place, the site of St Nectan's Well and the site of a church before the *burh* was built. After the *burh* was abandoned, the pull of this place was so strong that the church moved back here (Calder 2003).

The town of Watchet lies just to the east of Daw's Castle. In the 10th and 11th centuries it was a port and trading centre associated with the *burh* and also with the Saxon royal estate, centred at Williton, a few miles inland. Watchet was an important place by the 10th century. It had a mint, perhaps located at the *burh*, from *c* AD 980. Silver pennies were struck under moneyers called Sigeric, Hunewine and Godcild in the reigns of Ethelred, Cnut, Harold I, Harthacnut and Edward the Confessor (Fig 4.4). Coins from the Watchet mint have been found in Scandinavia (Blackburn 1974). They probably reached Scandinavia through trade and through payment of the Danegeld (a tax paid to protect England against Danish raids). Watchet suffered from many Viking raids in the 10th century and may have been at least partly destroyed in AD 997 (Gathercole 2003).

'Cantucuudu': a Saxon hunting ground?

The Saxon and the Norman kings used the more remote parts of Somerset as both a hunting ground and as a larder. Large parts of Exmoor, the Mendip Hills, the lowland moors around North Petherton and Ilminster, and Selwood Forest on the Somerset/Wiltshire border were designated as royal forest after the Norman Conquest, areas subject to forest law, and are well-documented in the 13th and 14th centuries (Bond 1994). Many of the royal forests seem to have originated within the royal estates of the Anglo-Saxon period, which probably contained extensive areas of woodland and upland and lowland moors – ideal terrain for hunting.

There is a substantial body of evidence that shows that the Quantock Hills were also a Saxon hunting ground but the area was not formalised as a royal forest after the Norman Conquest. This evidence comes from three sources: from documents, which indicate that the Quantock Hills used to be a forest, from the pattern of early Anglo-Saxon royal centres and the pattern of land ownership recorded at the time of the Domesday survey. The first mention of Quantock Forest is probably as early as the 7th century. King Centwine of Wessex granted land at Creech St Michael and West Monkton, described as near the famous wood called 'Cantucuudu', to Glastonbury Abbey. The charter is known only from a 16th-century transcription but it does seem to have been copied from a genuinely early original, which places the reference to AD 682 (Bond 1994, 121–2). In a similar vein, the Hundred Rolls of 1272–1307 refer to a pound that has been the property of the king since Canntock was a forest (Greswell 1900, 132).

A survey book accompanying a map of the Quantock Hills, drawn in 1609, describes a tract of land as 'wood and plain barren ground....reputedly a quarter of Quantock Forest....by tradition [descending] from their ancestors' (quoted in Siraut *et al* 1992, 13). This was 880 acres of land attached to the manor of Wick Fitzpayn in Stogursey and called Quantock Common. The estate can be traced back to the early 12th century, and there are references in the early 13th and 14th centuries suggesting that Quantock Common was part of a former royal forest. William de Falaise, between 1100 and 1107, granted to the monks of the Norman abbey of Lonlay 'firewood as needed in his wood called Canthoc'. John de Neville of Essex, lord of Stogursey, gave to the nuns of Cannington 'sufficient wood for their hearth in my forest of Cantoke' in the 1230s or 1240s and in 1301 a survey of Robert Waleraund's estate mentioned 'wood on Quantock in which the prior of Stogursey, the prioress of Cannington, William of Gryndham, John de Columbers and Margaret of Fairfield had grazing rights' (Quoted in Siraut *et al* 1992, 13). In the mid-12th century a holding in the parish of Stringston claimed 'housebote' and 'haybote' (the rights to take wood from the commons to build or repair houses and fences) in the wood of Quantock (Dunning 1992, 172).

The Quantock Hills are surrounded by probable early Anglo-Saxon royal centres: Williton, Taunton, North Petherton and Cannington (Fig 4.2). The pattern of land ownership at the time of the Domesday survey shows that the Quantock Hills were still surrounded by royal land and land owned by the church, the latter formerly royal land until given to the church in the 10th century by the Saxon kings. The 10th-century Charter of Privileges granted to the monastery at Taunton refers to a royal hunting lodge at Williton (Page 1911, 550). There are several instances of land in the parish of Broomfield that still had royal connections in the 12th and 13th centuries: the Kingshill estate paid rent to Somerton before 1204; Kingslands belonged to the crown before the Montacute family acquired it; Deadmanswell and Oggshole were anciently part of Somerton, and Melcombe, part of Creech manor, was of royal demesne in 1086, and remained so until it was given away in the 12th century (Siraut *et al* 1992, 13). One of the most intriguing references is to the king's *porcheria* (piggery) at Rooks Castle, Broomfield, in the late 13th century (Dunning 1992, 5).

The sequence of earthwork enclosures at Rooks Castle, perched high above the Kings Cliff valley, begins in prehistory (*see* Chapter 3). The D-shaped enclosure that overlies these ancient enclosures is probably associated with either Quantock Forest or with North Petherton Forest (Fig 4.5). Its location makes it unlikely to be a deserted medieval settlement, as the settlements in this area are scattered valley farmsteads, often with 'combe' or 'hole' elements in their names. The form of the enclosure at Rooks Castle is reminiscent of the small hunting lodges identified in a recent study of the earthworks associated with enclosure in the New Forest, Hampshire (Smith 1999). Like the site at Rooks Castle, these lodges are characteristically situated on ridge-top positions, remote from contemporary settlement. Robert de Odburville, the Forest Warden for the king's Somerset forests, who lived at Melcombe, 3km to the east of Rooks Castle, in the 11th century, may have built the hunting lodge here.

A second type of earthwork enclosure identified in the New Forest is the pound: small enclosures with a variety of forms. Most pertinent here are the so-called pig pounds, apparently relating to the right of a family to make ditches, hedges and houses in the forest every year for their hogs and pigs. These are generally about half the size of the Rooks Castle example, and of much slighter construction. The enclosure at Rooks Castle could be a pound, it could even be the royal piggery documented in the 13th century. Pigs were evidently important in the area, with Domesday recording 20 swineherds in the Hundred of North Petherton. There is also a strong tradition of using the Quantock woods for pannage, pigs were still to be seen roaming free in Shervage Wood in the early 20th century (Greswell 1903, 128) and names such as Swinage Wood and Lowsey Thorn (*see below*) also indicate the presence of pigs.

Fig 4.5

Rooks Castle: enclosure and quarries.

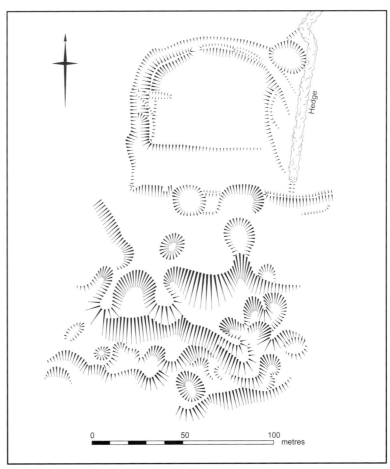

Rooks Castle was the county pound in the early 16th century and it was in use in the mid- 16th century, as attested by the account of the exploits of the Stawell family who used Rooks Castle to quarter stolen sheep (Dunning 1992, 5; Stawell 1910, 65). Pounds were commonly found in royal forests. Over on Exmoor, for example, there were two forest pounds, an ancient one at Withypool and a new one, built in the mid- 17th century, at Simonsbath (Riley and Wilson-North 2001, 92). A pound is marked on an early 17th-century map of part of the Quantocks (SRO 1609). Another pound is suggested at Lowsey Thorn at the head of Slaughterhouse Combe, as a common Somerset term for pig sties were pigs' looses (Greswell 1905, 128). If the D-shaped enclosure at Rooks Castle was originally built as a hunting lodge in the later 11th century, it could well have had a new use as an animal pound, first for the pigs, royal or common, then as a pound for any stray animals.

So where was the royal forest of Quantock, what was its character and when it did it cease to be a royal forest? Judging from the documentary evidence outlined above, the forest took in the whole of what is now common land and former common land (Fig 1.11). It probably extended as far as the sea to the north and as far south as the southern edge of the hills, as the land close to Quantock Forest that was given to Glastonbury in 682 was around West Monkton, north of Taunton. To the east, the whole of the area now occupied by the parish of North Petherton was once royal forest, so it is not hard to envisage the royal forest once extending unbroken up onto the hills. In fact, the addition of the uplands of the Quantock Hills to the North Petherton Forest area helps to explain the original location of North Petherton as a royal forest. The western boundary is hard to discern. It may have extended only as far as the present common boundary at the base of the steep west side of the hills. Alternatively, the forest could have extended as far as the flatter lands around the valley of the Doniford Stream, where its remnants may be seen in the former commons of Heathfield and Heddon in Crowcombe.

Quantock Forest as a Saxon hunting ground was an area of open heathland and pasture, with woodland on the west, east and south slopes. There is a certain amount of place-name evidence to substantiate this: a concentration of names with elements that refer to woodland or clearings in woodland has been noted around the slopes of the Quantocks (Costen 1988, 41). On the lower ground to the east, in what became North Petherton Forest, the marshy floodplain east of the River Parrett supported a variety of wild fowl and game birds. In the 1540s there were also plenty of deer in this area: 'There ys a great Numbre of Dere longing to this Park, yet hath it almost no other Enclosure but the Dikes to let the Catelle of the Commune to cum yn. The Dere trippe over these Dikes and feede all about the Fennes, and resort to the Park again' (Bates 1887, 91).

Quantock Forest was not designated a royal forest after the Norman Conquest. There are no references to such a forest in Domesday (but there are few generally, as royal forests were not liable for tax because they were already owned by the crown). Quantock Forest is not mentioned in any of the well-researched documents pertaining to forest law and forest courts of the 13th and 14th centuries and there are no perambulations that give its bounds. This suggests that Quantock Forest had ceased to exist by the time of the Norman Conquest. The Saxon hunting grounds on the Quantock Hills may have become fragmented as a result of the giving up of royal land to the church in the 10th century.

The Anglo-Saxon landscape

The Quantock Hills began to take on their present configuration by this time. The great expanse of Quantock Common in the northern hills was firmly established as part of the Saxon hunting ground and was essentially open heath, but the wooded slopes and combes were more extensive than we see today. The woods may have extended right up to the tops of the combes in places, perhaps around Shepherds Combe, Somerton Combe and Stert Combe, and along the steep western escarpment. Evidence for this comes from place names. Three holdings in Crowcombe parish, documented in the medieval period and probably in existence well before the Norman Conquest, have names showing that they were created from clearing woodland: Hurley, Cooksleigh and Leigh are derived from the Anglo-Saxon word *leah*, which means a clearing in woodland.

We have already seen the royal centres around the hills, with royal houses, service buildings, churches and places for trade and craft manufacture. As these large estates

began to fragment in the 10th century, other centres developed, the precursors to the well documented medieval manors at West and East Quantoxhead, Kilve and Kilton on the coast, for example. At such centres the lord built a manor house and often a church, adding to his status. Smaller again were individual farmsteads and their holdings, subservient to, and dependent on, the royal estates or independent manors (Fig 4.6). These were the precursors of many of the farms that are documented in the medieval period. Some were abandoned in the 16th and 17th centuries, others remained in use until the 19th and early 20th centuries, many remain as farms to the present day. It is easy to forget the people who lived and worked on the land at this time. We have a good reminder from a charter that lists the boundaries of Bishops Lydeard in the 10th century. *Motleah* – the place of assembly at the clearing – was the place on Merridge Hill where the people of the district met to deliberate and see justice done (Mayberry 1998, 16).

The later medieval period: lords of the manor

Evidence for the medieval landscape 1066–1540

The most direct evidence for the medieval landscape is an Ordnance Survey map of the Quantock Hills. It is easy to filter out the late 20th-century village bypasses and the 19th-century railway lines. The pattern of small, scattered farms and hamlets, manor house and church, enclosed fields, woods, lowland marsh and upland heath are part of a response to the landscape that began in the Anglo-Saxon period, but which we can grasp more clearly as documents and maps begin to bring the evidence into focus.

William the Conqueror was crowned in London on Christmas Day 1066. As well as a new king, the people had new local rulers: the estates of the defeated Saxon landowners were given to the new king's favourites. For parts of the Quantock Hills this had a profound effect on the landscape, where the

Fig 4.6
Coastal settlements and farmsteads on the common edge. (NMR 21902/29) (© English Heritage. NMR)

story of the landscape becomes the story of the changing fortunes of the great landowning families of the time. One visible reminder of the new Norman lords was the castle. In the years following the conquest, castles were built by the lords of Dunster and Stowey. Major castles were established by the Bishop of Winchester at Taunton in 1138 and by William Brewer at Bridgwater in 1200. Castles also made a statement about the importance and wealth of the new lords to the rest of the community. Many castles began life as earthworks, mounds or mottes, surrounded by a ditch, with an outer enclosure or bailey. The motte was topped with a defensive structure or keep, the bailey contained the lord's accommodation: a hall, chapel, stables, kitchens and lodgings. Most of the early buildings were wooden, and their traces are only found in excavations, but the remains of stone buildings, towers and walls survive either as romantic ruins – like Stogursey – or within the fabric of later building complexes as at Taunton Castle (Fig 4.7).

The great land-owning monasteries of the region were already established by the Norman Conquest: Glastonbury Abbey, an important monastic centre by the 10th century, owned land in a great block stretching from the River Parrett on the west to the foothills of the Mendips on the east, with an outlier at West Monkton on the south edge of the Quantock Hills (Rahtz 1993, fig 78). The core of the Manor of Taunton Deane was given to the Bishop of Winchester in 904. It grew into one of the largest and most prosperous estates in England in the medieval period, and included estates at Kingston St Mary, Cothelstone and Bagborough. The latter two were 'outfarings' or 'liberties' of the estate: the Bishop of Winchester was acknowledged as the overlord but, in typical Quantocks fashion, they func-

Fig 4.7
Stogursey Castle. (NMR 21200/10) (© English Heritage. NMR)

Fig 4.8
Sir Matthew de Stawell and his wife, Elizabeth. Church of St Thomas of Canterbury, Cothelstone. (AA048515) (© English Heritage. NMR)

tioned as independent manors and were governed by their own lords (Leach 1984, fig 2; Mayberry 1998, 19). Bishops Lydeard, however, was held by the Bishop of Wells, and was part of a gift of land by King Edward to the church in the early 10th century.

Other monasteries and chantry chapels were founded by the wealthy Norman lords: William de Mohun and his wife founded a Benedictine priory at Dunster in 1090 and William de Roumare, with the help of local landowning families, founded the Cistercian abbey at Cleeve in 1198. William de Falaise, lord of the manor of Stogursey, gave a grant of land on and around the Quantock Hills to the Benedictine abbey at Lonlay in Normandy at the beginning of the 12th century. Monks were sent from Lonlay to administer the new estates and Stogursey priory was formed (Ballard 1977). A priory of Augustinian canons at Minchin Buckland, Durston, was replaced by a nunnery in 1180 and the Benedictine nunnery at Cannington, founded in the 12th century, became notorious for delinquency and broken vows of chastity in the 14th century (Dunning 2001). The lord of the manor of Kilve had his own private chapel and the little chapel at Adscombe may have belonged to Athelney Abbey, but could also have been the private chapel of a high-status manor house (*see below*). A private chapel is mentioned in the will of Robert Stawell, lord of Cothel-

stone Manor in the late 15th century; a license for an oratory (a room set aside for private prayer) was granted to Plainsfield Manor in 1447, a chapel house was recorded there in 1511 and an oratory was noted at Spaxton Manor in 1408 (Anon 1908, 54; Dunning 1992, 162–3; 114). The finely-carved stone effigies of Sir Matthew de Stawell and his wife, Elizabeth, on their monument in the tiny church at Cothelstone, are a poignant reminder of the people who instigated all this activity (Fig 4.8).

Fig 4.9
Kingston St Mary Church. (Hazel Riley)

The parish churches themselves contain fabric that dates from the 11th and 12th centuries, from the simple carving on the stone font at Kilve to the superlative crossing at Stogursey. The churches at Bishops Lydeard and Kingston St Mary have stunning perpendicular towers. Built in the 15th century, they are particularly striking when viewed with the hills as a backdrop (Fig 4.9). Less grand and peculiarly intimate are a series of carved wooden pew ends, locally known as bench ends. The best executed of these are usually attributed to Simon Warman, who was working in the area in the early 16th century. The carvings depict scenes from everyday life, like the windmill at Bishops Lydeard and the textile worker at Spaxton, as well as the mythological, such as the Crowcombe dragons (Figs 4.36, 4.39 and 3.6).

Like churches, some secular buildings contain evidence of building techniques of this period. Court House, East Quantoxhead has a porch tower with a carved stone door surround of late 14th or 15th century

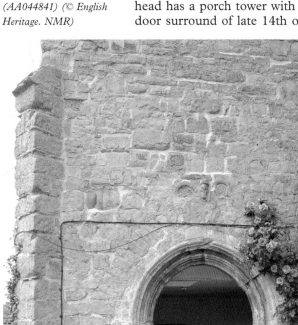

date and a wing with a garderobe or latrine that was built in the 16th century (Fig 4.10); the carved stone door surrounds at Manor Cottages, Cothelstone, date from the 15th century (Fig 4.23). Less grand buildings also preserve evidence of their early origins. The lowest layers of thick thatch and roof timbers may be stained black by smoke, which shows that the roof space was once open and that a fire burned without a chimney – evidence of a hall. At Hill Farm, Kingston St Mary, the farm house has jointed crucks, internal cob walls and heavy smoke blackening over what was once the hall of the medieval house, parts of this date from the 15th century (McCann and McCann 2003, 122–3). Other buildings have not survived the test of time. These can now be found in a range of states, from romantic ruin, as at Kilve, to humps and bumps in green fields, like Deak's Allers in East Quantoxhead, where the foundations of ruined and robbed out buildings leave a footprint on the landscape.

As elsewhere in England, the later part of the 12th century and the 13th century was a period of prosperity and growth in the southwest. A growing population meant a demand for food, such as corn, meat, fish and salt, and for the products of craftsmen, such as iron tools, pots, pans and woollen cloth. This prosperity is reflected in the growth of many small boroughs and market towns in southwest England, some on the sites of Anglo-Saxon *burhs* (*see above*), others growing up at sea and river ports. The manufacture of wool and woollen cloth, particularly important in southwest England, led to the creation of markets, fairs, guilds and urban centres around this industry. Other markets grew up to cater for the sale of agricultural produce. During the 13th century the use of water-powered fulling mills became widespread in cloth production. One effect was that cloth production began to move away from towns out into the country and the textile industry became a widespread rural industry as weavers and dyers settled around the new fulling mills located close to sources of water power. Towns were still important centres for the textile industry, however, and the rural industry did not replace the urban industry but, rather, seems to have been closely integrated with it (Palmer and Neaverson 2005, 29–32, 42).

The 14th and 15th centuries, however, mark the end of this long period of prosperity with its concurrent rural settlement

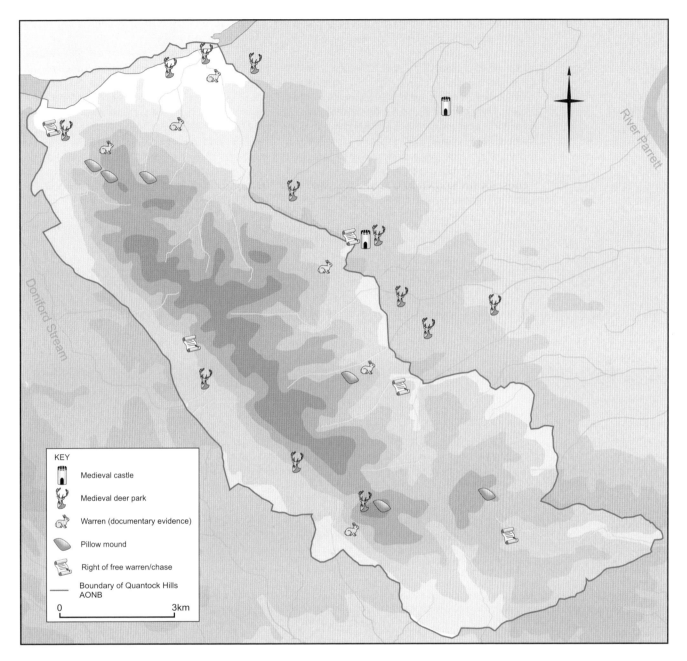

KEY

🏰 Medieval castle

🦌 Medieval deer park

🐇 Warren (documentary evidence)

Pillow mound

📜 Right of free warren/chase

— Boundary of Quantock Hills
    AONB

0   3km

growth, and expansion in towns and trade. The period 1300–1500 was a time of population decrease when poor weather (and thus poor harvests) combined with recurrent outbreaks of plague, which peaked with the infamous Black Death of 1348–9. The recession, already underway before the plague outbreaks of the mid-14th century, affected the area very badly; for example a survey of 22 of the manors belonging to Glastonbury Abbey in Somerset, Dorset and Wiltshire suggests that average death rates among their tenants were as high as 55% (Bettey 1986, 88) and in 1349 the rents received for Crowcombe manor were

so low because 'the tenants were dead from the plague' (Dunning 1985, 59). There was, however, still money to be made from trade and commerce, wool and cloth production and agriculture. This continuing prosperity is certainly seen in the Quantock Hills in the church towers, carved bench ends and houses that survive from the 15th and 16th centuries.

The general decline in population made arable farming less profitable. The expanding cloth industry and higher wool prices led to changes in farming practice and land tenure, with a decrease in arable land and a retreat from some upland areas, together

Fig 4.11

The Quantock Hills: medieval castles, deer parks, rabbit warrens and pillow mounds. (Based on an Ordnance Survey map, with permission. © Crown copyright. All rights reserved)

with an increase in large-scale sheep farming. This is seen particularly dramatically on the chalk downlands of Wiltshire and Dorset, for example. There was also a trend towards absentee landlords in the later medieval period, with a decrease in direct estate farming by major landowners and a subsequent increase in land leased to tenants. Some towns and cities continued to thrive. Ports like Minehead and Bridgwater exported woollen cloth and hides, with imports of wine, salt, iron, oil, dyestuff, alum and fish (Bettey 1986, 107–20).

Medieval manors and their estates

Life and the landscape of the Quantock Hills in the medieval period were dominated by several manor houses that lay at the heart of large estates. The best preserved and documented are those that form the whole of the coastal strip on the northern side of the hills (Fig 4.6). Here the parishes of West Quantoxhead, East Quantoxhead, Kilve and Kilton roughly equate to the medieval manors of the same names and the Victoria County History for Somerset

Fig 4.12
Nether Stowey and its castle. (NMR 21201/05) (© English Heritage. NMR)

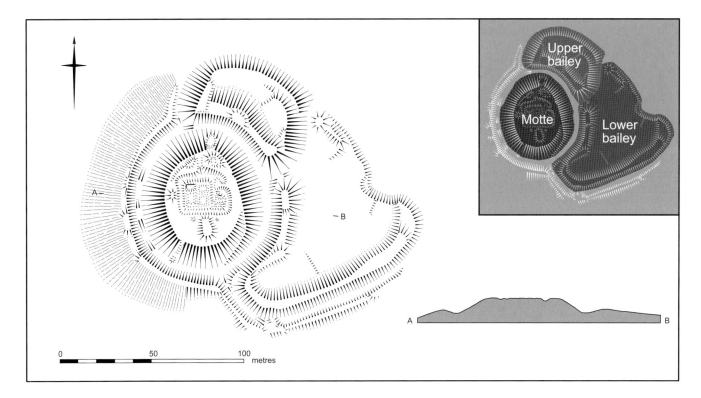

Fig 4.13
Nether Stowey Castle: earthwork plan.

has documented the history of these parishes in some detail (Dunning 1985). The remainder of the Quantock Hills, however, also contains much evidence for the medieval landscape (Fig 4.11).

There are several ways in which these medieval manors influenced the landscape of the hills. One way was by erecting high-status buildings of timber and stone – the castles, manor houses and churches. Another way was by laying out deer parks, often close to the manor houses, where wood pasture and more open grazing for deer contributed to a managed landscape around the lord's residence. A third was by the way in which agriculture was organised. There is some evidence for a certain type of open field farming on and around the Quantock Hills, but this is not an area of village and open field farming, as seen in the English Midlands, for example.

Nether Stowey Castle

One of the best ways to appreciate the location of the castle at Nether Stowey is from the A39, approaching the village from the south. The castle dominates the foothills of the Quantocks and commands the lower lying land to the north and east (Fig 4.12). The castle earthworks are very well preserved and, as we know very little about the castle from historical sources, we rely on the earthworks and clues in the surrounding

landscape to help tell its story (Fig 4.13). The castle was built in the late 11th or early 12th century when Isabel, daughter of Alfred d'Epaignes and wife of Robert de Chandos, held the Stowey estates. The castle earthworks are made up of a large motte, surrounded by a deep ditch, with two baileys on the east side. The motte was topped with a large building. The stone foundations, partially revealed by an excavation in *c* 1850, show that a substantial, square keep stood here, perhaps a timber building on stone foundations. This was the strongly defended heart of the castle, but the double bailey contained all the offices necessary for the lord of the manor to administer his estates. A hall and the rather elusive St Michael's Chapel probably occupied the upper bailey, while the lower bailey was for stables, lodgings and other accommodation. Philip de Columbers was evidently a figure of some importance. In 1248 he was granted a park with free warren in his home estate, and the park was stocked with deer in 1295, the park was probably to the west and south of the castle (*see below*), on a different site from the park that belonged to Stowey Court.

The site of the castle at Nether Stowey fell out of favour. The exposed and rather constricted site left little room to expand or rebuild the main accommodation, and by the end of the 15th century at least part of

Fig 4.14
The fantastic building on Castle Hill, drawn on a 1750 map of Nether Stowey. (SRO 1750a DD/SAS(a) C/1207) (Somerset Archive and Record Service)

Fig 4.14
The fantastic building on Castle Hill, drawn on a 1750 map of Nether Stowey. (SRO 1750a DD/SAS(a) C/1207) (Somerset Archive and Record Service)

the castle was abandoned. By 1497 work had begun on building a grand mansion house on a site close to St Mary's church, itself probably the site of the manor house of Budley. The idea of an imposing building on top of the castle mound remained, however. An estate map of 1750 shows a fantastic reconstruction of Nether Stowey Castle (Fig 4.14). There is a large, square building with an arcade, a domed roof and tower topped with a cross. This is flanked by two smaller towers of similar design and several smaller, less elaborate buildings cluster around the base of the three towers. The whole group is surrounded by a substantial curtain wall, studded with towers. The depiction must be a conceit on the part of the artist, Thomas England, who drafted this map of the land owned by Robert Balch of Stowey Court (SRO 1750a).

Manorial earthworks

A large, sub-rectangular flat-topped mound or platform lies in the corner of Castle Field, Over Stowey (Fig 4.15). It is 30m long, 25m wide and more than 2m high. The earthworks are very different in form from the castle earthworks at Nether Stowey. A geophysical survey showed that the platform had a ditch on its north and west sides and that the area had been subject to the deliberate building up of soil or other material (Sabin 2003); the area was

under arable cultivation in the 19th century (Over Stowey tithe map 1838). The platform in Castle Field is one of a number of medieval manorial earthwork sites that survive in the Quantock Hills (Fig 4.15). In lowland England such sites often take the form of rectangular platforms, enclosed by wide, water-filled ditches, usually known as moats or moated sites. The sites that survive on the Quantock Hills, however, are located on hillsides or small spurs and take the form of substantial rectangular platforms, terraced into the slope. Although the earthwork remains are all very similar, each site has a very different story to tell.

A castle at Stowey is first mentioned in a forged charter of before 1154 (Dunning 1981, note 14). Another charter, dating from the reign of Henry II (1154–89), records the grant of land from 'Staweye harpet near the old castle-precinct' (Ross 1959, 159–160). The reference to an old castle precinct, and the identification of the Stowey Herepath with a lane that runs by Castle Field, Over Stowey, has led to the suggestion that there was an early stronghold in Over Stowey, a precursor to Nether Stowey Castle (Dunning 1981, 125). The name Castle is often associated with the memory of an important building. The platform in Castle Field may well have been the site of a high-status building, probably with a defensible element, the home of Alfred d'Espaignes in the 11th century as Dunning suggests (1992, 160), and perhaps the home of Hugh de Bonville who held land in Stowey in the 12th century. The place name Courtway, a hamlet southwest of Merridge, is also suggestive of a high-status house. Courtway is today a straggle of cottages and a farm house on a sharp bend of the road between Aisholt and Fiveways Cross. An earlier route, now only a track, led up the valley to Waterpits, the main residence of the Merridge estate in the 18th century (Dunning 1992, 115). Close to this track is a platform, 40m long, 25m wide and more than 1m high, terraced into the hillside and located above a small stream (Fig 4.15). Much of the surrounding landscape has been disturbed by the construction of two ponds in the latter part of the 20th century, but the platform could be the site of the home of the Fichet family, who held the manor of Merridge in the 12th century (Dunning 1992, 114).

A puzzling landscape of narrow lanes with sharp bends, a glimpse of a tall, classical statue and a classically-modelled coach house

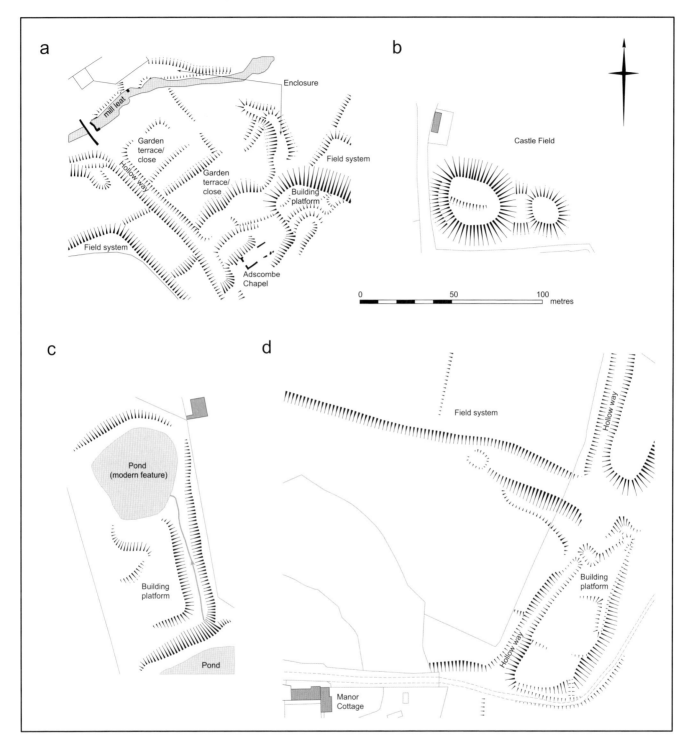

and stable block lies between West Bagborough and Cothelstone. This is the area of the old manor of East Bagborough. Hidden behind overgrown shrubberies are the remains of Cothelstone House, completed in 1820. Now divided into several cottages, this building was originally a substantial medieval house, with an open hall and a solar over the inner room. The main access, however, is a lane leading past 19th-century estate buildings to Manor Cottage and Terhill Cottages. The lane leads past the house, then turns sharply to continue as a hollow-way up the hillside. Here is a substantial earthwork platform with evidence that several buildings once occupied this spot (Fig 4.15).

There were a few cottages or farm buildings here in the 18th century, but the size and

Fig 4.15
Manorial earthworks in the Quantock Hills: Adscombe (a), Over Stowey (b), Courtway (c) and East Bagborough (d).

location of the platform and its name, Higher Court Meadow, shown on 18th-century estate maps (SRO 1778; 1792), suggest that a house of some substance was associated with this area. The house probably stood at the north end of the platform, where there are the remains of the footings of a substantial wall and some hollows that suggest that stone has been taken from the site. This may have been the original manor house of East Bagborough, with Manor Cottage either a later building or a second, high-status dwelling at East Bagborough. Certainly the location was a favoured one: to the north are the remains of an 18th-century house and landscape park, to the south the site of Cothelstone House and its park (*see* Chapter 5).

Adscombe Chapel

Until the 1960s a tall gable end wall, pierced with an elegant high window opening and a door beneath, was visible above a tangle of scrubby trees from the road to Adscombe Farm (Fig 4.16). This is Adscombe Chapel, a medieval building with two stories to tell. The first is that which the locals still tell today, that the chapel belonged to the monks of Athelney Abbey. Berta Lawrence captured the romance of former days:

These stones heard the monks chant mass, the hills gave pasture to the monks' flocks and wood for their fire .... After the

Dissolution .... the monks were never seen again on the hills, carrying axe or crook, and the sound of their prayers in the chapel no longer joined the murmur of the streams in Seven Wells Combe
(Lawrence 1952, 171).

The history of Adscombe and its chapel is complicated and not fully understood, but if the historical sources are used in combination with what remains to be read in the landscape, a rather different, but just as fascinating, story emerges. First is the long association of Adscombe with Athelney Abbey. The Cartulary of Athelney Abbey contains several references to Adscombe in the medieval period. There are grants of land in Adscombe to the abbey in the 13th century and a note of rents due to the abbey, for the monks' kitchen, from lands in Adscombe (Bates 1889, 150; 151; 163). There are, however, no known references to a chapel at Adscombe owned by the abbey (Dunning 1992, 170).

The names Fryron or Friarn may be derived from the Anglo-Saxon words *fran* or *fearn*, which mean, respectively, common land and fern or bracken, associations with the landscape rather than with religious foundations.

The first written reference to the chapel is in the early 16th century when the chapel is mentioned in two wills (Broadmead 1891, 239). At this point the story becomes tied up with the history of the manor of Over Stowey or Fryron (later known as Friarn). Hugh de Bonville granted land in Stowey to the church of Over Stowey in the mid- 12th century; his wife, Alice, granted her dower lands in Stowey to St John's Hospital, Bridgwater. This was part of the estate known as Over Stowey or Fryron, which was sold to Emmanuel Lucas, a London merchant, in 1544. A manor house or large house stood on the estate in 1538–9. Part of this estate was sold to the Rich family in 1646, who lived at Chapel House in the 17th and 18th centuries (Dunning 1992, 163); and there is anecdotal evidence of a grand house, which stood next to the chapel, with a date stone of 1519 and an oak staircase.

Adscombe today is a quiet hamlet, with a farm and a straggle of cottages along the lane opposite the chapel. Its location is typical of many of the Quantock settlements, in a combe and bordering former common land. Adscombe is recorded in the late 13th and early 14th centuries: in 1327 four peo-

Fig 4.16
Adscombe Chapel c 1903.
(Greswell 1903, facing
p. 187)

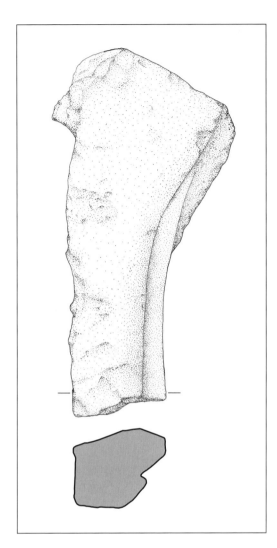

Fig 4.17
Adscombe Chapel:
fragment of window
surround. (Scale 1:10)

here suggest that a substantial house stood on the platform, close to the chapel and looking across to Over Stowey. The enclosure below the house may have contained stables and grazing for horses, terraced garden plots and an orchard (Fig 4.15).

By the 17th century a house here was called Chapel House, the home of the Rich family, and by the 19th century it was known as 'Chapples House and Barton', the chapel was used as a barn. But in the medieval period the house that stood on this platform, the manor house of Over Stowey and Fryron, must have been a high-status building and occupied by an important family, perhaps the de Lyf family. Walter de Lyf and his wife Lucia are mentioned in connection with a place that sounds very much like Adscombe, described as 'lying between the road from Ayly to Truscombe, and the hill of Cogerhulle, with the use and profit of the water at Cogercombe' (Greswell 1903, 190), and Lucia la Lyf is listed in the 1327 tax roll for Adscombe (Dickinson 1889, 140). Adscombe Chapel may have been part of the Athelney Abbey estate, but it could have been the chapel of the manor house, still a place of worship in the 16th century, but used as a barn by the 19th century.

The landscape for recreation and luxury: medieval deer parks

Medieval parks were different from the modern idea of spaces for public recreation or the 18th-century designed landscape parks that surrounded country houses. They were private game preserves, sometimes created under royal licence and enclosed by earthworks, walls, hedges or fences. Although there is a small amount of evidence for pre-Conquest and Domesday parks, the main period of park creation was in the 12th and 13th centuries, peaking in the second half of the 13th century, with a decline in numbers of new parks in the mid-14th century (Bond 1994, 133). There are many examples of medieval parks in Somerset, with a particular concentration to the south of the county, but the coast of west Somerset and the Quantock Hills are also notable for the number of medieval deer parks that they contain. The king and the church were important owners of deer parks in this period, examples being the royal park at Newton, North Petherton and the parks of the Bishop of Exeter at Norton Fitzwarren and the Bishop of Winchester at Poundisford, Taunton. The deer parks of the

ple were wealthy enough to be assessed for tax, in 1547 Adscombe had two houses and a ruined tenement (Dickinson 1889, 17; 140; Dunning 1992, 160). The chapel lies some way up a steep, north-facing slope and is reached by a deeply hollowed track, blocked by a tumble of fallen masonry. The foundations show that it was a small, rectangular, single-roomed building, with external dimensions of 16m by 7m. The chapel was built of local Devonian sandstone and the bases of substantial buttresses can still be seen at its west end. The west window was framed in a simple, carved stone surround and part of this lies in the ruins (Fig 4.17). The photograph and the surviving fabric suggest that the chapel dates from the later 13th or 14th century. The chapel is built on a levelled platform and 35m to the east is another platform, whose uneven surface suggests a building once stood here. Below the chapel is part of a curvilinear enclosure divided into plots or closes. The earthworks

Fig 4.18
The extent of the deer park at East Quantoxhead in the medieval period and in the 17th century. (Based on the Ordnance Survey 1st edition map, Somerset sheet 36 SE)

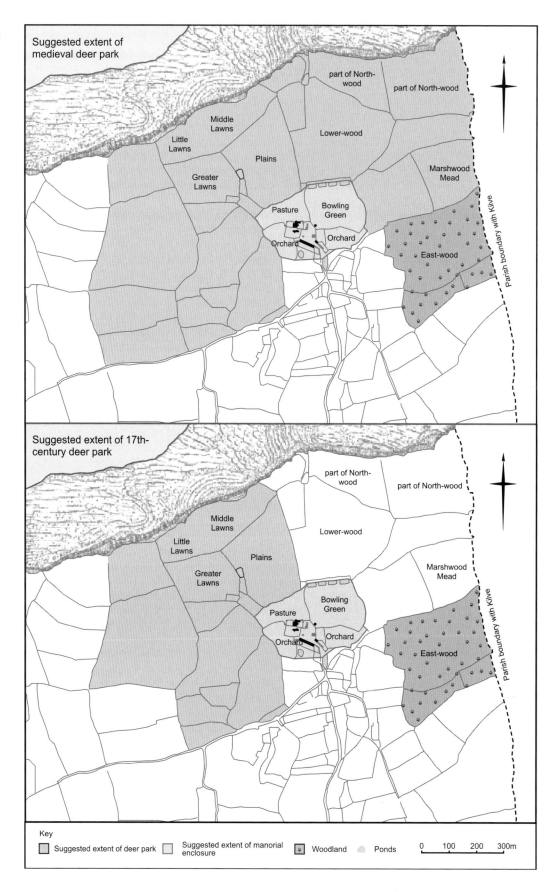

Quantock Hills were all owned by secular noblemen: the Luttrell family accounted for most of the parks on the west Somerset coast in the 15th century when they owned parks at East Quantoxhead, Marshwood, Dunster and Minehead.

The parks were stocked with both red and fallow deer, and the animals were hunted for recreation and to provide a luxury: venison. Fallow deer were a Norman introduction to Britain, and they were easier to keep in parks than the wilder red deer. There are, however, references to both red deer and fallow deer being kept in deer parks on the Quantock Hills. Red and fallow deer were kept in separate parks at Nether Stowey in the 16th century and red deer were recorded in the royal park at North Petherton (Dunning 1985, 191; Bond 1998, 23). Red deer antlers and bone were found in late medieval to early post-medieval contexts during an excavation in North Petherton, perhaps evidence of poaching from the park (Leach 1977, 39). As well as deer, domestic livestock, generally cattle and pigs, often grazed in the park and timber production was an increasing source of income from deer parks from the 13th century onwards. There are many records from Newton Park showing that the king granted oak trees for new buildings and for repairs to many of the religious houses in the area, including wood for the choir stalls at Cleeve Abbey and for the abbey church at Glastonbury (detailed in Bond 1994, 143). The medieval deer park landscape was a managed landscape and consisted of wood pasture, open pasture and meadow, stands of timber trees, areas of coppiced wood, together with ponds for watering deer and cattle, fishponds and rabbit warrens.

Medieval deer parks have been identified at 12 manors in and around the Quantock Hills (Fig 4.11). The evidence for these comes from a variety of sources, including contemporary documents that refer to the creation of a park or are concerned with the maintenance of the park and its boundaries; map or place-name evidence that indicates the location of a former park and the physical evidence of park boundaries in the form of earthworks. The parks have an interesting distribution (Fig 4.11). There is the concentration, already noted, along the coastal strip, with parks recorded at West Quantoxhead; East Quantoxhead; Kilve and Kilton. On the eastern edge of the hills there is also a concentration of medieval deer parks, all in similar locations on the flatter ground below the commons: at Currill near Holford, Nether Stowey, Aley, Plainsfield and Spaxton. The three medieval parks identified on the west edge of the hills are associated with the manors at Crowcombe, West Bagborough and Cothelstone. Where detailed research has made it possible to map the extent of the parks, the sizes range from c 60ha (Kilve) to c 100ha (Cothelstone).

Earthwork evidence for the park boundaries is scanty, but the impressive bank and ditch on the edge of Cothelstone Hill is a good candidate for a medieval deer park boundary work. On the north side of the park a bank 2m wide and 1.5m high runs for about 800m from Park End to the northern corner of Buncombe Wood. A ditch to the south, inside the park, is 4m wide and 2m deep. The bank was topped by a fence made of oak palings (hence the term park pale) and the ditch inside the park made it more difficult for deer to jump over the fence. Two banks in East Wood, East Quantoxhead, could be the boundaries of the East Quantoxhead and Kilve deer parks. The majority of the parks suffer some form of contraction in size or change in use in the 15th and 16th centuries. Parts of the extensive deer park at East Quantoxhead had gone over to arable cultivation by the mid-15th century. The park still contained deer in the early 17th century, but became farmland after the manor house was let as a tenanted farm in the mid-17th century (Fig 4.18). At Kilton the park was short lived. It was created by 1279 and by the end of the 14th century the park was divided into fields and partly ploughed. The park at Spaxton was let by 1440, partly ploughed by 1476 and wholly converted to farmland by the 17th century. Aley park fared rather better. It was about 100 acres in extent in 1275; in 1357 at least 36 people were accused of breaking into the park, hunting deer and killing a foal and cattle. Throughout the 15th century the pale was regularly repaired and the deer fed as necessary. By 1604 the park was divided up and let; it was ploughed for the first time in 1647 (Dunning 1985, 89; 1992, 112; 161).

Conspicuous consumption: pillow mounds, fish ponds and pigeon houses

The word warren was used in the medieval period in the legal term 'rights of free warren'. These were grants made by the king, allowing local lords to hunt small game animals on their own estates. Animals such as hares, rabbits, woodcock, partridge and pheasant were hunted and eaten, with other animals – foxes, wildcats, badgers, martens, otters and squirrels – considered vermin. Occasionally this grant of free warren was the precursor of making a deer park. The term 'coneygar' was used to mean a place for raising rabbits for their meat and fur (Bond 1994, 116), and pillow mounds – artificial burrows where rabbits could breed and be caught with dogs and nets – are the earthwork remains of this practice. Although recent excavations in Norfolk show that the Romans introduced the rabbit to Britain, the practice of breeding rabbits for food became popular after the Norman Conquest. The possession of a rabbit warren was another way to display wealth and status in the medieval period.

On and around the Quantock Hills there are several pillow mounds and a wealth of documentary evidence that can be used to show that many medieval manors had rabbit warrens in, or close to, their deer parks (Fig 4.11). The favoured location for the warrens was just below the edge of the commons, on more gentle sloping land, often looking

down over the deer park and manorial enclosure: this is seen at East Quantoxhead, Nether Stowey, Plainsfield and Cothelstone (Fig 4.19). At Kilve, however, the name Conygar is given to the area to the east of the fish ponds and close to the manor house (Kilve tithe map 1838).

At the head of Vinny Combe there are two small pillow mounds (Fig 4.20). The largest is rectangular, 9m long, 5m wide and 1m high with traces of a ditch on the south and east sides. The other pillow mound, also rectangular in shape, is 5m long, 3m wide and 0.5m high and has a ditch to the south and east. The head of the combe is criss-crossed with the ridges of a relict field system, and these ridges have encroached on the ditches of both pillow mounds, which therefore must be earlier than the field system. Philip de Cauntelo, lord of the manor of West Quantoxhead, was given a grant of free warren in 1267, and in 1418 the area around Stowborrow Hill was known as Conyger Hill (Dunning 1985, 130). The pillow mounds lie on the south slopes of Stowborrow Hill and can be confidently assigned to the 15th century or earlier on the basis of the earthwork and documentary

Fig 4.19
East Quantoxhead: medieval deer park (top) and rabbit warren (between the edge of the common and the A39). (NMR 21902/26) (© English Heritage. NMR)

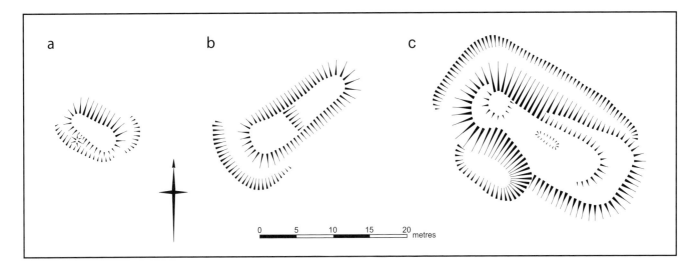

evidence. At East Quantoxhead the fields to the south of Townsend Farm were called Lower Coneyland and Higher Coneyland in 1687 (SRO 1687). A small, sub-rectangular mound, 5m long, 3m wide and 1m high with traces of a ditch to the west and east, at the head of Gay's House Combe could well be a pillow mound.

A good example of a pillow mound lies in the centre of the prehistoric enclosure of Plainsfield Camp (see Chapter 3) (Fig 4.20). It is a long, narrow rectangular mound, 15m long, 5m wide and 1m high, with a ditch to the southwest. There are irregular hollows on the top, which could be the remains of collapsed tunnels where the rabbits lived. The whole of the interior of Plainsfield Camp is covered in ridges – these could be the remains of relict field system, or they could be part of the process of planting the area as part of Great Wood in the early 20th century. These ridges run right over the mound. Plainsfield Manor had a medieval deer park, laid out to the east of the house and the fields below Plainsfield Camp were called Coney Close in the 19th century (Dunning 1985, 112; Over Stowey tithe map 1838). A small pillow mound lies on the edge of Broomfield Hill. This mound is 10m long, 6.5m wide, 0.5m high and has a ditch on its south side. Again, the appearance of the mound shows that it has been ploughed over. The lord of Broomfield manor, John de la Linde, received a grant of free warren in 1259 (Dunning 1992, 7).

At Cothelstone Manor the fields to the north of the church are called Lower and Higher Warren (Cothelstone tithe map 1838) and there is a large pillow mound on the top of Cothelstone Hill, within the area of the medieval deer park. This is one of the

best examples of a pillow mound on the Quantock Hills (Fig 4.20). It is 27m long, 12m wide and more than 1m high, with the remains of a ditch. A second pillow mound on the hill is twice as long. Cothelstone Manor was owned by an absentee landlord between the mid-17th century and the end of the 18th century, suggesting a medieval rather than a post-medieval date for the earthworks. In fact the earthwork evidence for most of the pillow mounds on the Quantock Hills suggests that they are of medieval rather than post-medieval date. This is significant given the claim that the majority of surviving pillow mounds are of post-medieval date (Williamson 1997, 99). The location of the surviving pillow mounds is also significant. They are on high ground, often on common land, in locations where they were highly visible and close to, or contained within, the deer park.

These managed, and, to a certain extent, designed landscapes related to their manorial enclosures. The deer parks at East Quantoxhead and Kilve virtually surrounded their respective manor houses and probably extended right out to the cliff edge (Figs 4.18 and 4.19). The backdrop to Cothelstone Manor is the great western scarp of the Quantock Hills. The medieval deer park took in Cothelstone Hill, but also swept right down the slopes towards the house (Fig 4.21). Philip de Columbers' deer park at Nether Stowey was also framed by the hills. Many of the parks were laid out on what was potential arable land, another way of showing wealth and status.

Another costly way to obtain protein was by keeping pigeons. A pigeon house (or, more recently, dovecote) was used to produce a supply of meat from squabs

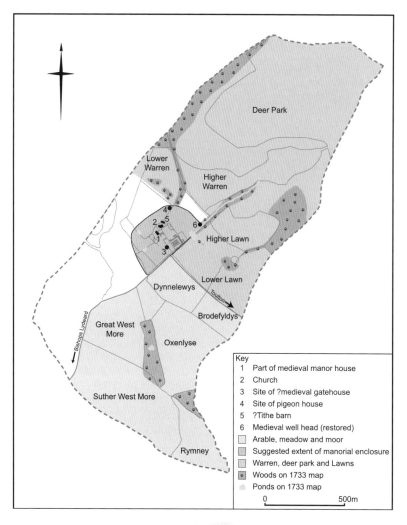

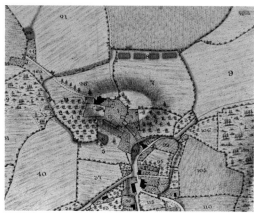

(unfledged birds) as a luxury for the rich. Until 1619 only the lord of the manor or the church could own a dovecote. It used to be thought that dovecotes provided fresh meat in winter as a welcome respite from salt meat. However, it is now clear that the wealthy had access to fresh meat throughout the year. This, combined with the fact that most squabs are produced during the late spring and late summer/early autumn, shows that the possession of a dovecote associated the owner with a luxurious way of life (McCann and McCann 2003, 21–2).

There is plenty of evidence to show that the lords of the manors of the Quantock Hills were leading a luxurious way of life. Although no dovecotes with medieval fabric are known in the area (McCann and McCann 2003), dovecotes are recorded in

Fig 4.21 (above)
Cothelstone: the medieval landscape. (Based on the Ordnance Survey 1st edition map, Somerset sheets 60 NW and 60 SW)

Fig 4.22 (above, right)
The 1827 estate map of East Quantoxhead shows the four fish ponds and the watery nature of the manorial enclosure boundary. (Colonel Sir Walter Luttrell) (AA044906) (© English Heritage. NMR)

Fig 4.23 (right)
Manor Cottages, Cothelstone: part of the medieval manor, a blocked medieval doorway can be seen in the centre of the south elevation. (AA046412) (© English Heritage. NMR)

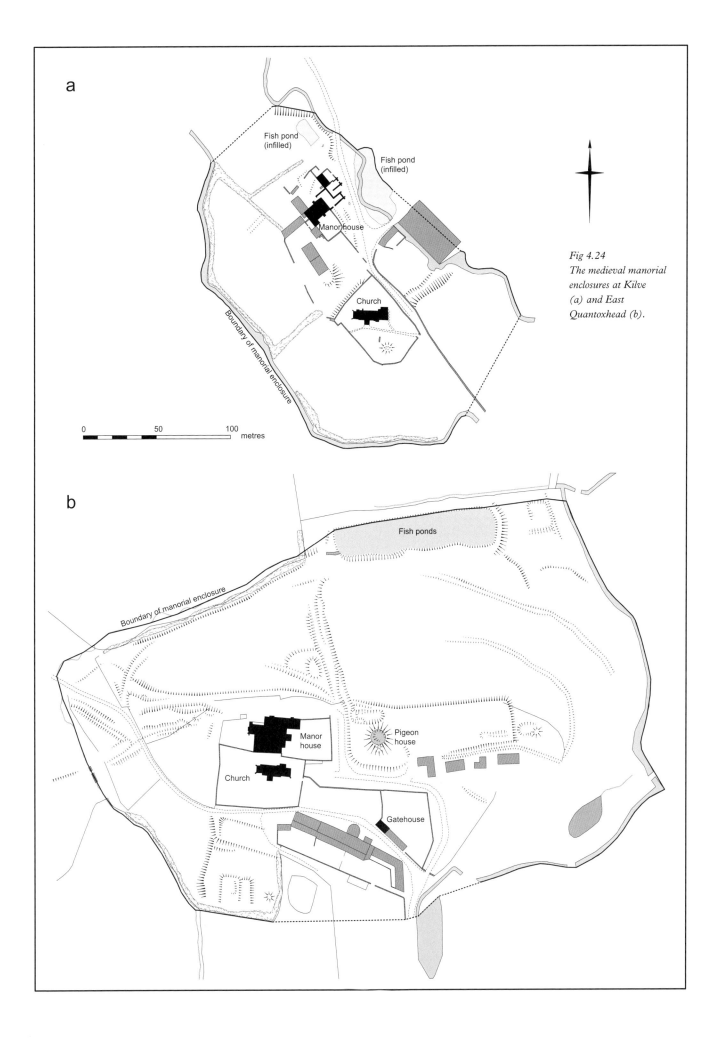

a

Fish pond
(infilled)

Fish pond
(infilled)

Manor house

Boundary of manorial enclosure

Church

Fig 4.24
The medieval manorial
enclosures at Kilve
(a) and East
Quantoxhead (b).

0   50   100
metres

b

Fish ponds

Boundary of manorial enclosure

Manor house

Pigeon
house

Church

Gatehouse

Fig 4.25 (this page)
Part of the medieval
gatehouse, Court House,
East Quantoxhead.
(AA044953) (© English
Heritage. NMR)

accounts from Crowcombe (14th century); Perry, East Quantoxhead (1407–8); Spaxton (1476) and Plainsfield (1511) (Dunning 1985, 57, 121; 1992, 114; 163). Place names such as Pigeon House Close near Cothelstone Manor and Culverhays, adjacent to Court House, East Quantoxhead, indicate the former sites of dovecotes ('Culver', the archaic word for pigeon, was commonly used in Somerset) (Cothelstone tithe map 1838; East Quantoxhead tithe map 1839). The name Kilve may be derived from Culver, and the site of the manorial dovecote is suggested by the watercolour by W W Wheatley, 1847, which shows a round, tower-like building between the church and manor house. Finally, the earthwork remains of a building to the east of Court House, East Quantoxhead, standing in the close known as Culverhays, are probably those of the medieval manorial dovecote (Fig 4.24).

Although there was an abundant supply of meat for the wealthy, there were many days in the church calendar when the consumption of flesh was forbidden. The alternative form of protein was fish and its supply was managed in artificial ponds. Larger breeding ponds were often constructed within deer parks, while smaller holding ponds can be found close to the manor house itself. Again, like dovecotes, the possession of fishponds was an important marker of status in medieval England – a symbol of lordship.

Some of the best evidence for medieval fishponds is at Court House, East Quantoxhead, where the estate map of 1827 shows a set of four regular, rectangular ponds on the edge of the medieval manorial enclosure: one is now dry and is preserved as an earthwork, the others have been made into one ornamental body of water (Fig 4.22). A pond in the northern part of the deer park is probably a breeding pond. The Ordnance Survey map of 1888 shows a set of ponds close to the manor house at Kilve, but they have now been filled in. The area known as the Grove to the southeast of Cothelstone Manor may have been the site of medieval fish-breeding ponds, like the ponds east of Flaxpool and southeast of Crowcombe, noted in c 1600 as the manor fishponds (Dunning 1985, 56). Although ponds are difficult to date on morphological grounds, the fact that the manors of East Quantoxhead, Kilve and Cothelstone were all owned by absentee landlords in the early postmedieval period strengthens the case for a medieval date for these ponds.

The manor house and its enclosure

At the heart of these designed landscapes was the engine house of the manor or estate, the manor house in its enclosure, accommodating the lord and his family, and his servants, and with all the buildings needed to service this extended household. Religious life ran hand in hand with the daily round and the manor house had a chapel or oratory; the larger manorial enclosures usually contained the parish church. At Cothelstone part of the medieval house is preserved as Manor Cottages. The roof of this building shows that it was built in the late 15th century as an open hall, perhaps the hall of an earlier manor house, or part of some rather grand service accommodation for an earlier manor house (Fig 4.23). At Kilve and East Quantoxhead detailed work has made it possible to reconstruct the medieval manorial enclosures (Fig 4.24). The enclosure at Kilve was 240m long and 160m wide, at East Quantoxhead it was 380m long and 250m wide. Water played an important part delimiting the enclosures, with streams and ponds forming many of the boundaries. Access into the manorial enclosure was controlled, and visitors had to pass through a gatehouse. At East Quantoxhead part of the medieval gatehouse is now a farm building (Fig 4.25).

The medieval manor house was built to impress, as the remaining buildings at Kilve show. Here the manor house of the de Furneaux family dates from the 14th century, but there was a manor house here in the 11th century. At the heart of the house was the hall, a communal space for meals and formal meetings, with private accommodation and a chapel for the family on the east and kitchens to the west (Fig 4.26). The manor house faces the church. In 1329 Simon de Furneaux paid for five chantry priests to pray for him and his family in perpetuity (Dunning 1985, 101). Their chapel was inside the church, where the remains of some arcading mark its site on the west side of the chancel. The manorial dovecote stood between the church and house. Farm buildings, a brewhouse, a bakehouse and stables all occupied the enclosure, but the area close to the house contained small garden courts and an orchard. Part of the enclosure survives today, and the importance of water in this landscape becomes apparent. The enclosure seems to have been surrounded by water, and the manorial fish ponds formed part of this watery landscape. The manorial enclosures controlled access to different parts of the landscape. The deer parks and warrens were restricted areas but access to the church was often through the manorial enclosure; so was access to the sea at East Quantoxhead and Kilve. Throughout the story of this managed, privileged and restricted part of the landscape, however, runs the thread of money, and it was (usually) agriculture that provided the driver for the maintenance and expansion of manorial estates. It is the story of that rather more mundane use of the landscape that has left the most lasting impression on the Quantock Hills.

Farms and fields in the landscape

The process of creating a farmstead, carving out the fields from woodland or heath, leaves an imprint on the landscape. It is during the medieval period that we can start to recognise this process across large parts of the landscape. As for the identification of medieval deer parks and rabbit warrens, a mixture of maps, documents and field evidence combines to tell the story.

The dominant form of settlement in and around the Quantock Hills is the farmstead or hamlet. As we have seen, many of these were established well before the Norman Conquest and many remain in use today. So the evidence for their form in the medieval period has been destroyed over hundreds of years of repair and rebuilding, and changing patterns of agriculture in the surrounding fields. Sometimes, for a variety of reasons, farms failed and the remains of these survive in the landscape as deserted farmsteads or settlements. This gives us the opportunity to examine the sort of buildings and farm layouts that were used in the medieval period. There are many deserted farms in the Quantock Hills, but most of them, although probably established by the 11th century, fell into disuse in the 19th and early 20th centuries (*see* Chapter 5). There are, however, two sites that have the remains of buildings that date from before the 16th century. These are near Durborough, west of Aisholt, and at the bottom of Smith's Combe, north of East Quantoxhead.

Hamme and Hulle: two deserted medieval farmsteads

A walk along the track that runs from Durborough Farm up onto Aisholt Common takes you past a well-built stone wall, enclosing a tumble of stone. Here, at the foot of Middle Hill, close to a stream and at an altitude of 200m, is a trapezoidal enclosure containing a stony mound on a platform 18m long and 10m wide, with a stone wall to the northwest (Fig 4.27). These are all that remains of Middlehill House and its barn (West Bagborough tithe map 1839). A little way to the east, a second track, leads up from the valley to nowhere in particular. At the top of this track, which now takes the form of a deep hollow way, are the remains of some buildings. The site is about a third of the way up a small combe that leads onto Lydeard Hill, at an altitude of 200m and on a north-facing slope. These remains are very different in character to the stony mound at Middlehill House. West of the hollow-way a rectangular platform 15m long and 7m wide lies above a spring. East of the track is a rectangular platform, also 15m long and 7m wide, which is overlain by a later field bank. Three smaller platforms lie to the southeast (Fig 4.27). This may be the remains of a single farmstead with outbuildings, or a hamlet of two houses, each with outbuildings.

There is a surprising amount of documentary evidence that has helped to identify these sites as deserted medieval farmsteads, and we can even suggest their early 14th-century names. 'Holt' (Aisholt) was a Domesday manor, with its focus around the church in Aisholt. Domesday also records an estate called Holcombe.

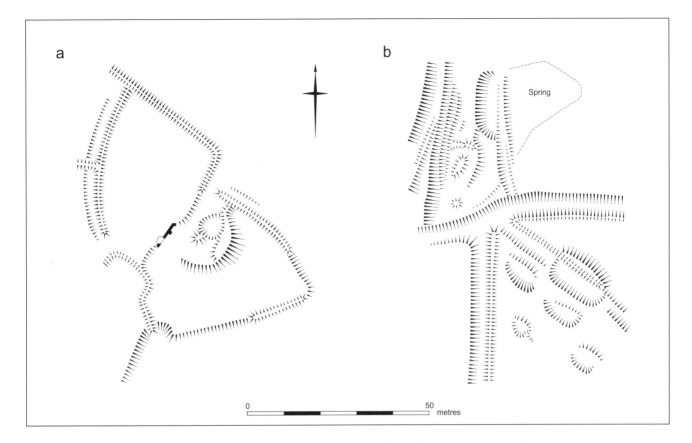

We can be fairly confident that Durborough Farm, named after 17th-century tenants, is medieval Holcombe, from place-name evidence (Aisholt tithe map 1842). The Lay Subsidy of 1327 lists the names of householders who were wealthy enough to pay tax. Some of their surnames have a Latin form known as the locative case. These names often coincide with present day farms or topographic features, indicating the antiquity of names in the landscape and showing that a holding existed at such a place in the early 14th century.

The list for Aisholt includes three such names: Radulpho de Holcomb, Waltero atte Hamme and Philippo atte Hulle (Dickinson 1889, 142). Place names suggest that Middlehill House was Hulle (hill) in the 14th century and that Hamme, in the corner of Old Home Meadow (West Bagborough tithe map 1839), was the other farmstead. Some more documents help to explain what happened in this valley in the medieval period. Hamme was probably in existence by the 11th century as the Domesday estate of Holcombe had land for two ploughteams, divided equally between the demesne (land that was part of the main farm of the manor) and another holding. In the early 14th century Waltero atte Hamme

lived here. By the early 15th century this farm had probably fallen into disuse as lands at West Holcombe are conveyed to Sir Edward Hull in 1443 but no house is mentioned (Dunning 1992, 70). Hulle was a more viable place to live and the West Holcombe land may have become part of Hulle.

It is hard to imagine how the farms at Hulle and Hamme functioned. The site at Hamme is on a steep, north-facing slope, receiving little sun, particularly in the winter months. Hulle is on the valley floor in a sunnier location but again surrounded by the steep slopes of Aisholt Common and Lydeard Hill (Fig 4.28). There is some flatter land on the lower slopes that could have been used for meadow or arable, and this is borne out by the information in the 19th-century tithe awards, which show that several of these fields were meadows, probably belonging to each holding in the medieval period: Middle Hill Meadow; Old Home Meadow and Holcombe Meadow. The relict field systems on Lydeard Hill are complex (*see* Chapter 5) and the earliest phases of these may well have been used by the two farms. Similarly, Middle Hill and land above Durborough Plantation have traces of a relict field system, with Aisholt Common and the Slades (enclosed from common in

Fig 4.27
Deserted farmsteads:
Middle Hill (a) and
Durborough (b).

Fig 4.28
Holcombe and Aisholt
Common, Middle Hill is
at the bottom, Durborough
Farm towards the top.
(NMR 21958/12)
(© English Heritage.
NMR)

Fig 4.29
Ring-fenced holding of
Higher Aisholt Farm.
(Based on the Ordnance
Survey 1st edition maps,
Somerset sheets 49 SW
and 60 NW)

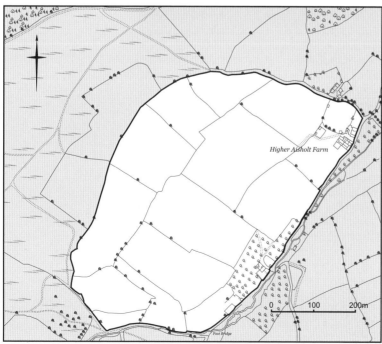

Higher Aisholt Farm

0   100   200m

Foot Bridge

the early part of the 17th century) providing pasture and potential arable land.

The wider landscape around these deserted farmsteads shows, in the pattern of the fields, how many of the farms are created from enclosing a block of land in a single operation from waste – heath or woodland. This can be seen in the fields around the farms of Durborough, Higher and Lower Aisholt, Muchcare, Luxborough and Bishpool (Fig 4.29). South of Broomfield, Oggshole and Rows Farm are good examples. Some of the farms were in existence by the 11th century (Durborough) and by the 13th century (Lower Aisholt and Oggshole) (Dunning 1992, 68; 69; 12).

Domescombe and Deak's Allers: medieval holdings in East Quantoxhead manor

Two more examples of these sorts of farmsteads can be seen on the northern end of the Quantock Hills, between East Quantoxhead and the edge of Quantock Common

(Fig 4.19). Just south of the commons boundary, at the foot of Dens Combe, is a ruined barn. By the end of the 19th century the barn was part of an outbarn, a shelter shed and a barn used for over-wintering cattle. The site, however, is recorded in documentary sources as early as the early 14th century. It is known as Domescombe in 1327, Dennaryscombe in 1394 and in 1687 the farm was held by Giles Sweeting and called Dunscombe (Dunning 1985, 121). The description from this time gives a clear picture of a small farmstead. The farm covered 54 acres and included 38 acres of arable contained in four fields; one meadow of 13 acres and three acres of woodland. This holding, which probably reflects the original medieval pattern of land use, can be seen fossilised in the current field boundaries together with the slight earthworks of former fields and cultivation ridges. The ruined barn lies on top of some earthworks, these are part of the 17th-century farmstead, itself on the site of the medieval farm (Fig 4.30).

A very similar site lies only a kilometre to the northwest. Again, a barn marks the site. This barn is a fine example of an 18th-century estate farm building (*see* Chapter 5), and is important here as it signposts the site of a deserted farmstead. Again, the 1327 Lay Subsidy and the locative surnames help to unravel several mysteries. One is the origin of the name Gay's House Combe, a combe that leads from Smith's Combe up onto the heath. In 1327 Willelmo Gouz lived in the parish of East Quantoxhead (Dickinson 1889, 165), very probably in the farm that is now marked by an earthwork enclosure and building remains (Fig 4.31). There were three or four buildings – the farmhouse and outbuildings – close to a stream and associated with an enclosure, part of which is marked by an earthen bank. The farm was reached by a track, still visible as a hollow-way. We can say that these are the remains of the medieval farm buildings as a map of 1687 shows a farm to the south of this area, where the barn stands today. In 1687 the farm was known by the splendid name of Deak's Allers (Deak's alder trees – several alder trees grow close to the site today) and was much smaller than Dunscombe, with 21 acres of arable, three acres of meadow and, very specifically, six oak trees, nine ash trees and four elm trees. Like Dunscombe, Deak's Allers functioned as an outbarn by the end of the 19th century.

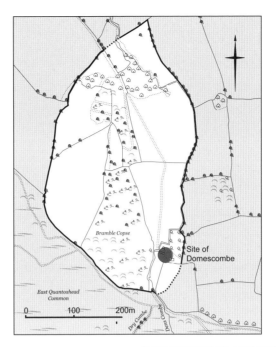

Fig 4.30
The holding of Domescombe. (Based on the Ordnance Survey 1st edition map, Somerset sheet 36 SE)

Fig 4.31
The deserted farmstead of Deak's Allers: earthwork plan.

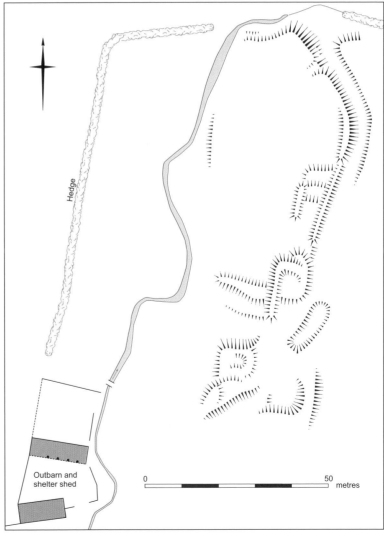

Fig 4.32
Reconstruction of the
medieval open hall
farmhouse and barn at
Middle Halsway Farm.

The buildings in the farmstead

We have already seen how high-status buildings – manor houses and churches – contain the remains of medieval fabric. There is some evidence from the detailed recording of cottages and farm houses as to the size and layout of the houses of ordinary people. A study of some of the oldest buildings in the parish of Crowcombe gives an insight into the sort of buildings that stood at the farmsteads described above in the medieval period (RCHME Building Files). At Middle Halsway Farm a thatched barn lies close to the farmhouse (Fig 4.32). The barn has a roof construction that can be no later than the 15th century and the house was originally an open hall house roughly contemporary with the barn, its central hearth replaced by a chimney stack in the early 16th century. Quarkhill Farm, Forge Cottage and the Old Rectory were also open hall houses, but Carew Cottage began life as a longhouse, a building that housed both people and animals. Carew Cottage was built of cob in the late 15th or early 16th century. It had a hall and small inner room with a byre for the cattle on its east end. Flaxpool Cottage may also have originated as a longhouse. The buildings were all originally three bayed and were roughly the same size, about 13m long and 7m wide.

Common fields and common pasture: medieval field systems

Open field or common field agriculture, where farmers held unenclosed, individual strips of land in two or three large fields located close to the villages where they lived, was widespread in the medieval period in parts of England, particularly in the Midlands. This system of agriculture has received much attention from both historians and archaeologists. The field systems of southwest England, however, have not been studied in such depth.

Some parts of Somerset do contain examples of common field villages, with a particular concentration to the south and east of the county, but a recent study of the available documentary evidence showed that there was a range of agricultural economies in west Somerset, with both common field villages and scattered settlements with enclosed land (Aston 1988).

Most of the fields that surround the farms and hamlets of the Quantock Hills have their origins in a farming system known as infield/outfield farming. In this system a field close to the settlement was used for arable, this was often communally farmed and there was also abundant pasture, common and waste ground available for periodic arable use. Some of the manors on the coastal strip do, however, seem to have operated common field agriculture, for example at Kilton and Lilstock. Both common fields and some infields began to be enclosed or consolidated from as early as the 13th century. This was the process whereby single strips or blocks of strips were exchanged between individual farmers or tenants to make more convenient blocks of land. A detailed study of the process in east Devon showed that it was the result of a shift away from arable farming to a livestock based economy (Fox 1972). The process of consolidation and enclosure can be seen in the landscape, either on historic maps or fossilised in the modern field pattern. At Bicknoller bundles of enclosed strips can still be seen on the edge of the village to the northeast of Trendle Lane and to the north of Dashmoor Lane (Fig 4.33). A few 'furlong' (a block of strips) field names are recorded in the 19th century (Bicknoller tithe map 1838). At Nether Stowey there is documentary evidence that names North Field and South Field, two common arable fields that were in the process of consolidation by the 15th century (Dunning 1985, 191; 195). Some of the enclosed strip fields can still be seen today, around Blindwell House (South Field) and sandwiched between the A39 and, presently, a chicken factory (North Field) (Fig 4.12). However, the tithe map of 1841 and a plan of the town drawn in 1750 show many more of these

strip fields still in existence, and the tithe award shows that many of the strips were owned and tenanted by a variety of people and put to a number of uses (Fig 4.34) (SRO 1750a).

Kilton Field and Sessons (from 'selion' meaning a cultivated strip), named in the 16th century, suggest former open fields around the village, as do East and West Field, recorded in the early 17th century. Kilton gives us some of the best evidence for the farming regime in the late 14th century, when, for the period 1377–81, the crop was mainly wheat, grown in a three year cycle, with small areas of beans and peas, and barley for just one year. There were 50 pigs and 25 cattle, 17 of these were draught animals. The farm workers were two ploughmen, two drovers and a swineherd (Dunning 1985, 89; 93).

The importance of arable cultivation is reflected in the survival of two windmill mounds on the East Quantoxhead estate.

Fig 4.33
Enclosed strip fields at Bicknoller to the north (left) and east (top) of the village. (NMR 21958/02) (© English Heritage. NMR)

Fig 4.34
Enclosed strip fields at
Nether Stowey, drawn on a
map of 1750. (SRO 1750a
DD/SAS(a) C/1207)
(Somerset Archive and
Record Service)

The earliest windmills in England, dating from the late 12th century, were post mills. The sails, gearing and millstones were carried by a timber framed structure that revolved around the head of an upright post. This caused the sails to turn to face the prevailing wind (Watts 2000). The substructure of the post mill was usually buried in a substantial earthen mound for stability and these mounds survive in the fields between East Quantoxhead and Perry (Fig 4.35). Just north of Underhill Lane – the hollow-way linking these two settlements – lies a large, rectangular mound (21m long, 18m wide and 2m high) with ditches to the north and south, on a small hilltop. To the north of Perry Farm, one kilometre to the west, there

is a similar mound, 16m long, 11m wide and 1.5m high, now partly obscured by a hedge bank. Windmills were built to supplement water powered mills. At East Quantoxhead the manor mill is mentioned in the 11th century (Dunning 1985, 125).

These two windmills on the coast must have provided another source of income for the manor in the medieval period, as mills were built for the lord, not the peasant. Unfree tenants were obliged to have their grain milled at the manor mill and to pay a toll in kind. The windmills may have been built as early as the 13th or 14th centuries. A similar mound on the line of the M5 at Chedzoy, near Bridgwater, was excavated and was found to be the base of an early 15th-century post mill (Dawson *et al* 2001, 44–5). A fine bench end carving at Bishops Lydeard church showing a post mill, some rather hungry looking pigeons, and the miller and his horse, dates from the mid- 16th century (Fig 4.36). By the 19th century the mound at Perry lay on the edge of 'Windmill Piece' and it could have supported a post-medieval windmill (East Quantoxhead tithe map 1839; Dunning 1985, 121).

With common field farming there was the right to pasture on the manor commons for the tenant farmers. There is plenty of documentary evidence to show that this occurred in the medieval period. For example, tenants and landowners in Stogursey had grazing rights in pasture and wood on the Quantock Hills by the late 13th century, there were general rights to graze and dig turf on the common of East Quantoxhead at this time and the manor court supervised repair of a common way in 1340 and 1379 (Dunning 1985, 58, 125). There was, however, pressure on the common land. As early as the 14th century and 15th century there was some cultivation on the commons. In Bicknoller in the 1330s the Chapter of Wells held an area of waste on the hill for sheep pasture, with a further area there under cultivation. Small plots of 'common on Quantock' were ploughed in 1405 in the parish of Crowcombe; in East Quantoxhead areas of common were cultivated in 1454–5 (Dunning 1985, 15; 58; 125). The commoners of Stogursey had small areas of arable on the hills by the late 15th century; in the early 16th century rye and oats were grown; and in 1515 14 acres of common land on Broomfield were brought under cultivation. Areas of the lowland commons were also being enclosed and cultivated at this time,

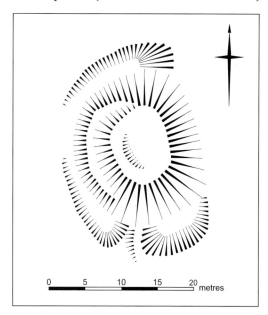

Fig 4.35
Windmill mound,
Underhill Lane, East
Quantoxhead.

0 5 10 15 20 metres

for example parts of Heddon and Heathfield Commons in Crowcombe parish were under cultivation by the 1430s (Dunning 1992, 166; 12; Dunning 1985, 58).

As we have already seen, large areas of the commons are covered with relict field systems. The relict fields as we see them now in their latest, most developed form probably date from the late 16th century onwards, and so are described below (*see* Chapter 5), although some of these fields may well have their origins in the medieval period, as suggested by the documentary evidence of small-scale, periodic cultivation on the commons in the 14th and 15th centuries. These outlying fields were probably worked in common by the holders of the small farmsteads, described above, who grew rye and oats in small plots on the commons, allowing for a period of fallow for the more intensively cultivated lowland arable fields. East Quantoxhead, for example, grew 55 acres of rye and 166 acres of wheat in the 1570s (Dunning 1985, 124).

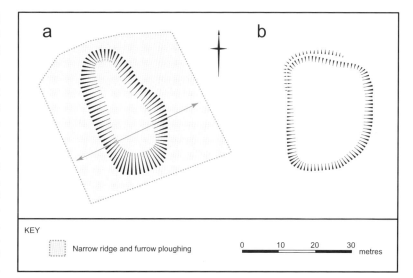

KEY

Narrow ridge and furrow ploughing

0   10   20   30 metres

The remains of these plots survive as earthworks on West Hill and the Greenway.

The main use of the commons in the medieval period, however, was for pasture, both cattle and sheep. A reliable water supply for the stock, particularly cattle, was essential and ponds were constructed on the commons to ensure this. The remains of three of these ponds can be seen on Woodlands Hill, at Withyman's (or Wilmot's) Pool below Black Hill and on Black Ball Hill (Fig 4.37). The ponds are all substantial features in the landscape. The largest, Withyman's Pool, is 40m long, 30m wide and 1.5m deep (Fig 4.38). All three ponds have evidence of relict field systems running over their edges and the pond on Black Ball Hill has been ploughed right over. Withyman's

Fig 4.36 (left)
Post mill and miller on bench end, Bishops Lydeard Church. (Hazel Riley)

Fig 4.37 (top right)
Stock ponds on the common: Black Ball Hill (a) and Woodlands Hill (b).

Fig 4.38 (above)
Withyman's Pool. (Hazel Riley)

Pool is named Wilmot's Pool on the 1609 map of Quantock common (SRO 1609). A small pond in Duke's Plantation, bisected by later woodland boundary banks, may be a similar survival.

Small-scale and local: industry in the medieval period

The Quantock Hills could provide many of the raw materials needed for the establishment of industries based on a rural way of life. The streams and the upland sheep pastures provided the power and raw materials for woollen cloth manufacture, as water-powered fulling mills were established close to fast-flowing streams. An abundant supply of wood and local sources of clay meant that pottery manufacture was possible and tanning and leatherworking depended on a supply of oak bark and hides.

Nether Stowey was an important centre for the production of pottery in the post-medieval period (*see* Chapter 5), but there was also a pottery industry here in the medieval period. A pottery kiln dating from the 13th and 14th centuries was excavated to the south of Nether Stowey Castle (Nesbitt 1970; Ponsford and White 1971). Medieval pottery from this kiln has been identified in assemblages from excavations on the island of Lundy and from the deserted medieval settlement at Leyhill, near Porlock. Three sherds of the fabric were found in Dissolution and post-Dissolution contexts at Cleeve Abbey (Allan 1998). Documentary evidence suggests a well-established pottery industry in the area by the end of the 13th century. In 1275 a group of potters in Nether Stowey paid 20s for the right to make pottery *ab antiquo* (as formerly) (Patourel 1968, 108). A potter from the continent was living in the neighbouring parish of Over Stowey in 1591 and by the early 17th century a potter held land beside the Stogursey road in Nether Stowey parish (Dunning 1985, 195; 1992, 167). A local pottery industry was also established in the medieval period at Little Quantock Farm, Crowcombe, where kiln wasters were found (Allan 1998, 47).

Although the physical evidence for the textile industry dates from the post-medieval period (*see* Chapter 5), there is some evidence from documentary sources to show that this industry had its roots firmly in the medieval rural landscape of the Quantock Hills. Flaxpool, where flax was prepared for making linen, and a fulling mill at Crowcombe are both mentioned in 1355 (Dunning 1985, 61; 54).There were fulling mills at Ivyton and Adscombe in the 15th century (Dunning 1992, 13; 167). Spaxton was important for finishing and dyeing cloth by the 16th century and a fulling mill is documented here from the 13th century through to the 16th century. The image of a lively textile worker decorates a bench in Spaxton church (Fig 4.39). A flaxpit, a dye-house and a tucker's rack are all documented in Nether Stowey in the 16th century (Dunning 1992, 119; 121; 195). The presence of the cloth industry, together with the products of agriculture, including leather, must have acted as stimuli for the growth of Nether Stowey and Crowcombe, both of which had borough status, a market and a fair by the 13th century (Dunning 1985, 59; 195; 196).

There is some evidence that the mineral suites on the east and south of the Quantock hills were worked before the 18th century (*see* Chapter 5). Most of the early references are to iron mining or smelting. In the early 14th century tenants in Crowcombe who used common pasture on the Quantock Hills had to pay an annual render of 12 slabs of iron to Stogursey Castle and the tenants in Bicknoller and Thorncombe owed slabs of iron to their landlord (Dunning 1985, 58; 15). Quantities of iron slag were noted during building work at Combe Cottage, Crowcombe, but their exact context is unclear (S Henson, pers comm). Slag from Ebsley Farm near Spaxton has been identified as being of Roman or medieval date (Somerset HER 10804). East of the Quantock Hills at Lexworthy, Enmore, three mills paid rent in iron blooms or iron ore in the 11th century, indicating that iron was being mined or smelted in this region in the medieval period. The place names Kingslode and Loads in Kingston St Mary date from the medieval period and suggest early mining in the area (Hamilton and Lawrence 1970, 69).

The stone quarries at Rooks Castle

Below the complex of enclosures at Rooks Castle is a wedge-shaped area of pits and spoil heaps (Fig 4.5). These are the remains of an industry that grew up here in the medieval period, when outcrops of Morte Slates were dug as a source of roof tiles. The presence of quite extensive spoil heaps suggests that at least some initial dressing of the slate tiles was carried out on site, and this is borne out by the fact that Hugo le Helier (the tiler) lived here in the 14th century (Dickinson 1889, 162). Tiles from these quarries were used on high-status local buildings. The accounts of the church wardens of St Mary, Bridgwater, for 1394, list as expenses '4250 stone tiles bought at Rookscastle, 5s 8d at 16d per 1000' (Dilks 1938, 228–32). In the late 14th century Bridgwater Castle and its dovecote were roofed with stone tiles brought from Rooks Castle. In one year the chapel roof lost its tiles twice due to gales, and the repair of these roofs is a frequent charge in the castle accounts (Dilks 1940, 103). The excavators of Taunton Castle suggest that the broken slate roof tiles found in a well, backfilled in 1659, may have come from the Rooks Castle quarries (Radford and Hallam 1955, 80; 88). As later quarrying often destroys the remains of earlier extraction sites, the earthworks here represent an important survival from the medieval period.

The medieval landscape

The medieval landscape of the Quantock Hills has survived in remarkable detail in some places. On the coastal strip the buildings at Kilve and the deserted farmsteads of Dens Combe and Deak's Allers are visible survivals of a way of life, centred on the manor and its lord, that has persisted through the centuries in certain places. Many aspects of the managed and designed landscapes that surrounded the manors can be found, both from maps and surviving as features in the landscape. The commons, too, contain fragments of the medieval way of life: the remains of small plots of arable land above the settlements that lie to the north and west, and the ponds, carefully dug and maintained to provide water for cattle.

It is in the quiet combes of the southeast side of the hills, however, where patterns of the medieval landscape are pervasive. Many of the hamlets and farms around Aisholt and Merridge, connected by narrow lanes and tracks, have their origins in the 11th century or earlier. Broomfield parish, too, contains much evidence for the medieval landscape.

Many of the farms and hamlets are documented by the 13th century, but it is the distribution of these holdings together with the later prehistoric enclosures that must be considered one of the most special aspects of the historic landscape of the southern part of the Quantock Hills (Fig 3.19). Large prehistoric hill-slope or hilltop

Fig 4.39 (opposite)
Textile worker with the
tools of his trade, bench
end, Spaxton Church.
(Hazel Riley)

113

enclosures (*see* Chapter 3) lie close to existing farms and hamlets at Lydeard Farm, Broomfield, Ivyton Farm, Rows Farm, Downs Farm, Oggshole Farm, Rooks Castle Farm and, in Kingston St Mary, Volis Farm and Hestercombe. The most outstanding example of this is at Rooks Castle. Here the medieval and later prehistoric are side by side. Rooks Castle is one of the most intriguing sites in the Quantock Hills: it may well be the site of a hunting lodge associated with the pre-Conquest Quantock Forest or the forest of North Petherton.

Is the presence of the former royal forest of Quantock the clue to the survival of these large prehistoric enclosures and their propinquity in space to the historic settlements of the area? To the north, the commons remained open heathland, partly due to the topography, but also to the presence of a few large manors that preserved a way of life using lowland and common into the modern period in some instances. To the south, enclosure of common and downland was early and went hand in hand with the establishment of scattered farmsteads in the valleys – land that was granted from the Crown as the forest ceased to exist. This part of the Quantock Hills was favoured for settlement in the 1st millennium BC. The same areas were chosen as the land was settled again in the historic period.

5
A Romantic landscape?
The Quantock Hills in the
post-medieval period

A changing landscape: enclosure, improvement and industry

The beginning of the post-medieval period in Britain is marked by the dissolution of the monasteries in *c* 1540. It ends in 1900 when Britain can be finally called an industrial nation. The pace of change over these 360 years was rapid and unrelenting, and the period is, of course, well documented by historical narratives. The landscape, however, is another document, which has often not been read. The aftermath of the dissolution of the monasteries saw the great monastic buildings, symbols of ecclesiastical authority, left as ruins or rebuilt as the houses of the secular gentry. Medieval manor houses were rebuilt and grand designs for new houses and grounds were planned and executed. Some of this wealth came from overseas as this was the age of colonial expansion; some came from the estates of the gentry.

A broad theme runs through English agrarian history in the post-medieval period. It is of steady growth to feed an expanding population. The population of England doubled in size in the earlier part of the period, from about 2.4 million in 1540 to about six million in 1750. This sort of growth was sustained by improvements in agricultural practices, particularly in enclosure of common and waste land, the enclosure of common fields in the English Midlands, the use of new crop breeds and rotations, and in southwest England in particular the increased use of outfield cultivation on the commons. The idea of an Agricultural Revolution, with dramatic and far-reaching change concentrated in a short period of time in the later part of the 18th century has been replaced by the idea that the process of change was more gradual, beginning earlier and continuing later than was previously thought. English agriculture

expanded just about continuously in the 300 years from the later 16th century to the late 19th century. The success of the colonies, ironically, led to the period of depression in the 1870s when competition from imported foodstuffs led to the collapse of prices for the English farmer. The new territories in the Americas, New Zealand and Australia supplied both meat and grain at prices that undercut the English farmer (Barnwell and Giles 1997, 3–7).

For most of the post-medieval period, however, the story of English agriculture was a success story and farmers supplied the rapidly increasing population with a range of foodstuffs. This had a profound impact on the landscape. By 1900 the process of enclosure of former common fields was complete and huge areas of former wastes and commons had been enclosed and 'improved'. The new canal and railway networks meant that many vernacular building materials were replaced by mass-produced brick and tile. Large areas of countryside were affected by widespread and large scale extractive industries: metal ores, coal and stone. New industrial towns developed and there was a market in these towns hungry for new, mass produced consumer goods, manufactured in large factories.

Gardens bright with sinuous rills: designed landscapes on the Quantock Hills

Geometric and formal: early post-medieval gardens

The gardens of the gentry in the 16th and early 17th centuries had their origins in the small closes and courts of the medieval manor house (*see* Chapter 4). These early post-medieval gardens were formal spaces, clearly separated from the world outside by high hedges, fences or walls, and their design was dominated by geometry, seen in

Fig 5.1
Cothelstone Manor: the
gatehouse. (AA048455)
(© English Heritage.
NMR)

Fig 5.2
Cothelstone Manor: the
early post-medieval layout.

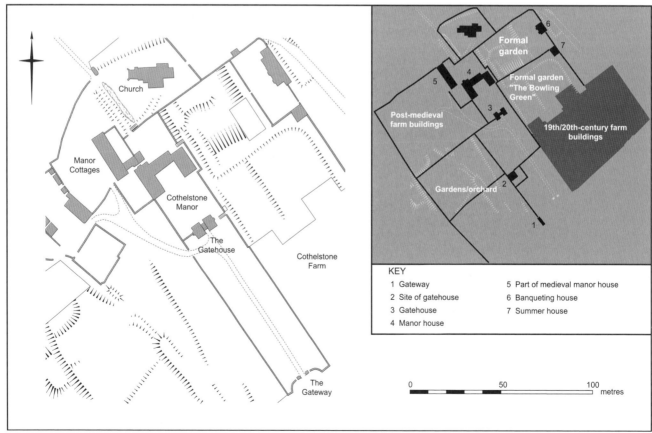

KEY

1 Gateway   5 Part of medieval manor house
2 Site of gatehouse 6 Banqueting house
3 Gatehouse   7 Summer house
4 Manor house

the elaborate knot gardens of the period. Garden buildings were important features in these spaces, providing another opportunity to display one's wealth and taste. The final course to a formal meal was taken in the banqueting house, where elaborate and often quirky food was served. The remains of such gardens can be seen at Cothelstone Manor.

Sometime about the middle of the 16th century, the old manor house at Cothelstone and its outbuildings were completely remodelled, probably by the second Sir John Stawell, lord of the manor between 1541 and 1603. A new house and gatehouse were built close to the old hall range (Fig 5.1). Parts of this house had been left in a ruinous state after the Civil War and the house was thoroughly restored in the 1850s by Edward Jeffries Esdaile. His diaries and some 18th-century estate maps help to interpret the buildings and earthworks at Cothelstone. The approach to the new manor house was very elaborate. Esdaile takes us on a journey from the front of Cothelstone Manor out into open countryside. 'Passing through an archway [the extant gatehouse] we find ourselves in a wide open space, all walled, and another porter's lodge before us. At the time of writing this [1855] not a vestige remained to mark the site of any such, but very old people....remember heaps of stones lying about' (Stawell 1910, 460). In fact, the location of this gatehouse is shown on the estate map of 1733 and it was directly opposite the lane from Toulton, making it a good candidate for a gatehouse to the medieval manorial complex, retained to add another element to the formal approach to the new manor house. Esdaile also records that a white-stoned, semi-circular arch finally led one out of the confines of the manor. This arch was moved from its original location spanning the road from Bishops Lydeard to its present location framing both gatehouse and manor house. The approach to the new house at Cothelstone was thus very grand indeed. The visitor passed under an arch, then into a courtyard, through a gatehouse and into another enclosed court. Finally, the visitor passed through another gatehouse into the inner court to face the house itself.

A new house, in a new position and with a new gatehouse, needed new surroundings. The formal gardens consisted of three large rectangular enclosures, one in front of the house, the other two on each side. High walls, with evidence of much repair over the years, and earthworks show how each enclosure was divided into smaller garden courts (Fig 5.2). The banqueting house stands at the highest point of the garden layout, with views across the Vale of Taunton to the hills beyond.

Fig 5.3
Cothelstone Manor: the early post-medieval formal gardens and banqueting house. (AA048460) (© English Heritage. NMR)

117

There was a passion for bowls at this time: by 1541 the game was so popular that the government, alarmed by the betting it attracted and the neglect of archery it supposedly encouraged, made it illegal to play the game anywhere apart from private gardens (Williamson 1995, 34). There was a bowling green at Cothelstone Manor and Esdaile records that workmen found the bowls and their jack (Stawell 1910, 461). At the corner of the bowling green, at the end of a terraced walk, stands a little summer house, probably on the site of an earlier garden building. When these gardens were built, the manor still had its adjoining deer park (*see* Chapter 4), providing a pastoral setting for the formal gardens and new house (Fig 5.3).

The earthwork remains of gardens that probably date from the 17th century can be seen at Parsonage Farm, Over Stowey; Court House, East Quantoxhead and Crowcombe Court (Figs 5.4 and 5.5). The evidence for the layout of smaller gardens of the early post-medieval period often comes from documents and pictures. The vicarage at Nether Stowey, for example, had a garden and orchard in 1571 and a hop yard by 1613 and in 1690 the vicar of Yeovil planted apple trees, artichokes, asparagus, gooseberries

Fig 5.4
The Quantock Hills: early post-medieval gardens, landscape parks, tree rings and shooting butts. (Based on an Ordnance Survey map, with permission.

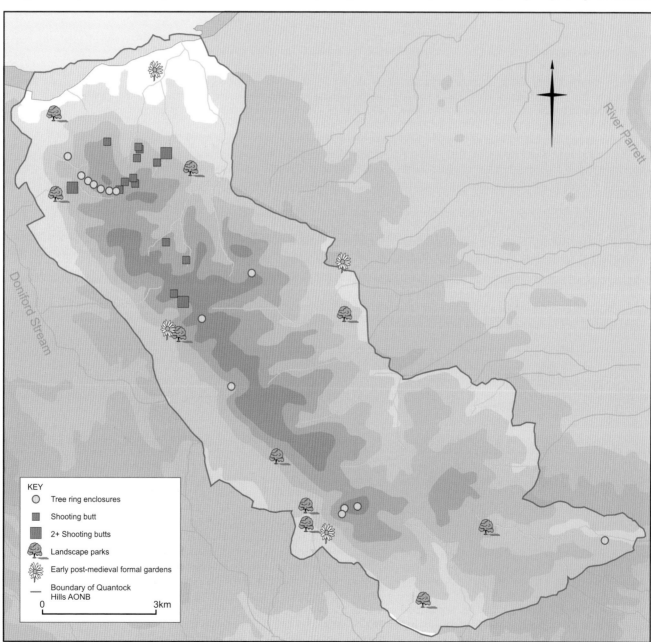

KEY
- ○ Tree ring enclosures
- ■ Shooting butt
- ■ 2+ Shooting butts
- 🌳 Landscape parks
- 🌼 Early post-medieval formal gardens
- — Boundary of Quantock Hills AONB

0   3km

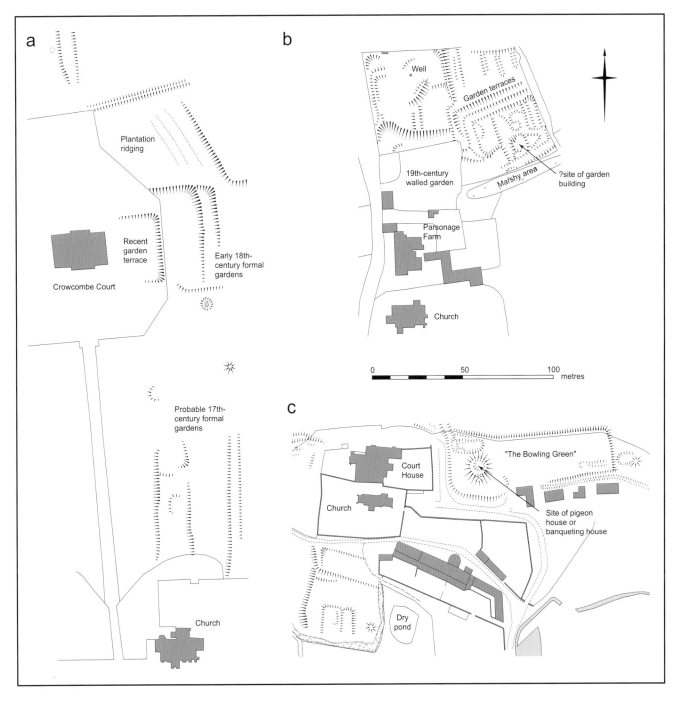

and cherries (Dunning 1985, 198; Bond 1998, 73–4). The 17th-century garden earthworks to the north of Parsonage Farm are therefore important survivals from this time. The garden was pleasingly formal in design, with two wide terraces sheltering an area for flower beds and perhaps a summer house. Above the terraces were more garden beds. The terraces offered the ideal environment for growing hops, vines or espaliered and cordoned fruit trees, as well as providing a way up through the garden area (Fig 5.5).

At Court House formal gardens were laid out both to the south and east of the house, probably in the earlier part of the 17th century when the house was remodelled. The gentle slope to the south of the house and church contains the earthwork remains of a small, formal garden, recorded on a map of 1687 (SRO 1687). The earthworks show that the garden consisted of a rectangular area, some 50m long and 40m wide, aligned with the churchyard. A small terrace lay at the top of the garden; below it

Fig 5.5
Seventeenth-century formal gardens: Crowcombe Court (a), Parsonage Farm (b) and Court House (c).

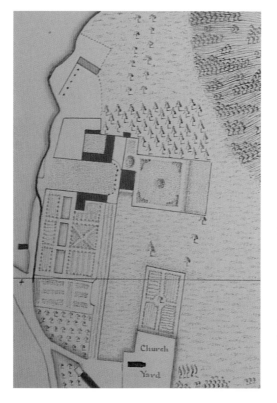

site of a banqueting house, sited to afford spectacular views across the deer park with the Bristol Channel beyond.

The exact location of the medieval manor house at Crowcombe is not known, but it was still in existence in 1676 when John Carew laid out a court and garden (Dunning 1985, 57). This may be the detached garden between the 18th-century house and the church, portrayed on a map of 1767 and now just visible as slight earthworks to the north of the churchyard (Figs 5.5 and 5.6). The garden was a simple plat, divided into four by paths with a tree at the centre. The medieval house was pulled down in 1724 and replaced by Crowcombe Court. Thomas Carew sold six manors to pay for his new house, which gradually acquired the requisite setting, clearly shown on the map of 1767. Kitchen and ornamental gardens lay to the south of the house and a square garden was laid out before the east front of Crowcombe Court. The earthworks of this garden, together with ridging for a formal, very regular plantation and a long avenue linking house and park can all be seen (Fig 5.5).

were two rectangular garden beds (Fig 5.5). To the east of the house is a level area of ground – the Bowling Green – with a large circular mound at its western end. This may be the site of the manorial dovecote (*see* Chapter 4). Equally, it may have been the

Contriving the natural: landscape parks

The remains at Crowcombe Court bridge the gap between the geometric formality of the late 17th and early 18th centuries and

the natural settings favoured by Brown and his contemporaries in the latter part of the 18th century (Williamson 1995). The avenue to the north of the new house, leading out into the park, and the areas of geometric gardens to the south and east of the new house were seen as old fashioned by the 1760s. The ornamental gardens were removed some time after 1767 to achieve a naturalistic 'modern style' (Dunning 1985, 58), integrating the existing park with the setting of the house. By 1800 everybody who was anybody had a landscape park as a setting to their country house (Fig 5.4). Such parks echoed the wood pasture of the late medieval deer park, indeed, some had older parks at their heart. When a landscape park was laid out, existing mature trees were kept and new planting had soft edges. The serpentine lake was a ubiquitous feature; it was created by constructing a dam across the valley of a stream or river. A curving carriage drive took visitors through the park to the house, often crossing the river close to the lake and carefully placed buildings drew one's eye across the landscape.

The landscape park at Crowcombe has its origins in the park laid out by Sir John Carew in the early years of the 17th century (Dunning 1985, 56). This park took in some of the lower slopes of the Quantock Hills and, by 1767, contained a mixture of open woodland and ornamental planting (Fig 5.7). A warren occupied the ground above it, echoing the arrangements of medieval deer parks observed in the Quantock Hills (see Chapter 4), and the remains of at least one pillow mound still survive as a rectangular mound, 11m long, 6m wide and 0.6m high. By the end of the 18th century Crowcombe Park contained a cascade of eight ponds and a gothic folly, reached by a path leading through a rusticated arch and across the cascades by a rustic bridge (Fig 5.8).

The importance of water in the 18th-century landscape park is demonstrated at Fyne Court, Broomfield, a small landscape park laid out in the late 18th century by Richard Crosse. Here were a cascade of ponds and a small serpentine lake. These were created, unusually, by constructing a long dam along the edge of a stream, so that the body of water is perched above the house and drive. The sight of a punt gliding gently through the trees, seemingly in mid air, was a surprising element in the walks through the park. The most was made of a small space. Walks were punctuated by

views across the park to Broomfield Church, which acted as an eye catcher, as did the decorative boat house at the end of the serpentine lake. Most eye-catching of all, however, was the Folly built by the lake edge at the point where the drive swings sharply towards the mansion house (Fig 5.9). A deeply rutted lane cutting through bare rock in places, part of an old route up to the church, and several overgrown quarries were used to give the landscape a fashionable picturesque element. Here were parts of the existing landscape brought into the designed landscape park.

Fig 5.8
Crowcombe Park: some of the masonry in this gothic folly is medieval and may come from the old manor house at Crowcombe or from Halsway Manor. (Hazel Riley)

Fig 5.9
The Folly at Fyne Court is placed as an eye-catcher by the drive to the mansion house. (Hazel Riley)

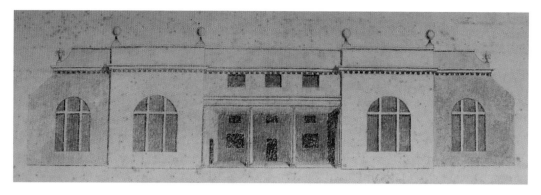

Terhill Park

Thomas Slocombe built a new mansion house at Terhill, between West Bagborough and Cothelstone, evidently completed by 1778 (SRO 1778). The house was a substantial, three-bayed building, facing south, with large windows to take advantage of the wonderful views across the Vale of Taunton afforded by the site (Fig 5.10). Only a hollow, some 25m long, 20m wide and 1.2m deep, now marks the site of Terhill House (Fig 5.11). When Edward Jeffries took over the estate he was unimpressed with the house, describing it as 'in a ruinous state being built of bad materials and by bad workmen' (quoted in Nicholas Pearson Associates 1998, 17). The new owner was also rather scornful of what he considered to be the rather parochial landscape park that Slocombe laid out around Terhill:

> Mr Slocombe was a character, offering as instance of a strong mind left to itself, he spent his money and his time in what he considered adornments of his Estate, but in fact follies, to show this it need only be mentioned that to reach his house you had to cross two Canals, or narrow shallow ponds over a Draw Bridge, the said Pond running thus the centre part which formed the division, about 3 feet wide, was a strawberry bed!!!
> *(quoted in Nicholas Pearson Associates 1998, 17).*

In fact, the map evidence and earthwork evidence combine to show that Terhill Park is an excellent example of a small landscape park dating from the middle of the 18th century (Fig 5.11). The park covered an area of some 21ha (52 acres), taking in the very steep ground to the north of Terhill, as well as more gently sloping ground to the south, and contained areas of formal planting, carriage drives, a canal and several ornamental buildings.

One of the most important buildings in Terhill Park is the grotto (Fig 5.12). This lies to the southeast of Terhill House and occupies a prominent position. The building is shown on the estate map of 1778, and the same map shows how the grotto was the destination for a walk from Terhill House, through the formal gardens and across a canal. The grotto is built of local slatey sandstone with quartz detailing and is remarkably well preserved. Built into the base of a slope, it is 5m wide, 3m deep and 3.5m high and contains five stone lined niches, each 1.8m high and 1.1m wide, the central niche has a further niche above. Two arches, divided by a central pier, form the entrances into the grotto. A small niche is built into the front elevation above the central pier. The front elevation is capped by a large boulder and traces of external pilasters can be seen. A small fragment of rusticated stone survives at the top of the western pilaster.

An elevation of a grotto on the estate map of 1778 is very similar to this grotto (Fig 5.13). The drawing shows the pilasters capped with goat skulls, deer skulls above the arches, and a satanic figure standing above the central pier. No figures, however, survive on this building, if, indeed, they ever existed.

An obelisk and a summer house, now only marked by a ruined wall and a level stance, once stood at the top of the park, in positions where they could be seen from inside and outside the park. Classical statuary was very fashionable in the early 18th century, indeed advice was proffered: Jupiter or Mars for large open areas, Neptune for canals, and fauns and sylvans for wilderness (Williamson 1995, 39). Only one statue of the ten that originally graced Terhill Park remains. This is a striking figure of Jupiter, placed at the very top of the park. His companions in the 18th century included an 8ft high Venus, as well as Minerva, Mercury, Atlas and Apollo (SRO Esdaile Manuscripts).

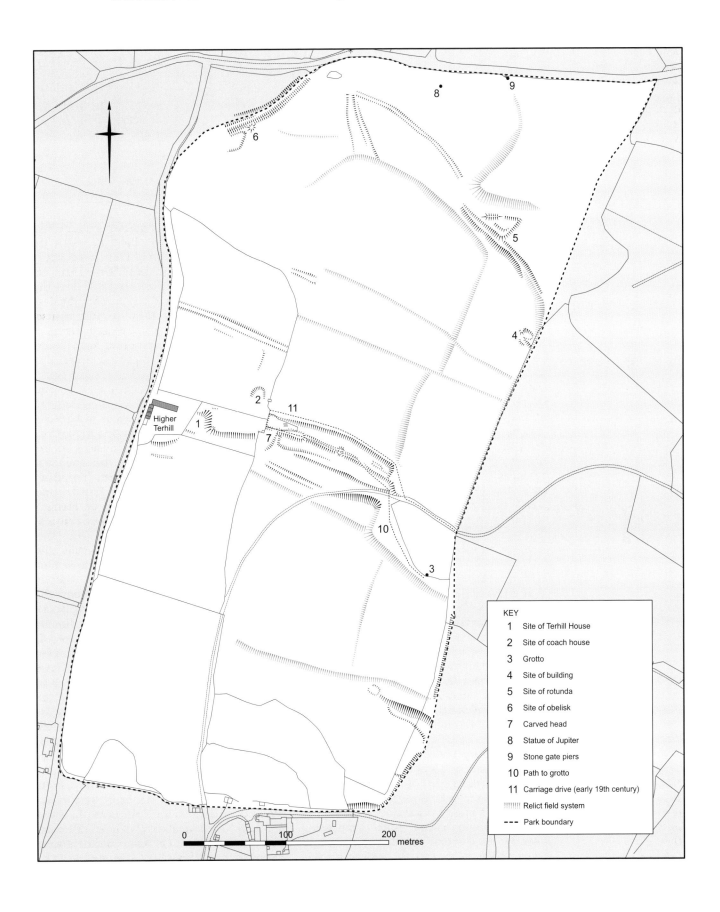

Higher
Terhill

KEY

1 Site of Terhill House
2 Site of coach house
3 Grotto
4 Site of building
5 Site of rotunda
6 Site of obelisk
7 Carved head
8 Statue of Jupiter
9 Stone gate piers
10 Path to grotto
11 Carriage drive (early 19th century)

|||||||| Relict field system
- - - Park boundary

0   100   200
                         metres

Fig 5.12
Terhill Park: southern
elevation of the grotto.

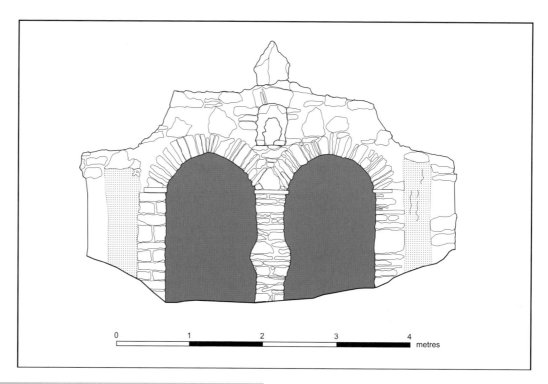

Fig 5.13
Terhill Park: southern
elevation of the grotto as
drawn on a map of 1778.
(SRO 1778 DD/ES
C/2217) (Somerset
Archive and Record
Service)

A carriage drive through the park was lined with trees and passed an ornamental canal. The remains of the drive and the canal are preserved as earthworks. A path led from the formal gardens by the house, across the canal, giving the impression of crossing a large body of water or moat. Here, the path is carried on a substantial earthen and stone bank, 40m long, 5m wide and 1.2m high, and a revetment wall is decorated with a finely carved stone head representing Neptune. The walk continued, following the course of the drive, then diverging south towards the grotto, all the while flanked by water. As well as the canals close to Terhill House, the landscape park contained a number of other water features. Two ponds in Kiln Close were to become part of a series of ponds that fed the lake at Cothelstone House.

A very large pond is shown on the 1778 estate map at the bottom of Terhill Meadow, east of Pilgrims' Cottages. This pond became incorporated into the large orchard that lay between East Bagborough and Pilgrims' Cottages in the 19th and early 20th centuries. It was this pond that became the centre of a dispute between Thomas Slocombe and Frances Hamilton of Bishops Lydeard. In 1791, rival workmen spent the whole day diverting a stream that flowed down to Pilgrims' Barn, first to Mrs Hamilton's fields, then to Mr Slocombe's pond, and so on. The dispute was finally settled by Mr Gibbs, the tenant of Cothelstone Manor, who said that both parties were in the wrong, and that most of the water should flow down to East Bagborough, for the stream was the village's water supply (Allen 1983, 268).

One of the most striking features of Terhill Park is the way in which the remains of an extensive relict field system have been preserved in the park. The fields were in use until the middle of the 18th century, when the park was created (Nicholas Pearson Associates 1998, 17). Some of the oldest trees in the park are hedgerow trees retained when the park was created, for example the large oaks towards the top of the park, while a group of lime trees on the southern edge of a large quarry north of Terhill House appears to be a survival from the 18th-century planting regime. Some planting was also carried out in the 19th century, when Terhill Park became part of Cothelstone Park.

The ornamental landscape

Viewed from the Great Road descending Beacon Hill, the house at St Audries, as the manor of West Quantoxhead was known after *c* 1540, has a fairytale quality. This sylvan setting was only achieved after more than 100 years of diverting roads, planting trees and moving the old village of West Quantoxhead from between the manor house and the medieval church to its present site. This process culminated in the rebuilding of the church in 1855–6, leaving it in splendid isolation at the top of the old village street, now the main drive to the manor house. Both church and house were rebuilt to designs by John Norton, architect of Tyntesfield, the gothic mansion in north Somerset.

The extensive emparking around St Audries began in the early 18th century by James Smith and was carried on with vigour by subsequent owners. Much of the 19th-century work was done under the ownership of Sir Peregrine Fuller-Palmer-Acland and his successors. One of the 18th-century designers evidently had a grand vision that actually included a large part of the common in an ornamental scheme. This was intended to be seen not just from St Audries Park but also from the Brendon Hills, perhaps from the parks at Nettlecombe and Combe Sydenham and, most likely, from the park of nearby Orchard Wyndham.

Six very regular, circular banks, all *c* 27m in diameter, march along the northern edge of Weacombe (Fig 5.14). A seventh, recorded on 19th-century maps, fell victim to the large stone quarry in Vinny Combe in the 20th century. The highest, at nearly 300m, is on a steep slope at the very top of the combe and all are close to the track known as the Great Road, the track over the hills linking West Quantoxhead and Holford. These are tree rings, circular hedge banks, planted with thorn to keep browsing stock and deer away from newly planted clumps of trees. These tree rings are about 250 years old. About 100 years ago they contained groups of ornamental conifers, indeed a couple of fallen conifers can still be

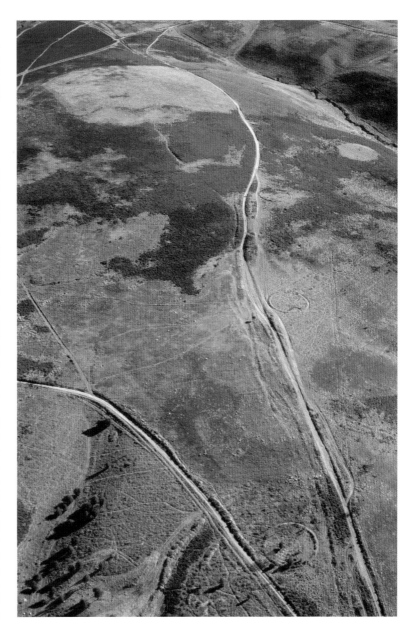

seen in one of them, although originally they may have been planted with beech trees. Beeches were certainly widely planted in the hedge banks that formed the boundary with the commons by the late 18th century, and are now a familiar part of the Quantock landscape (Fig 2.22).

Tree rings can be found elsewhere on the Quantock Hills on common or open ground (Fig 5.4). On Great Bear scrubby oak woodland has engulfed two tree rings, both planted to be seen from the Fairfield estates. A map of 1825 shows these as well established (probably) beech clumps (SRO 1825). At Kingscliff the tree ring is marooned in a conifer plantation. The prehistoric burial cairn at Crowcombe Gate was

Fig 5.14
Six 18th-century tree rings line the way up the edge of Weacombe. Narrow ridge and furrow ploughing, medieval pillow mounds (bottom left) and practice trenches from the Second World War (centre left) can also be seen. (NMR 15858/30) (© Crown copyright. NMR)

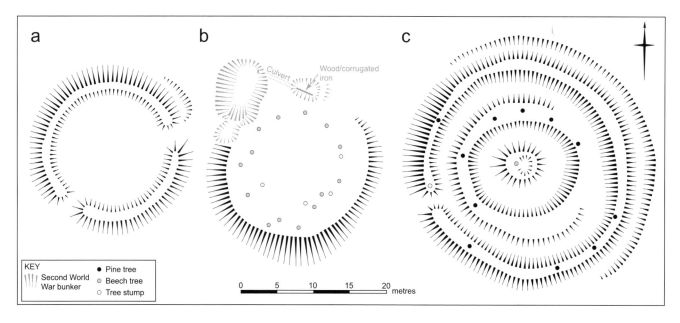

KEY

||||| Second World War bunker

● Pine tree
⊙ Beech tree
○ Tree stump

0 5 10 15 20 metres

Fig 5.15
Tree rings: Cothelstone Hill (a, b) and Marrow Hill (c).

Fig 5.16
Cothelstone Hill: a school treat at the Beacon Tower, 1893. (Somerset Archaeological and Natural History Society)

planted as an ornamental tree clump in the 18th century and the Seven Sisters, originally a clump of 15 beech trees planted on a prehistoric burial cairn (see Chapter 2), now reduced to five, is a well known landmark on Cothelstone Hill. Two more tree rings lie to the west on the summit of the hill, one with its tall beeches hidden in regenerating woodland, the other now an empty earthwork (Fig 5.15). The most ornate of these features is the Devil's Ring at the bottom of Marrow Hill. Here, two concentric banks were planted with conifers and a beech tree stood at the centre on a circular mound (Fig 5.15). Very little is known about these features, which made such a bold statement out on the commons and hills. Sometimes the trees themselves or tree stumps enable us to recreate their original intent, and they are often

shown on 19th-century maps. Most of the tree rings on the Quantock Hills seem to have planted in the 18th century (OS 1802) and were planted with beech or conifers, or, occasionally, both, as at the Devil's Ring. On Cothelstone Hill the ornamental tree planting was embellished with a building, the Beacon Tower. The spot where the tower stood until it succumbed to a storm in the early years of the 20th century is now marked by a large stony mound on the hilltop. The tower was built by Lady Hillsborough, later Baroness Stawell of Somerton, between 1768 and 1780, just before the family sold their Cothelstone estate (Kemeys-Tynte 1920). Photographs of the tower show a substantial, circular building, about 10m high, with two doors and a heavy buttress, the whole perhaps originally conceived as a ruin (Fig 5.16). Throughout the late 18th and 19th centuries the summit of Cothelstone was marked by a tall stone tower and three large tree clumps, visible from the Vale of Taunton and beyond.

Both unenclosed tree clumps, particularly conifers, and small plantations were also laid out on the commons. By the 19th century unenclosed clumps of conifers had been planted in a line, which drew the eye from Court Farm up to the head of Smiths Combe, where two rectangular enclosures once contained plantations of conifers (Fig 5.17). A clump of conifers lies at the head of Stert Combe. Such planting was not only ornamental but gave cover to deer. Stag hunting was just one of a range of recreations carried out on the commons by owners of large estates in the 19th and early 20th

Fig 5.17
Conifer plantations and plantation enclosures at the head of Smith's Combe. (NMR 21190/14) (© English Heritage. NMR)

centuries. On the north part of the hills 20 shooting butts have been recorded. These have a specialised distribution, occurring at the heads and edges of combes. Shooting butts have been found overlooking Dens Combe, Gay's House Combe, Weacombe, Stert Combe, Slaughterhouse Combe and the un-named combe in Crowcombe Park (Fig 5.4). The shooting butts are simple earthwork features, usually 3–5m long and 2–4m wide, constructed by digging a rectangular stance into the slope and placing the spoil downslope to provide shelter and a rest for the gun. There is no evidence for any stone or timber revetting like those elaborate structures of 19th-century date found on the grouse moors of northern England (Newman *et al* 2001, 11). As well as black grouse, the guns were seeking snipe, curlew, woodcock, pheasant and partridge (Page 1906, 140–162; Sandford 1888, 61; 300).

A working landscape: farms, farming and industry in the Quantock Hills

Cultivating the common land: relict field systems

The late winter sun throws the faint traces of cultivation ridges and field banks into sharp relief on much of the unenclosed heath of the Quantock Hills (Fig 5.21).

These are the remains of relict field systems. The most extensive areas of relict field systems are on the west side of the hills, on Beacon Hill, Weacombe Hill, Bicknoller Hill, Thorncombe Hill, Halsway Hill, Firebeacon, Great Hill and Marrow Hill (Fig 5.18). These fields occupy common land, now open heath (*see* Chapter 1). They are mostly confined to the flatter land of the hilltops, but in places the fields occupy more extreme topography, such as those on the very steep lower slopes of Marrow Hill. All of the fields on the west side of the hills are at a height of more than 300m OD and as high as 340m on Firebeacon and Great Hill. To the southwest relict fields are found on Bagborough Hill, Lydeard Hill, Aisholt Common and Middle Hill. Again most of the fields are at a height of more than 300m OD, with those on Lydeard Hill at more than 350m OD. There are fewer relict fields to the north and east, with some on West Hill and the Greenway, a few areas on Longstone Hill and larger areas on Lower and Higher Hare Knap, Woodlands Hill and Black Hill (Fig 5.18). Generally, these fields are found at a lower altitude than those to the west and southwest, between 200 and 300m OD, although those on Black Hill are at 330m OD.

The relict fields on the west side of the hills are regular and organised. The fields are rectangular and measure, on average, 140m long and 70m wide. Good examples

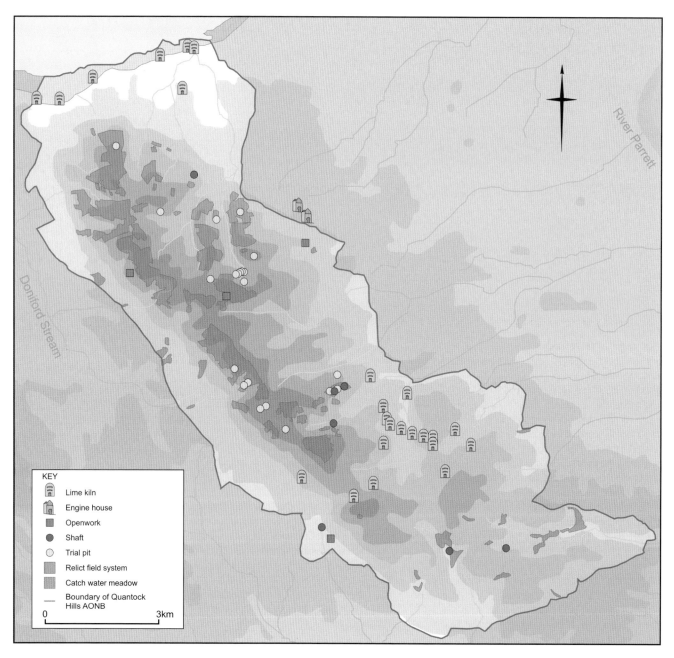

Fig 5.18
The Quantock Hills: relict field systems, catch water meadows, lime kilns and mining sites. (Based on an Ordnance Survey map, with permission.
© Crown copyright.
All rights reserved)

can be seen on Weacombe Hill, Beacon Hill and around Thorncombe Barrow. To the east, in contrast, on Woodlands Hill and Higher and Lower Hare Knap, there is little evidence of individual fields but rather large areas of narrow ridge and furrow (Fig 5.19). The cultivation ridges measure, on average, 3–5m from ridge to ridge and are 0.3–0.6m high. Some of the banks that separated individual fields have themselves been ploughed over, for example on Lydeard Hill, suggesting that these areas have been cultivated over a considerable number of years. The layout of the fields has been influenced by existing features in the landscape, such as

parish boundaries and tracks. This is seen on Weacombe Hill where fields are laid out on either side of the boundary between the parishes of West Quantoxhead and Bicknoller, and on Beacon Hill where fields are laid out on either side of the Great Road.

Only one area of relict field system has produced evidence of structures associated with outfield cultivation. This is on Lydeard Hill where two small structures, one built into the side of a prehistoric burial cairn, were probably used for shelter and storage (Fig 5.20). Similar structures have been noted on the edges of outfields on Mill Hill, Exmoor and on Bodmin Moor, where ancil-

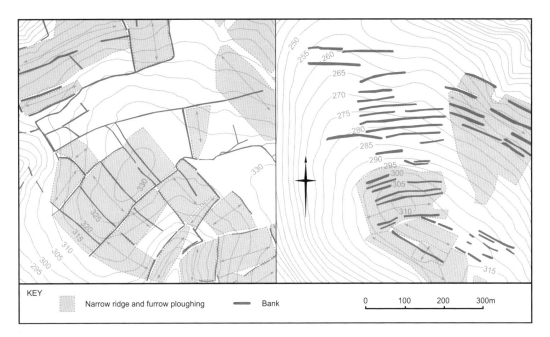

KEY

▨ Narrow ridge and furrow ploughing   ▬ Bank

0   100   200   300m

Fig 5.19
Relict field systems:
Thorncombe Hill (left)
and Lower Hare Knap
(right). (Based on an
Ordnance Survey map,
with permission.
© Crown copyright.
All rights reserved)

lary buildings found at some distance from deserted medieval settlements probably functioned as field barns and stores (Riley 2003; Johnson and Rose 1994, 90). The remains of a small stone building lie about halfway up Bicknoller Combe. This is not directly associated with the relict field system that covers much of Bicknoller Hill but it may have been a store or shelter for people working the outfields or using the commons for grazing livestock.

Such fields are difficult to date. There has been little systematic study of the archaeological remains of relict field systems in southwest England in general and this type of cultivation in the uplands in particular. The relict field systems on the Quantock Hills are dated here by considering the documentary evidence for cultivation on the commons, the evidence from the landscape itself and by comparison with similar traces of cultivation elsewhere in southwest England. The documentary evidence suggests that small-scale cultivation of the commons occurred in the medieval period (*see* Chapter 4), and that this continued into the later 16th and 17th centuries. Rye was grown on Bicknoller Hill in the late 16th century and on East Quantoxhead Common in the late 16th and early 17th centuries. Tillage was permitted on the Quantock ridge by the Stogursey commoners and tenants in the early 17th century and 23 acres of Aisholt Common were ploughed in 1603 (Dunning 1985, 15; 124–5; 1992, 166; 68).

None of the relict field systems are shown on the Ordnance Survey mapping of 1802. The same is true for the Ordnance

Survey 1st edition maps, with the exception of a few boundaries on Lydeard Hill. A visitor to the Quantock Hills in 1796 wrote that the hills 'resemble, in surface, soil, and present produce, the hills of East Devonshire;

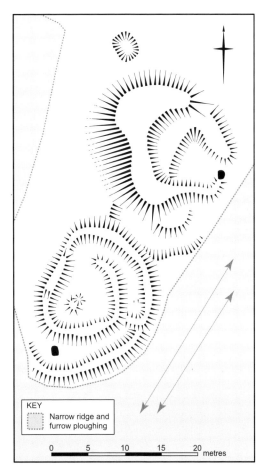

KEY

▨ Narrow ridge and
furrow ploughing

0   5   10   15   20 metres

Fig 5.20
Lydeard Hill: shelters built
into prehistoric cairns.

and, like those, have been heretofore culti-vated (in whole or in part): the vallies or breaks between them, being now in a state of cultivation' (Marshall 1796, 172–3). This evidence shows that the fields were not in use in the 19th or late 18th centuries.

Several landscape features are constructed on top of areas of relict field system, for example the 18th-century tree rings on Weacombe Hill and the Second World War searchlight battery at Crowcombe Gate (*see* Chapter 6). The relict fields overlay other landscape features. Many of the prehistoric burial cairns have been ploughed over, such as the small cairns at the head of Ramscombe; incorporated into the field systems, as on West Hill; or ploughed over as on Beacon Hill, where the edge of the large platform cairn has been clipped by the plough ridges (Figs 5.21 and 2.18). Most of the pillow mounds recorded on the Quantock Hills show that they have been ploughed over and all of the ponds on the commons, constructed to ensure a supply of water for grazing live-stock, have been ploughed over (*see* Chapter 4). Hurley Beacon, the top of Crowcombe Combe, Firebeacon, Great Hill and Marrow Hill were all enclosed from common in 1780 under an act of 1776 (SRO 1776), suggesting that the relict fields here had gone out of use before this date. A large infilled shaft, a copper mine dating from 1716–19 (*see below*), cuts through relict fields on Aisholt Common. The pillow

mounds in the enclosures above Crowcombe Park, probably of early 17th century origin, have relict fields overlying them. This gives a precise (for landscape history) date for the relict fields here: between the mid-17th and the early 18th centuries. For the Quantock Hills generally, the documentary and landscape evidence taken together suggest that the relict field systems in their present form date from the later medieval and post-medieval periods, more specifically from the 16th and 17th centuries.

These dates concur with evidence from Dartmoor, where Fleming sees narrow rig cultivation as a post-medieval phenomenon, specifically from the 16th and 17th centuries. On Dartmoor the remains measure from *c* 3m to 8m (or more) furrow to furrow and there is considerable variation in size. Fleming observed these ridges overlying medieval cultivation remains and running right up to medieval longhouses and they occur at altitudes from 250m to more than 400m OD (Fleming 1994). Relict field systems similar to those on the Quantock Hills are widespread on the Exmoor commons. Documentary evidence indicates that this sort of cultivation was practised in 16th and 17th centuries on Dunkery Hill and Withypool Common (Riley and Wilson-North 2001, 126).

So what do these relict field systems represent? They are not the abandoned field systems of long-deserted farmsteads, nor are they the remains of abandoned attempts

Fig 5.21
Relict field systems cover the summit of Beacon Hill; two prehistoric burial cairns lie to the east (top). (NMR 15858/29) (© Crown copyright. NMR)

to enclose and improve large areas of the commons. They are the remains of outfields – that is, areas of temporary cultivation that were worked either in common, or, where individual farms had access to waste, by individual holdings. On the Quantock Hills we can see the outfields of the inhabitants of West Quantoxhead and Bicknoller on Beacon Hill and Bicknoller Hill, for example, and perhaps the individual outfields of Little Quantock Farm, Combe Farm and Triscombe Farm on Firebeacon, Great Hill and Marrow Hill. Detailed work on the manor of Kenton in south Devon has shown how these outfields functioned over many years (Fox 1973). They were cultivated only sporadically at intervals, rather than annually and regularly, and it is this irregular cultivation that holds the key to their function. The outfields provided a bonus arable crop every now and again, without losing the resources of the common – pasture and fuel. The relict fields we see on the Quantock Hills represent the very last time that this system of agriculture was practised.

The principal crop from the outfields on the Quantock Hills was rye. We have seen many references to the cultivation of rye in documents of both the medieval and early post-medieval period. Rye was certainly a widespread crop in southwest England until the mid- to late 18th century. Charles Vancouver, an early 19th-century agricultural commentator, wrote that rye was cultivated to a considerable extent in Devon and he noted the:

vast quantity of rye-straw that is to be found to form the lower layer in all the ancient thatched buildings, and the vestiges of an ancient cultivation, which are to be clearly traced on all the extensive moors and commons that occupy so large a proportion of the county. Here large fields of rye are said to have been cultivated
(Vancouver 1808, 170–1).

Rye straw was commonly used with wheat straw in thatch in Devon, where it has been found in medieval and later contexts. Small amounts of rye were still grown especially for thatching in east Devon in the mid-18th century and on Dartmoor in the early 20th century (Cox and Thorp 2001, 45; 77). On Exmoor anecdotal evidence suggests that rye was a frequent crop on the commons, where the old fields are known locally as 'the rye-beds' (Fleming 1994, 106). It seems that the outfields on the Quantock Hills provided not only a source of grain, but also rye straw for thatch, the most common roofing material for buildings of all kinds until the 19th century.

Ordering the land: settlement desertion and contraction

An abandoned farm has a peculiarly poignant atmosphere, perhaps because it is so easy to imagine the last family who lived there. There may even be tattered wallpaper hanging down in strips from the remaining gable end, or a long cold fireplace. As we have seen (*see* Chapter 4), the process of

Fig 5.22
The large threshing barn at the centre of the farm buildings at Court House, East Quantoxhead, is built on the site of a medieval barn. (AA044962)
(© English Heritage. NMR)

Fig 5.23
This 18th-century outbarn is all
that remains of Deak's Allers
deserted farmstead. (H Riley)

Fig 5.24
Combe Farm in 1797: arable
fields (yellow), medow land
(green). (SRO 1797 DD/TB
51/3) (Somerset Archive and
Record Service)

farm or hamlet abandonment began as early as the 15th century, and the reasons for such an event are manifold, ranging from personal misfortune to a grasping landlord. Many of the abandoned farms in the Quantock Hills seem to have fallen foul of a trend that is still happening in the 21st century, that of amalgamation of holdings to form larger units, which can be farmed more efficiently. We can see this in action in the Quantock Hills in the 18th and 19th centuries.

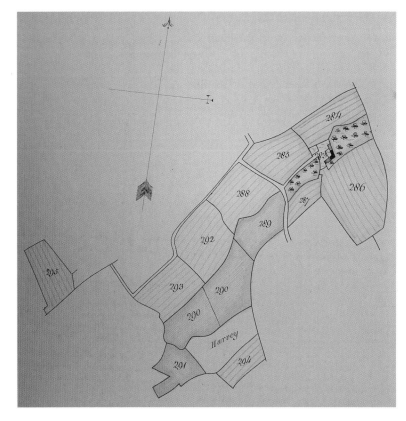

The effect of this process on the landscape is profound. It can be seen around Kenley Copse where the small fields of Muchcare Farm were grubbed out in the late 19th century. The process is well illustrated by the estates on the coastal strip. By the late 17th century Dunster Castle became the main residence of the Luttrell family and Court House, rebuilt only a few decades before, became a farmhouse and grain store – the centre of estate farming for the next 200 years. This is evidenced by the agglomeration of farm buildings at the entrance to Court House, now mostly of 18th- and 19th-century date, but on the footprints of older farm buildings, as evidenced by the survival of a single timber cruck in one of the two threshing barns (Fig 5.22).

Several of the oldest of the East Quantoxhead estate farms suffered an ignominious end during this time. The old holdings of Denscombe and Deak's Allers became part of Townsend Farm by the early 19th century, their existence only acknowledged by the presence of outbarns in the old farmyards (Fig 5.23). Outbarns are usually found in more remote places than the edge of the Quantock Hills, where they provided a place to overwinter cattle with a fodder store away from the main farm. In this case it seems to have been a pragmatic arrangement, utilising the existing buildings of the abandoned farmsteads for another century, until this practice, too, ceased. By 1827 most of the agricultural land in East Quantoxhead was divided between just four farms: Court Farm (now Court House) (381 acres), Baker's Farm (now Court Farm) (253 acres), Townsend Farm (179 acres) and Perry Farm (196 acres). These four holdings had been created by the amalgamation of 19 smaller holdings documented in the 1670s.

The same process happened in Crowcombe. In 1724 the Crowcombe Studley estate had 69 tenant farmers, all with holdings of less than 50 acres. The need to address this was recognised at this time: the surveyor of the estate recorded both holdings of Slocomb and Brewers together as they were 'so intermixed and convenient to be thrown together when in hand' (SRO 1724). The small farms of the estate were amalgamated during the next 40 years: by 1761 the manor had reduced its tenant farmers to only 19.

This process continued right through the 19th century. Combe Farm, one of the ancient holdings of Crowcombe Biccombe

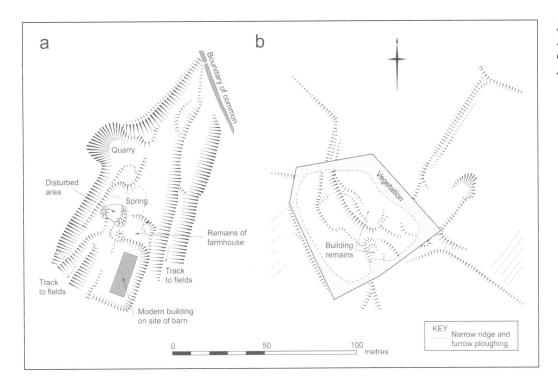

a

Quarry

Disturbed area

Spring

Remains of farmhouse

Track to fields

Track to fields

Modern building on site of barn

Boundary of common

b

Vegetation

Building remains

KEY
Narrow ridge and furrow ploughing

0   50   100
                                metres

Fig 5.25
Deserted farmsteads:
Combe Farm (a) and
Muchcare Farm (b).

Manor, recorded in 1327 as the home of Rogero de Comb (Dickinson 1889, 166), was a small farm of 37 acres in 1797. A house and barn lay at right angles around a tiny yard at the very edge of the commons in the shadow of Great Hill (SRO 1797). Combe Farm had access to a range of land: two large orchards lay to the north and south of the farmstead, there were arable fields and meadows below the farm (Fig 5.24) and pasture above on Great Hill, which also provided occasional arable as the remains of relict field systems show (above). Sometime during the early 19th century the farm was abandoned but the foundations of the farmhouse survive, as do the ways up to the arable fields each side of the farm and up to the pasture and outfields on Great Hill (Fig 5.25).

One of the most melancholic of these deserted farms is Muchcare Farm, located at the head the combe on the east of Lydeard Hill. Muchcare Farm was a small holding carved out of waste on the edge of open heath. It is called Muchcare Farm on a map of 1802 and if this is its original name then it was a late enclosure, perhaps as late as the 16th or 17th century. By 1838 the land was all part of Tilbury Farm (Bishops Lydeard tithe map 1838). The small fields that marked the original holding of Much-care Farm were grubbed out and only the names Muchcare Moor, Muchcare Mead and Muchcare Plantation lived on. The farmyard and its three buildings, however, can be seen as earthwork platforms in a small copse (Fig 5.25). Like Combe Farm at the foot of Great Hill, Muchcare Farm was close to the outfields on Lydeard Hill.

The southern part of Broomfield parish shows this process in action in the 19th century. This is the area between Broomfield, Kingston St Mary and Thurloxton, only a few miles north of Taunton yet surprisingly remote, a landscape of long, steep sided combes and few settlements. Before the 19th century, however, the land was populated with several hamlets and many dispersed farmsteads (Fig 5.26). Ivyton, at the head of a deep combe north of Tetton, was once a major focus of settlement, comparable in size to Broomfield. It consisted of three farms, Ivyton Farm, Higher Ivyton and Lower Ivyton, with a possible fourth to the south. By 1835 these farmsteads had been amalgamated under the Tetton estate into one farm, Ivyton Farm, and the landscape is still littered with the remains of the old farms (Fig 5.27).

Raswell, east of Ivyton, was once a hamlet of two or three farmsteads, but was a single farm by the end of the 19th century. Raswell House was once the farmhouse, and has features that date from the 16th century. Another farm lay a few hundred metres to the east, where its site is marked by a few overgrown walls. Similar settlement foci were at Westleigh Farm, Oggshole Farm,

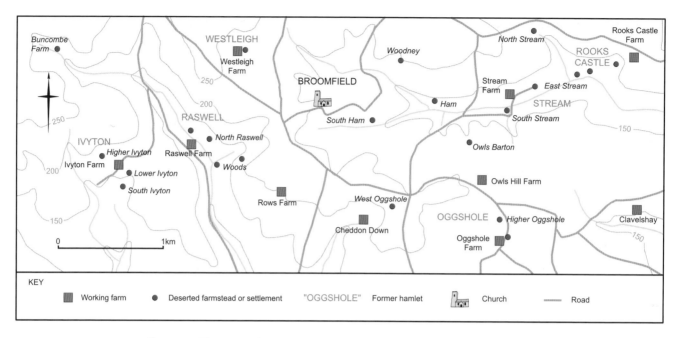

Fig 5.26

Broomfield: former hamlets and deserted farmsteads. (Based on an Ordnance Survey map, with permission. © Crown copyright. All rights reserved)

Fig 5.27

Ivyton Farm and the former settlements of Lower Ivyton (top) and South Ivyton (right). (NMR 21408/35) (© English Heritage. NMR)

Stream Farm and Rooks Castle Farm. Stream Farm is a new farmstead, built of brick in the early 19th century. Three earlier farmsteads to the north, south and east were all abandoned and their land amalgamated with Stream Farm by 1835 (Dunning 1992, 12–13). The same pattern is seen at Rooks Castle Farm, where the early 19th century farmstead is on a new site on the ridge top above three settlements, all seemingly deserted by the late 19th century.

Some farmsteads and hamlets were completely abandoned. Buncombe Farm, high up the combe above Raswell Farm and on the east of Cothelstone Hill, probably a tenement of Buckland Priory, is mentioned in documents of 1544 and 1604 (Dunning 1992, 10). At the beginning of the 19th century it was a small farm, but only a cottage in 1890. Now the ruined farmhouse and its barn lie within Buncombe Wood and its fields can still be traced on the surrounding land. The site of Woods, a medieval farmstead, has been engulfed by Woods Copse, but the remains of a farmhouse and small enclosure can still be found. Johanne and Martino atte Ham lived in the parish of Broomfield in 1327 (Dickinson 1889, 162). Ham was east of Broomfield, at the head of a combe, close to the edge of Broomfield Common, where Ham Cottages stood in 1890.

Improving the land: catch-water meadows and lime kilns

Catch-water meadows were a common feature in the west Somerset landscape in the 17th and 18th centuries, and their utility was praised by 18th-century agricultural commentators (Marshall 1796; Billingsley 1797). Irrigation of meadows was practised to provide early grass for sheep and lambs in early spring and to boost the summer hay crop.

There were two ways of doing this. Where an existing stream flowed close to a meadow, a channel was dug to divert the stream across the top of the meadow. Further channels were dug below this. When the water was needed the stream was diverted to fill the channels and flood the hillside with the stream water, which contained both dissolved minerals and organic matter. If no stream was available, then a pond was built to collect rainwater and runoff from the farmyard, so again nutrient-rich water flooded the meadow. The first watering started in November and continued until February. The meadows provided grass for ewes and their lambs until May, when they were watered again and a summer hay crop was taken six or seven weeks after this.

The practice may well have begun in the medieval period, as shown by fields called Waterleets above Perry, East Quantoxhead, recorded in the 13th and 16th centuries (Dunning 1985, 122). Catch-water meadows were certainly widespread in southwest England by the 17th century and in 1797 those in west Somerset are 'as good as any in the county' (Billingsley 1797, 264). The practice was encouraged by the agricultural improvers of the 19th century: Sir Thomas Dyke Acland was a great advocate of catch-water meadows, both on enclosed farmland and as a way of making heath or waste land more productive (Acland and Sturge 1851, 157–8). A catch-water meadow at East Nurcott Farm near Winsford on Exmoor was still worked in the late 20th century. Most catch-water meadows, however, went out of use by the mid- 20th century when the widespread use of tractors and a shortage of agricultural workers led to their demise (Francis 1984, 12; 49).

The earthwork remains of catch-water meadows often survive in the hill country of west Somerset. Those on the Quantock Hills have been mapped from aerial photographs (Fig 5.18). There are a few examples on the north and west side of the hills, particularly around Halsway, Crowcombe and Little Quantock Farm. The main concentration of catch-water meadows is to the south of the Quantock Hills. There are good examples at Kenley and Bishpool Farms, but it is in the area around Broomfield that nearly every farm has a catch-water meadow (Fig 5.28). The topography of the hills has a certain effect on the distribution of such works, but a major factor in the concentration in this area is probably best explained by the fact that the two largest estates in the neighbourhood – Tetton and Petherton Park – were both owned by the Acland family in the 18th and 19th centuries.

Applying slaked lime to agricultural land increases both soil fertility and soil texture. Slaked lime is the final product of the lime burning industry. When limestone is burnt at 900° C carbon dioxide is released, leaving quicklime behind. Quicklime reacts violently with water to produce slaked lime, which was used not only in agriculture but in the building industry where it was used in mortar, plaster, floors and lime wash. Limestone was burnt in lime kilns and there are references to such kilns in the medieval period, together with the physical remains of lime kilns in several medieval castles (Williams

Fig 5.28
Catch-water meadows northeast of Stream Farm. The deserted farmstead of North Stream lies at the head of the combe (bottom left). (NMR 21406/28) (© English Heritage. NMR)

2004). Lime was used as a soil improver from at least as early as the 16th century and the 18th century saw a rapid growth in the number of lime kilns built in rural locations to produce lime for agriculture. By the mid-19th century, however, this rural industry was in decline due to competition from large commercial burners and the introduction of Portland cement for building.

The rural lime industry developed where there was a source of limestone, a source of fuel and a market. The Quantock Hills had all of these requirements. Roadwater limestone (*see* Chapter 1) outcrops in narrow bands around Cothelstone, Merridge, Aisholt and Bincombe and the distribution of lime kilns reflects this underlying geological structure (Fig 5.18). The exceptions to this are the lime kilns at West Quantoxhead, East Quantoxhead and Kilve, which lie on the coast with access to the sea. Although the Lias rock on the foreshore did contain lime, by the late 18th century imports of Welsh culm (anthracite) was the preferred fuel and limestone from the quarries of south Wales was imported with the coal (Dunning 1985, 97; 121). Prior to this brushwood, furze and timber were used for fuel, all of which the Quantock Hills could supply in abundance. The industry is documented in the 18th and 19th centuries in the Quantock Hills and as early as 1652 in Aisholt, where a woman was granted a licence to continue burning lime (Dunning 1995, 68).

A lime kiln was a simple structure, usually built into a slope in or close to the limestone quarry. It consists of the pot, essentially a circular hole, lined with brick or stone and tapering to the bottom, and thick kiln walls, providing insulation for the process. At the base of the pot is the draw hole, providing draught and the way for extracting the burnt lime, accessed by the large, distinctive, draw arch. The pot was loaded from the top with a mixture of broken limestone and fuel in the proportions of four to one. The burning process lasted for three or four days and was carefully controlled by the lime burner (Stanier 2003, 25–6).

There is documentary and field evidence for some 23 lime kilns on the Quantock Hills (Fig 5.18). Those kilns that do survive occur in various states of preservation, ranging from the bramble-covered mound in Kiln Close on the edge of Cothelstone Hill to the newly restored structure on Hawkridge Common. Where the surviving remains enable a distinction to be made, the kilns all seem to be of the draw type, which could burn over a period of several days or even weeks. The kilns are all built of local stone and there is some evidence for the use of brick in finishing details. As the lime burner had to be on site over a number of days to control the burn, small shelters are sometimes located close to the kilns. These are rare on the Quantock Hills, but a good example survives by the top of the kiln on Hawkridge Common (Fig 5.29).

The limestone quarries are a testament to hundreds of years of manual work with pick, shovel and cart. The quarries on Hawkridge Common and at Kiln Close are substantial. The quarry behind the restored kiln on Hawkridge Common is 120m long, 35m wide and more than 10m deep and the extensive quarry at Kiln Close covers some 3ha and is more than 5m deep in places. Other quarries were not so large and suggest more periodic working, perhaps by a single farm or family. Examples of these occur in the parish of Aisholt, at Tuck's Barn and around Luxborough Farm. The lime kiln north of Tuck's Barn is a good example of a kiln, built into the hillside, by a small quarry. The pot is lined with local stone and the kiln walls, also of local stone, are 4.6m high and 0.5m thick, with a wooden lintel and brick relieving arch over the (damaged) draw hole. The draw arch is of stone. Other surviving details include a stone-lined pigeon hole where the lime burner could keep his bread and cheese and his tinder box clean and dry (Fig 5.30). Just to the north of the kiln is a linear quarry, 80m long, 20m

Fig 5.29
Hawkridge Common: lime burner's shelter. (Hazel Riley)

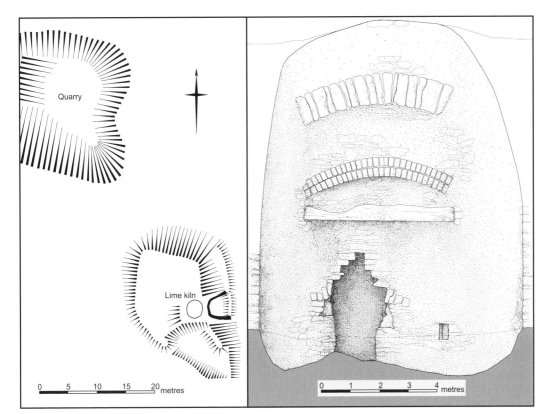

Fig 5.30
Aisholt: plan of the lime kiln and quarry (left) and elevation of the east side of the kiln (right).

wide and nearly 5m deep, cutting into a narrow band of Roadwater limestone.

The larger estates had their own kilns. The coastal kilns at East Quantoxhead and Kilve burnt limestone and coal imported from south Wales in the late 18th and 19th centuries, reflecting the drive to improve on these large estates. Limestone quarries and kilns on Cothelstone Hill and in the park supplied the Cothelstone estate. One of the most interesting areas with evidence for rural lime burning on the Quantock Hills is around Merridge. This is an area of dispersed farms and hamlets, mostly part of the Stawell estates, which had an absentee landlord from the mid-17th to the late 18th century.

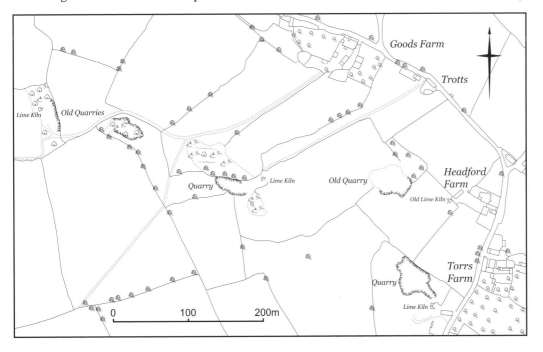

Fig 5.31
Merridge: lime kilns, quarries and farms. (Based on the Ordnance Survey 1st edition map, Somerset sheet 60 NE)

A small outcrop of Roadwater limestone has been exploited for at least 200 years. On the southwest side of Merridge Hill, between Lower Aisholt, Courtway and Merridge, are four lime kilns, each with its own quarry (Fig 5.31). The quarries themselves are remarkable features, at first glance a clump of trees and a single strand of barbed wire marks the edge of a field, but closer inspection reveals great trenches into the hillside, some as deep as 15m and only 30m wide. Each farm had its own quarry and kiln, and tracks linked the more remote kilns to the farmsteads, as at Good's Farm and Trotts.

Lime burning continued in parts of the Quantock Hills into the early 20th century. The farmer at the Old Rectory, Aisholt, recalls how the fine kiln by Tuck's Barn was damaged when a bullock fell down the pot, and that it was still in use in the 1920s or 1930s. The limekiln and quarry to the north of the Traveller's Rest Inn, Merridge, were not opened until after 1888 and remained open in the first decade of the 20th century. Many kilns, however, were disused by the later part of the 19th century or the early years of the 20th century when they are recorded as such on the first edition and second edition Ordnance Survey maps.

Managing the land: woodland industries

The oak trees that hug the steep sided combes of the eastern side of the Quantock Hills have a skeletal appearance and lichen decorates the tall, gnarled trunks (Fig 5.32). Their distinctive character is the product of the cessation of their management for the production of coppice wood and oak bark. The woods have not been regularly coppiced for about 100 years, as demand for traditional products such as broom handles, thatching spars and hurdles fell throughout the 20th century. Coppice wood was also burnt to produce charcoal. Charcoal burning was carried out in the woods, usually from spring through to late autumn. Charcoal is produced by the slow burning of wood in an oxygen free atmosphere. The wood stack was built up around a central upright pole and sealed with a layer of bracken and turf then covered with fine soil. The charcoal burner pulled out the central pole and the gap acted as a flue. Burning charcoal thrown down into the flue ignited the stack and the burn continued for a number of days. At the end of firing, the clamp was dismantled and the charcoal removed. On flat ground the clamp was built in an

Fig 5.32
Oak woodland, Holford
Combe (AA053330)
(© English Heritage.
NMR)

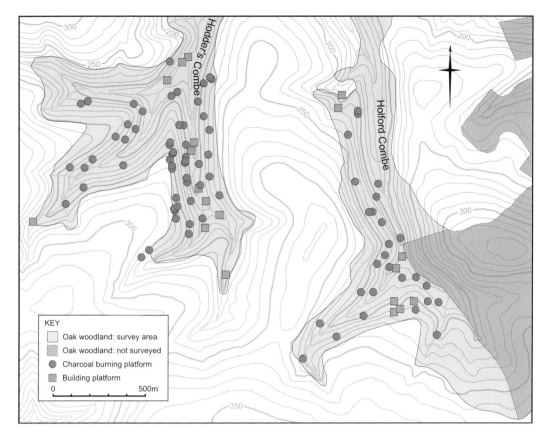

Fig 5.33
Hodder's Combe and
Holford Combe: charcoal
burning platforms and
building platforms. (Based
on an Ordnance Survey
map, with permission.
© Crown copyright.
All rights reserved)

area cleared of woodworking debris but on steep slopes a level platform to take the clamp was terraced into the hillside – a charcoal burning platform.

At the beginning of this survey there were no charcoal burning platforms recorded in the Quantock Hills. Detailed survey work in two areas, Hodder's Combe and Holford Combe and their associated combes, has resulted in the recording of more than 100 structures associated with charcoal burning or oak bark collection (Fig 5.33). Charcoal burning platforms are also found in the woods to the north of Dowsborough, in Bin Combe, Ramscombe, Quantock Combe and Cockercombe (information from Quantock Orienteers). The charcoal burning platforms recorded in the study area are oval and are fairly uniform in size, with an average measurement of 5–6m long and 3–4m wide. They are terraced into the hillside to a depth of 1–1.5m (Fig 5.34). The platforms are often found in pairs and one of these platforms may have provided the level stance for a timber and thatch shelter (Fig 5.35). Tom Poole described John Walford, a charcoal burner who worked in the Quantock Hills in the late 18th century as living in 'a little cabin, built with poles and turf, in the form of a cone' (Worthy

1998, 48). The small platforms or stances, less than 3m long and 2m wide, often found just upslope from the charcoal burning platforms could have been used as a shelter, or provided extra level areas for storing tools or piles of sieved earth for covering the stack (Figs 5.34 and 5.35).

Very little is known about the people who carried out this work, the way the woods were managed or what the final product was destined for. The most famous (indeed infamous) charcoal burner of the Quantock Hills is John Walford who was hanged for the murder of his wife in 1789. He worked both as an agricultural labourer and as a charcoal burner, living in a cottage in Bin Combe but spending days on end out in the woods when he was burning charcoal. The documentary evidence suggests that blocks of woodland were sold to itinerant charcoal burners. In Over Stowey parish, for example, wood from the Quantock commons was sold to charcoal burners in 1605 and in the late 17th century coppice wood from Friarn Wood was sold to charcoal burners at £4 an acre (Dunning 1992, 167). In the study area there is little evidence for the division of areas into compartments or blocks for coppicing. The blocks may have been separated by natural features such as streams and

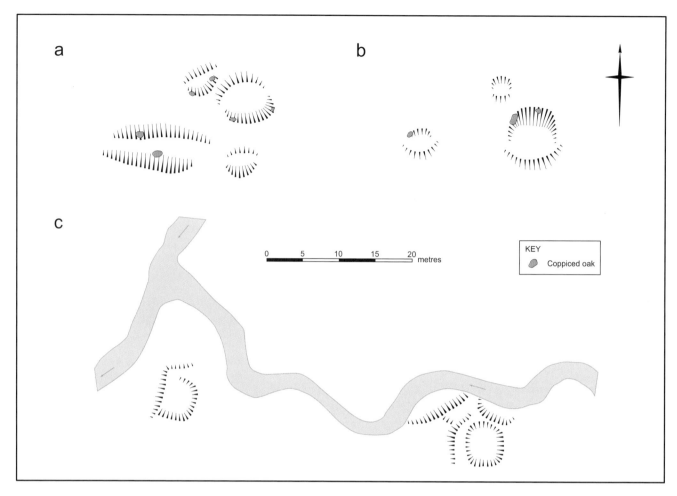

a

b

c

0   5   10   15   20 metres

KEY

Coppiced oak

Fig 5.34

Charcoal burning platforms and building platforms: Slaughterhouse Combe (a), Somerton Combe (b) and Short Combe (c).

Fig 5.35 (opposite)

Charcoal burning in Slaughterhouse Combe in the 18th century. (© Jane Brayne)

combes or by footpaths and tracks, distinctive trees such as pollards or even by heaps of stones, which have long since vanished. Perhaps the most difficult problem is the lack of boundaries between open heathland and the woods, suggesting that deer and grazing livestock could freely enter the woods and browse on the regenerating coppice stools.

This must also have been a problem in the areas of outfield cultivation (*see above*) and may have been overcome by a number of methods. Newly coppiced areas could be protected by timber fences and hurdles, probably effective for grazing livestock but not effective against deer unless they were substantial barriers. Where outfield cultivation came down to the woodland edges, as occurs on Lower Hare Knap and Woodlands Hill for example, then hedges or fences around the arable plots may have also acted to exclude stock from the woods. Pollarded trees and the consequent landscape of wood pasture would eventually emerge from long-term management of the woods with browsing stock, but this is not the case

in the Quantock Hills, where there are surprisingly few pollards in the woods that have been studied. The pollards that remain seem to mark routes through the woods and up onto the heath, such as along the north side of Lady's Edge. Some wooded areas, however, seem to have been deliberately managed for grazing. Dowsborough Wood and the heath around it were let for sheep pasture in *c* 1620 (Dunning 1992, 172).

The production of charcoal is a well documented forest industry. Charcoal was used in large quantities in ironworking until the introduction of coke in the 18th century and as late as 1788 one third of the blast furnaces in Britain were still using charcoal as a fuel rather than coke. Charcoal burning platforms in oak woodland are often associated with a relatively local and early metal-smelting industry, such as those found in association with the medieval iron-smelting industry in Furness and those found close to the Roman iron-smelting site at Sherracombe Ford, Exmoor (Bowden 2000; Riley and Wilson-North 2001). The copper ore from the well documented mines of the late

18th and early 19th century at Dodington was smelted at Swansea. There is, however, some evidence to suggest that copper and possibly iron was mined in small quantities in and around the hills in the medieval and early post-medieval periods (*see below*). Charcoal from these woods may have been used in small scale local metalworking. The density of the platforms in the areas subject to detailed survey work does suggest that the charcoal was being produced for a specific industry rather than for general use.

James Brydges, duke of Chandos, established a glassworks in Bridgwater in 1721, part of his initiative to stimulate local manufacturing industries (Dunning 1992, 222). Glass making at this time required copious quantities of charcoal. Although the glassworks in Bridgwater were relatively short lived, glass was produced until 1733 and the charcoal required for this enterprise must have come from the Quantock Hills. The foundries in Bridgwater and Taunton may also have used charcoal from the hills, as well as the local smithies. Although the metalworking industry was the largest consumer of charcoal in the medieval and early post-medieval periods, charcoal was also an important ingredient in the manufacture of gunpowder. There were gunpowder works at Taunton and Wells in the 17th century (Cocroft 2000, 283).

The function of one of the charcoal burning platforms in Swinage Wood has been confirmed by finding charcoal fragments brought to the surface by an animal burrow. There are several earthwork sites on the flatter ground towards the valley floors and at the heads of some of the combes. These have the appearance of building platforms rather than charcoal burning platforms. These are typically 4–6m long, 4–5m wide and are sub-rectangular in shape (Fig 5.34). If these are the level stances for buildings rather than the remains of charcoal burning platforms then they could be associated with bark peeling or bark ripping.

Oak bark was used in large amounts in the tanning process (*see below*). Thomas Hardy gives a typically vivid description of the process in *The Woodlanders*. Bark stripping was carried out in spring and early summer. Before the tree was felled its base was stripped of small twigs and moss, then the trunk was stripped of bark using a barking iron to as high as a man could reach. Then the tree was felled with an axe and cross saw and 'as soon as it had fallen the barkers attacked it like locusts' (Hardy

1887, 184). The oak bark was useless if it got wet since the tannin leached from it. These platforms on the valley floors, close to the routes up the combes, may be sites where bark heaps were stored, under a temporary roof of turf, bracken or heather thatch, before it was taken down to the tannery by packhorse or cart. The tanners leased areas of woodland for oak bark. In 1676 a tanner in Crowcombe parish leased the 40 acre Waterman's Wood (Dunning 1985, 60). Oak bark from Great Wood was sold to the tannery in Langport in 1910 (Mead and Worthy 2001).

Oak bark was used in the many tanneries that grew up on the edge of the Quantock Hills. Tanning, the process where hides and skins are converted to leather, became an important rural industry in the 17th and 18th centuries when it was closely linked to agriculture. The process is split into three distinct activities. First the hides are prepared and limed, then the hides are tanned, finally the leather is dried and finished. The final stage could be carried out at a different location, although often all three stages were carried out on the same site. The basic raw materials needed for liming hides, oak-bark tanning and leather finishing are: a supply of cattle hides, water for washing and mixing lime solutions and tan liquors, lime, oak bark, valonia (a type of acorn husk with a very high tannin content, grown in Turkey especially for the industry) and cod oil (Jones 2001). A tan yard contained a range of buildings, including those for storing oak bark, skins and leather, and a range of pits for both liming and tanning the hides. Tanning was a lengthy process: a hide could take as long as a year to pass through all of the stages. The first two activities were particularly noisome and produced large quantities of filthy water.

There were perhaps as many as 12 tanneries in the Quantock Hills in the 17th, 18th and 19th centuries. All are now closed and many of the tan yard sites have disappeared. The tan yard at Crowcombe, now only marked by the street name Tanyard, occupied an extensive area behind the Church House in the 19th century and there were two other tanneries in the parish, both disused by the mid-19th century (Dunning 1985, 60). The tan yard at Marsh Mills, also disused by the mid-19th century, was surprisingly close to Marsh Mills House for such a noxious activity (Over Stowey tithe map 1838). Tanning and gloving were carried out in the parish of Bicknoller in the 16th and 17th centuries, there was a tanner at Kilve in 1851 and there were tan yards at Postridge near Spaxton and at Dyche near Holford in the 18th and 19th centuries (Dunning 1985, 16; 100; 1992, 70; 176).

The remains of 18th- and 19th-century tannery buildings survive at Bin Combe, Nether Stowey, Holford and Tanyard Farm near Kingston St Mary. Close to the stream that flows along the bottom of Bin Combe and to the north of Bincombe Farm there is a ruined and overgrown building. It lies on a platform that has been terraced into the hillside. It is 6.5m long, 5.5m wide and has walls – of lime mortared, roughly coursed, local stone – that are 0.5m thick and stand to a height of 1.5m. This may well be all that remains of the tannery at Bin Combe, disused by the early 19th century but in existence by 1716, when the owner left on his death 111 calfskins, horse hides and leather worth more than £66, together with equipment worth £39 (Over Stowey tithe map 1838; Dunning 1992, 167).

The same stream that supplied the tannery at Bin Combe was used by the tan yard at Nether Stowey. There was a slaughterhouse in Nether Stowey by 1593, which produced both meat for the town market and skins for the local tanners and glove makers. This was probably in the vicinity of Butcher's Lane to the north of the castle.

By the 18th century tanning in Nether Stowey was carried out on one site, the tan yard owned by the Poole family behind Castle Street. A map of the town in 1750 shows how the tanning was carried out in the old burgage plots behind the street frontage (Fig 5.36) (SRO 1750b). These plots were by this time mostly used as gardens, but behind the Poole family house was the tan yard. The long, narrow building was probably a drying loft with a working area below, with a large yard in front.

Tom Poole, friend of Coleridge and a man so steeped in the tanning business that the young wits of Taunton nicknamed him 'Lord Chancellor Hyde', took over his father's tanning business in the late 18th century. By 1838 the tan yard had expanded considerably and it was Tom Poole and his partner and successor in the business Thomas Ward who were responsible for this (Fig 5.36). Behind Tom Poole's house in Castle Street were a garden, the main tan yard buildings and the liming and tanning pits, described by Coleridge as 'Tartarean' (Mayberry 2000, 63). A new building with a combined leat and header pond lay some 100m west of the tan yard.

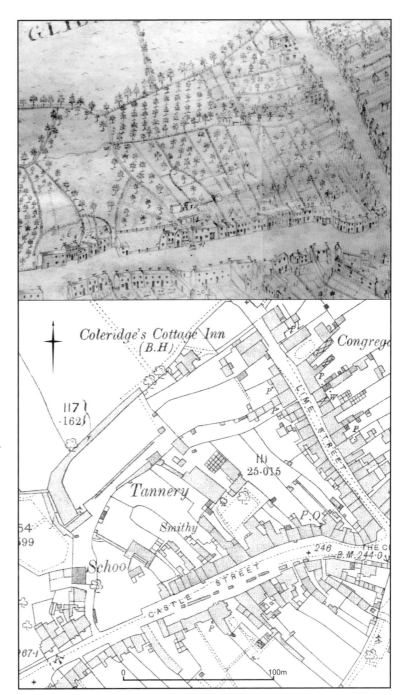

Tom Poole was building a 'new house for grinding bark' in 1795 and in 1796 the new bark mill was at work (Sandford 1888, 100). The building known as Tom Poole's Bark House is now a house, but it retains some features showing that it was originally part of the tan yard (Fig 5.37). The building is characterised by five large openings on the upper floor, now blocked but originally fitted with wooden louvres (Mead and Worthy 2001). These louvres are characteristic features of drying lofts. Drying was an impor-

Fig 5.36
Nether Stowey: the tan yard in 1750 (top) and 1888 (bottom). (SRO 1750b DD/AH 66/27) (Somerset Archive and Record Service) (1st edition Ordnance Survey map, Somerset sheet 49.6)

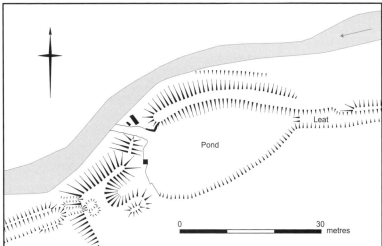

tant part of the tanning process. Oak bark needed to be dried before it could be ground up, hides and leather needed to be dried and stored at various stages of the process (Jones 2001). A water wheel, removed in 1957, was installed in this building in 1812. The wheel drove the oak bark mill but water power may also have been used to drain the liming and tanning pits.

The tannery at Holford was south of the village, at the point where Holford Combe begins to open out, on the site of the Holford Combe Hotel. The tannery was established here by 1825, when it was named 'Mr J Hayman's Tan yard' (SRO 1825). The Hayman family ran the tannery at Holford until 1900 when it closed and the house was converted to a hotel. By the mid- to late 19th century Holford tannery was a substantial enterprise. There were three sets of pits, a shed, drying loft and a range of outbuildings, one of which housed the waterwheel. Sometime between 1840 and 1888 a large header pond was constructed some 400m to the south of the tannery. A leat ran off the stream above the pond and water was carried from the pond to drive the waterwheel at the tannery. The pond no longer holds water, but the earthworks that survive around the pond show what a massive undertaking this was (Fig 5.38). The pond is 35m long, 15m wide and was probably well over 2m deep. Water was retained by a substantial earthen and stone dam, 35m long, 5m wide and 1.2m high on the north side of the pond.

A massive rectangular mound, 18m long, 15m wide and as high as 2m, lies on the west edge of the pond. It contains a deep rectangular pit, 9m long, 6m wide and 1.6m deep with sloping sides. This could be part of the tannery processing area. When the hides arrived at the tannery they were stained with dirt, dung and blood from slaughtering. In the 19th century at Grampound tannery in Cornwall the hides were washed in a large pit, the soaking pit, which had one sloping side to enable the hides to be removed more easily. The water quickly became contaminated and soaking required access to a plentiful supply of clean water. At Grampound the initial soaking and liming process was carried out some distance from the main tan yard buildings, close to the stream (Jones 2001). Some of the initial soaking may have been carried out by the header pond in Holford Combe although there was extra work involved carting the hides to and from the tan yard. The water-

wheel provided power well into the 20th century, when it powered a stone crusher, a circular saw and even a boot cleaning machine for the hotel.

A small tannery north of Kingston St Mary utilised the water that was leated down Buncombe to drive the mill at Bradford Mills, some 100m to the north. All that remains of the tan yard is a small storage building and a drying loft, now used as a barn but recognisable by the blocked openings on the upper floor (Fig 5.39). The tithe map shows that the tanning pits lay on the east side of the drying loft, with a combined leat and header pond above the yard, similar to that serving Nether Stowey tan yard, and a further range of buildings to the east (Kingston St Mary tithe map 1838).

Power from the land: the silk industry at Holford and Marsh Mills

The fast flowing streams that drain the Quantock Hills were also responsible for the growth in the rural textile industry. All textile sites relied on water both for power and for processes such as scouring the wool and dyeing the finished cloth. There is a wealth of documentary evidence to show that the textile industry was well established in and around the Quantock Hills by the 16th century (*see* Chapter 4). This early rural textile industry was based around hand spinners and hand weavers, working from home, who brought their cloth to the fullers for finishing. By the 17th century the Somerset/Devon border country became the centre of a successful serge trade centred at Taunton, Tiverton and Exeter, with cloth often finished at, and always exported from, Exeter (Ponting 1971). By the late 18th century the woollen textile industry in Taunton was in decline, as new machines took over from the hand spinners and weavers, although hand

spinners at Creech St Michael, Kingston St Mary and West Monkton still supplied the looms in Taunton in the 1780s.

A ban on the import of finished silk goods was introduced in 1776 and this encouraged manufacturers to set up silk factories in rural areas with access to water power and cheap labour. Imported raw silk was brought to the mills and water-powered machinery was used for the process of silk throwing. The throwsters used an engine to wind skeins of silk onto bobbins before the thread was twisted or thrown. In Taunton the first silk throwing and silk weaving took place in 1780 and by 1820 there were 1000 silk looms in the district and 500 people employed in throwing mills. By 1866 the industry had virtually died out in the area, with only one silk factory remaining (Stanier 2003).

In the Quantock Hills there are two places connected with the textile industry where buildings remain. These are in the village of Holford and at Marsh Mills, Over Stowey. The silk factory at Marsh Mills marks the final phase of a long history of milling in this locality. Marsh Mill, established between 1648 and 1676, was occupied by a clothier in 1681 and included a fulling mill (for finishing woollen cloth). The clothier was Matthew Poole (an ancestor of Tom Poole of Nether Stowey), a wealthy man with goods worth more than £300, including cloth and wool, and a flock of sheep worth £90. Equipment such as yarn, racks, cards and shears show that wool carding, spinning and weaving were all carried out at this site in the 17th century (Dunning 1992, 166–7).

The exact site of this early textile mill is not known, but it was probably south of Marsh Mills House, close to the stream before that was diverted to power the silk factory. In 1812 a new enterprise was begun

Fig 5.37 (opposite top)
Nether Stowey: Tom
Poole's bark house.
(AA053366) (© English
Heritage. NMR)

Fig 5.38 (opposite centre)
Holford Combe: Hayman's
Pool.

Fig 5.39 (opposite bottom)
Tanyard Farm, Kingston
St Mary: drying loft.
(Hazel Riley)

Fig 5.40
Marsh Mills: the early
19th-century leat and
silk mill.

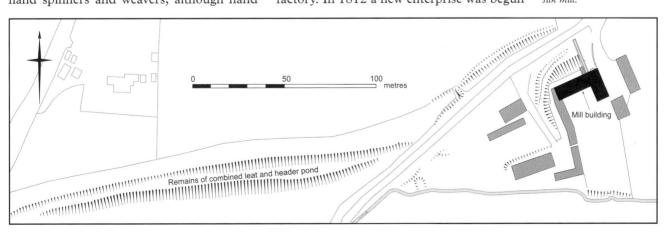

0   50   100 metres

Remains of combined leat and header pond

Mill building

Fig 5.41
Marsh Mills: the silk factory. (Hazel Riley)

Fig 5.42
The dye house in Holford Glen. (Hazel Riley)

at Marsh Mills by Thomas Ward, business partner of Tom Poole of Nether Stowey. This was still based on the textile industry but instead of using local wool to produce cloth, now imported raw silk was made into silk thread at Marsh Mills. A new building was constructed and the local streams were captured to provide power for the silk-throwing machines (Fig 5.40). The water wheel was powered by the streams that flowed down Seven Wells Combe. Water was collected in a small pond between Over Stowey and Aley and flowed into a combined leat and header pond, held in by a massive earthen dam. This pond was some 300m long and 10m wide and its dam still survives as a massive scarp, more than 2m high. A culvert ran under the road and water was taken via a leat into the back of the factory.

It seems that the factory produced silk thread, which was taken to Taunton for weaving. The factory provided employment: Thomas Ward gave evidence to a parliamentary committee in 1838 when he said that 'from 1812 to 1838 I was employing several hundreds of the female children and adults of this neighbourhood in throwing silk' (quoted in Warren 1996, 24). Weaving may also have been carried out at the factory, which could have incorporated a weaving loft. The building still stands on the site and is now domestic accommodation. Thomas Ward's silk factory at Marsh Mills was a substantial building, originally three storeys high. Built of local stone with brick detailing, the building is impressive and is one of only a few purpose-built industrial buildings to survive in the Quantock Hills (Fig 5.41). It reflects, on a small scale, the philanthropic spirit of some early 19th-century factory owners. The local parson, however, took a dim view of the place: 'there is a sad collection of girls from the Silk House in this parish….and sad work there is, I am told, among the young men and them' (Ayres 1984, 270).

The silk industry in this area has become the stuff of local legend. In the winter a ruined building catches the eye at the head of Holford Glen. This is part of the 'Silk Factory (Disused)' shown on the Ordnance Survey map of 1888. There is anecdotal evidence that silk was made here in the past from silk thread supplied by silk worms that were kept at Over Stowey. There is a long history of textile making in the area. Weavers, clothiers and dyers lived in the parish in the 16th, 17th and 18th centuries and a tucker is mentioned in 1609. A clothier who died in 1688 left cloth, racking and finishing equipment, together with raw materials and dye, indicating organised production. There was a linen house in Holford in 1721, a dye house in 1756, and two fulling mills in 1664 (Dunning 1985, 4). The ruined buildings in Holford Glen date from the late 18th or early 19th century and one, in the 1830s, was a dyehouse (Fig 5.42) (Kilve tithe map 1838). The tithe map also shows groups of dye pits in the area. Although both of the buildings are close to the stream there is no evidence of any wheel pits or other provision of water power to either of them. The dyeing process required plenty of water and the hills not only provided this but also some of the raw materials. Alder bark, nettles and ragwort produce yellow hues, lichen gives a range of browns, and bramble and bracken shoots give grey (Feltwell 1990). The upper storeys of one or both of the buildings may have been used for silk weaving, or even for silk throwing, as parts of the late 18th-century silk industry were still based on manual machinery for silk throwing, spinning of silk yarn and for patterned silk weaving. Ward's silk factory at Evercreech, Somerset, for example, had no evidence for the use of powered machinery or shafting (Williams 2002). A silk throwster living in the neighbouring parish of Nether Stowey in 1851 (Dunning 1985, 196) may have worked at Holford, as by this time the silk factory at Marsh Mills had become a corn mill.

Mining the land: the copper mines of the Quantock Hills

The Devonian rocks of the Quantock Hills contain a small suite of metalliferous minerals, mostly copper ore together with some iron, lead and silver ores (*see* Chapter 1). In the later part of the post-medieval period there were two main areas of copper mining: around Dodington and in the Broomfield area. There is both documentary and field evidence to suggest that there was some earlier working in parts of the Quantock Hills and a surprising amount of field remains connected with mining and prospecting for metal bearing rocks survive on the hills (Fig 5.18). The history of mining on the Quantock Hills has been told in *Men and Mining on the Quantocks* (Hamilton and Lawrence 1970). This is the story of the optimism and perhaps foolhardiness of the 18th-century adventurers and mine captains as none of the Quantock mines seem to have been very profitable.

The 18th-century accounts of the mines provide evidence for earlier mining activity on the Quantock Hills. In 1725 Henrik Kahlmeter wrote of a copper mine at Stowey that was no longer worked and John Woodward described rich deposits of copper ore at Dodington in 1728. These early attempts to mine copper in the Dodington area were made by miners from Derbyshire and are marked on a plan of 1801, where they are named as Derbyshire Old Workings and were apparently quite substantial: a 38-yard-long adit and six shafts. This mine was some

300m to the east of the Glebe engine house (*see below*) but the workings have been filled in and nothing can now be seen of them. Later miners deliberately sought out areas of old workings and this can be seen at the Beech Grove mine where the engine house is built in an area of older mining. Two linear trenches, both running northwest-southeast, lie to the southwest of Dodington Hall. The smaller trench is 90m long, 15m wide and 1.5m, the larger is 150m long and 20m wide and nearly 2m deep. Both are rather irregular in plan suggesting that they were formed from a series of trial pits.

There is field evidence showing that the search for copper went on over most of the Quantock Hills (Fig 5.18). Large pits or infilled shafts have been recorded on Woodlands Hill, in Alfoxton Park, on Aisholt Common and on Wills Neck. These pits are circular with a small rim of spoil around the edge and measure 8–18m in diameter and 2–5m deep. Linear trenches or small openworks have been found on Black Hill, to the north of Halsway Manor and at Cothelstone Manor (Fig 5.43). These are substantial features in the landscape. On Black Hill a trench 15m long, 10m wide and 1.5m deep has spoil on each side and a small trial pit at its north end. In the north corner of the enclosure behind Halsway Manor is a trench 30m long, 5m wide and 1.5m deep with spoil along its northern edge. A rectangular hollow to the north of Cothelstone Manor is 60m long, 17m wide and 2m deep. Areas of trial pits lie on Wills Neck, Robin Upright's Hill, Aisholt Common, Great Hill and Marrow Hill, and

Fig 5.43
Trial pits and openworks at Halsway Manor (a) and Black Hill (b).

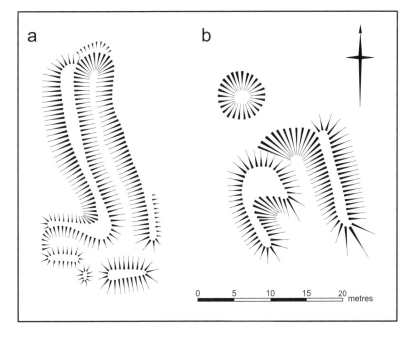

in Frog Combe. Similar pits are also found dug into the later prehistoric earthworks of Dowsborough Camp and Plainsfield Camp. These pits are generally sub-rectangular, 4–6m long, 2–4m wide and up to 1m deep, with spoil mounds to one side and may well date from the medieval or early post-medieval period. Two areas of trial pits and two large pits or shafts lie on Aisholt Common. The larger of the pits is 18m in diameter and 5m deep and seems to be an in filled shaft. A similar large pit, 8m in diameter and 2.5m deep, lies just above the deserted medieval settlement of Hamme. This is probably the remains of an early 18th-century enterprise. In 1714 a licence for mining copper and other ores in Aisholt was granted and mining in Aisholt and Over Stowey made £45 for the lord of the manor between 1716 and 1719 (Dunning 1992, 70). A single trial pit on the north side of West Hill seems to be the only feature to show that copper was ever sought here after a lease was granted to mine copper on Perry Hill in 1714 (Dunning 1985, 125).

The copper mines at Dodington

Copper mining in the Dodington area is documented from as early as the late 17th or early 18th century. In 1762 the Dodington estate was inherited by the Marquis of Buckingham who had mining interests in Cornwall. William Jenkin, agent for the Marquis' Cornish mines, was given the task of developing mining on the Dodington estate and work on the Buckingham Mines began in earnest in 1786. One of the first tasks was to drive a drainage adit west of Dodington Hall running south to an area where a lode had been found, subsequently the Garden Mine. Soon after this initial work, specific mine setts (mineral leases) were outlined and leased to companies of adventurers. One of these new setts was the New Hall Mine, leased by the Mines Royal, who drove an adit and several shafts in a line from New Hall to a point east of the Castle of Comfort. This was apparently a wasted effort as no lodes were ever worked in this sett. A third sett, known as Dodington Mine, was located west of the Counting House. Sporadic work continued at the Buckingham Mines during the 1780s and 1790s, but ore production was uneconomic. This mining was all quite shallow but to dig deeper a steam engine was needed to pump water from below the level of the adit. Despite Jenkin's best efforts, the capital needed to buy the engine was not found and the mines were all closed in 1801. The energetic Tom Poole spent several years trying to

Fig 5.44
Engine houses and shafts at Beech Grove (a) and Glebe (b).

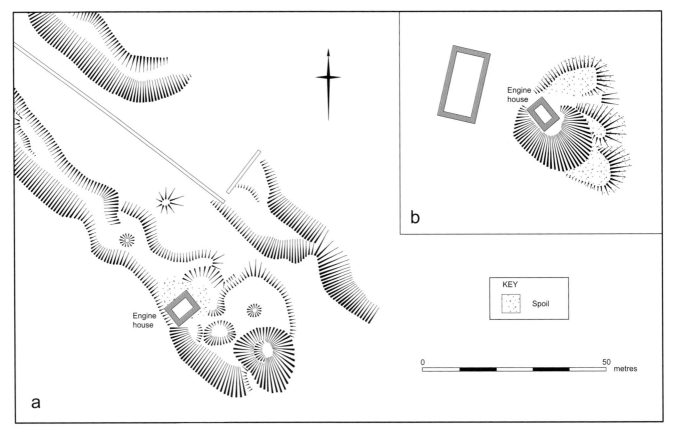

re-open the old Buckingham Mines. In 1817 Tom Poole and his associates signed a lease for 21 years and a steam engine was finally installed. However, the mines remained uneconomic and closed for the last time in 1821.

The engine houses, a few other buildings and some shafts and spoil heaps are all that remains of these mines. The Garden Mine is now within the gardens of some modern houses and no traces of its shafts survive. At New Hall the adit has been filled and the shafts capped and levelled. A stamping and ore dressing area was built at New Hall by 1791 but nothing now remains. The main drainage adit to the east of Dodington Hall was open as recently as 1954 but it is now blocked as are all the associated shafts in Shutt's Close and the Downs. There are, however, the remains of a pit near Walford's Gibbet, which is probably that documented in 1791, and some much degraded earthworks east of the Counting House, which are the remains of the activity recorded on Durborough Common in 1789–90.

The most striking remains are the two engine houses at Dodington. The engine house to the south of Dodington Hall, known as Beech Grove engine house, was built between 1817 and 1820 in the remains of older surface workings (Figs 5.44 and 5.45). The building housed a steam engine:

Fig 5.45
Beech Grove engine house.
(Hazel Riley)

Fig 5.46
Glebe engine house:
industry in a rural setting.
(Hazel Riley)

149

a Boulton and Watt single acting beam engine with a 47-inch diameter cylinder, a 12-ton cast iron beam and enough pump rods to make it possible to sink the shaft about 200ft below the surface (Hamilton and Lawrence 1970, 61). The engine house, built of local stone, is an ivy-covered ruin. It was originally a tall, three-storeyed building, standing to a height of more than 11m. Enough of the fabric survives, however, to show how it functioned. The northeast wall is 1.6m thick; this is the bob wall upon which the beam pivoted. The shaft next to the northeast side of the engine house was the engine shaft where the pump rods descended the shaft. Opposite the bob wall was the cylinder opening for the engine. Some 350m to the southeast is the second engine house, the Glebe (or Sump) engine house (Figs 5.45 and 5.46). The engine from Beech Grove was moved to this building, possibly in 1820. The Glebe engine house survives virtually intact to its original roof level. The scatter of red tile fragments around its base shows that it originally had a tiled roof. A large infilled shaft, some 16m in diameter, lies to the south of the engine house and spoil heaps lie to the east. The thick bob wall was on the southeast, the cylinder opening, with a brick arch, was in the northwest wall. Some good quality copper ore was raised from these deeper levels: 100 tons of ore from the Buckingham mines was sampled and shipped from Combwich in 1820 when it was described as 'rich and of prime quality' (Hamilton and Lawrence 1970, 62). The engine houses are remarkable testaments to the business acumen of Tom Poole and the practical enthusiasm of Matthew Grose, the mine captain. The Glebe engine house is the oldest intact beam engine house in southwest England (Stanier 2003).

The mines of the southern Quantock Hills

The activity at Dodington spurred on other land owners to search for copper. Edward Jeffries granted a lease with permission to carry out mining operations on his Cothelstone estate in 1791. An infilled shaft and some spoil dumps to the north of the lake in Cothelstone Park are all that remains, but a large openwork close to the manor house could be earlier, and may be the site of the old workings referred to in a letter of 1792. Andrew Crosse of Fyne Court, whose experiments with electricity earned him the sobriquet the 'Wizard of Broomfield', worked a small mine at Raswell Farm, north of Kingston St Mary in the early 19th century.

Small-scale mining operations were carried out in the 1820s, 1845–6 and in 1853 the Broomfield Consols Copper and Silver-Lead Mining Company was set up, with plans to work three lodes but only a year later the mine closed. The waste dumps from these operations can be seen south of the lane that links Raswell Farm and Broomfield. Two other mines in the area are not documented and probably represent small-scale 18th or 19th century attempts to strike it rich. These are at Wort Wood, Broomfield – where there are spoil heaps and shafts – and east of Courtway, Merridge.

Wild simplicity? The post-medieval landscape

'Wherever we turn we have woods, smooth downs and valleys with small brooks running down them through green meadows, hardly ever intersected with hedgerows but scattered over with trees. The hills that cradle these valleys are either covered with fern and bilberries, or oak woods, which are cut for charcoal….Walks extend for miles over the hilltops; the great beauty of which is their wild simplicity: they are perfectly smooth without rocks' *(Hill 1981, 23–4)*.

So wrote Dorothy Wordsworth, describing the Quantock Hills to Mary Hutchinson in 1797. Dorothy, her brother William and Samuel Taylor Coleridge walked for miles in and around the hills and used the landscape for inspiration. We have found evidence of a manmade landscape along the paths that they took from Stowey and Alfoxton up onto the heathland. Dorothy herself mentions the charcoal burners and 'the manufacturer' in Holford, perhaps a textile worker. Once the heath was reached the remains of the last ploughed fields of outfield cultivation would have been plain to see. People also used the heath for gathering furze and wood, cutting turf and grazing livestock and the present day steady stream of cars across the heath from Stowey to Crowcombe would have been a steady stream of pedestrians and packhorses in the 18th century. The Wordsworths and the Coleridges lived less than two miles from the Dodington mines and were great friends with the self confessed tradesman Tom Poole, with his tanyard and his mining interests. Coleridge's 'dear gutter' of Stowey had powered at least two water mills and supplied water to tan yards at Bin Combe and Nether Stowey before it flowed past his cottage door.

The creation of landscape parks was at its height in the late 18th century and Dorothy Wordsworth had strong feelings about these attempts to manipulate the landscape. She visited Crowcombe Park in April 1798 and wrote of it in her journal:

'Quaint waterfalls about, about which
Nature was very successfully striving
to make beautiful what art had deformed –
ruins, hermitages, etc. etc. In spite of all
these things, the dell romantic and
beautiful, though everywhere planted
with unnaturalised trees. Happily we
cannot shape the huge hills or carve out
the valleys according to our fancy'
(Moorman 1971, 13).

The contrived landscapes at Crowcombe, Fyne Court and Cothelstone are seen by us, 250 years after they were laid out, as wild, forgotten and hidden landscapes. Surrounded by young trees and newly built cascades and follies, Dorothy gives an account of the impact this sort of landscaping must have had when it was first carried out. Sydney Smith kept two donkeys in his garden at Combe Florey (Virgin 1994, 235). The donkeys occasionally appeared on the lawn sporting antlers strapped onto their heads. This was Sydney Smith, like Dorothy Wordsworth, scorning the pretension of his neighbours at Combe Florey House who had the genuine article – a landscaped deer park.

6

A remembered landscape?
The Quantock Hills in the
20th century

A rural idyll? The Quantock Hills in the early 20th century

At the beginning of the 20th century parts of the Quantock Hills were still 'twelve miles from a lemon'. The catch water meadows at Ivyton were still flooded every winter and farmers in Aisholt and Merridge still burnt lime in their own kilns to spread on the fields. Mr Wilkins of Friarn could remember oxen ploughing the land and the last charcoal burners working in the woods behind Over Stowey in the early decades of the 20th century and in 1901 the bark rippers still worked in Great Wood (Lawrence 1952, 165; Mead and Worthy 2001, 65). Mills at East Quantoxhead, Spaxton, Kingston St Mary and Bishops Lydeard used water power to grind corn and most of the farms had a water wheel for powering machinery. The same water wheel often provided electricity in the 1950s and 1960s.

The poet Sir Henry John Newbolt lived in the Old School House at Aisholt from 1927 until his death in 1938. He was aware that this part of the Quantock Hills was a very special place and wanted to save it both from progress and from the depredations of another war. Newbolt wrote that 'the country too is so unspoiled by the conveniences of today – it gives a great deal of that sense of safety, of the absence of the Enemy'. He found in Aisholt a respite from the political anxieties of the 1930s, hoping that Aisholt would remain forever in its untroubled seclusion: 'Let no one hear of it while the moon endureth' (quoted in Lawrence 1952, 161–2).

An industrial interlude: the Kilve oil fields

Picnicking on the beach at Kilve was, and still is, a popular pastime. At the beginning of the 20th century a perfectly ordinary beach bonfire was sometimes enlivened by the accidental ignition of some of the rocks on the cliffs and foreshore. During the Great War a mining engineer discovered oil-rich shales in the cliffs and in the 1920s Dr W Forbes-Leslie, a geologist, set up some experimental retorts at Kilve (Wright 1967). He travelled southwest England from Plymouth to Bristol on a lecture tour with bottles of oil and petrol from Kilve.

Joining forces with two other scientists, he established from boreholes that the oil-bearing rocks were 1000ft deep, covered an area from Watchet to the mouth of the River Parrett, and could produce five million gallons of oil a year. A new branch line of the

Fig 6.1
The oil retort at Kilve, built in the 1920s, part of an unsuccessful venture to win oil from the local rocks. (AA048466) (© English Heritage. NMR)

Great Western Railway from Bridgwater to Kilve was proposed at a cost of more than £250,000. The Shalime Company was formed and at least one commercial retort replaced the earlier experimental ones at Kilve. A few hundred barrels of oil were produced, probably in 1924, but the whole operation folded shortly after this and Kilve was left with a fine example of an early 20th-century industrial building.

The retort stands on the edge of Kilve Pill (Fig 6.1). It is a brick tower, 3m by 2.2m and about 4m high, with a cast iron neck, which apparently functioned as a combined condenser and flue. Crushed shale and, presumably, coke, was loaded into the retort via an opening on the eastern side. A second opening at the base of the northern side allowed slag and ashes to be removed. The vapour was collected from the iron retort neck via the flange about halfway up the condenser. The holes on the north side of the retort took scaffolding, which supported the extensive system of pipework through which the distillate flowed before it was collected in wooden barrels (Mead and Worthy 2001, 38).

The Second World War and the Cold War: the Quantock Hills in the later 20th century

Some of the most recent buildings and landscape features are the least well studied and documented. Without the memories of the men and women who lived and worked on the Quantock Hills in the Second World War and the Cold War they remain as bleak, empty shells and objects of local curiosity (Figs 6.2, 6.4 and 6.9). When the stories of the people who used these buildings are told, the buildings have a renewed sense of place in the story of the landscape.

Training ranges

The tranquillity of the hills that Newbolt valued was soon to be shattered. After the First World War it became apparent that one of the biggest threats to Britain in a future conflict was from long-range strategic bombing. Aircraft had dropped bombs on London in 1917; fighter aircraft, early-warning systems and anti-aircraft gunnery were needed. In the early 1920s an anti-aircraft unit was formed with guns at Hunstanton in Norfolk. Local people, however, complained loudly that the shooting interfered with their fishing and a War Office colonel was sent on a reconnaissance of the Bristol Channel coast for a new artillery range site.

The fishermen of Watchet were made of sterner stuff than those from Hunstanton and in 1925 the first gunners and searchlights moved to the cliffs at Doniford. The artillery range at Doniford trained thousands of artillerymen. In the early years eight guns fired from the cliff top at a small aircraft towing a target, later a radio-controlled plane carried the targets (Hurley 1978). The artillery range and camp at Doniford closed in the late 1950s and the site is now a holiday park. A few miles to the east are the remains of a tank training range at West Kilton Farm. West Somerset took its share of evacuees, it had coastal defences and took hits from bombs dropped as planes returned from raids on south Wales or Bristol, but arguably its most important roles during the Second World War were to provide artillery training ranges and areas for the concentration of American troops and equipment during the run up to D-Day.

The coastal path from Lilstock to Kilve affords stunning views across the Bristol Channel. Turn inland, however, and some small brick buildings can be seen in a sea of arable land (Fig 6.2). These are part of the remains of a tank training range at West Kilton Farm (Fig 6.3). It was built in 1942 and was used by American troops until just before D-Day in 1944. Most of the actual buildings were sold after the war but the brick buildings still stand in good condition and the concrete bases for other buildings and the concrete roads all remain. The tanks fired from a stationary position, marked by a large area of concrete hard standing, across to a target railway, more than a kilometre to the north on the edge of the cliffs. The railway was protected by a massive earth and stone bank constructed from topsoil taken from nearby fields. This was dismantled at the end of the war and the material spread back onto the fields. The three brick buildings that can be seen from the cliffs mark the southwest and northeast ends of the target railway, these were communication posts (Fig 6.2). The tanks were kept under cover in Kilton Park Wood. There were approximately 30 to 40 staff manning the range, as well as a steady stream of GIs arriving for training. The staff accommodation was in Nissen huts to the south of the tank firing position. Here was a dormitory for the men, wash rooms, kitchens, a mess room and officer's accommodation.

Fig 6.2
West Kilton Farm:
communications post at the
end of the target railway.
(Hazel Riley)

Fig 6.3
West Kilton Farm: the
tank training range.
(Based on an Ordnance
Survey map, with
permission.
© Crown copyright.
All rights reserved)

KEY

CP	Communication post
W	Workshop
H	Hardstanding for tanks
AB	Accommodation buildings
—	Banks

0   300m

Life went on as usual at West Kilton Farm, even though there were tanks firing only 200m from the farmhouse. The household was kept well supplied with cigarettes, sugar and pig swill by the American troops.

Kilton was not a peaceful place during the Second World War. Not only was there a tank training range at West Kilton Farm but a few kilometres to the north was a practice bombing range in the Bristol Channel. Originally HMS Heron, part of RNAS Yeovilton, it is still in use as RAF Gunnery Range, Lilstock. The large concrete building that stands on the cliff edge to the north of Lilstock was a blast-proof shelter (Fig 6.4), manned by the Home Guard for part of the war and connected to the small communication building on the cliff edge at Kilve, itself in turn connected to the target railway communication posts (J Ash, pers comm).

American camps

Thousands of American troops were concentrated in Somerset prior to D-Day, with the US Corps Headquarters around Taunton. Hestercombe House was the Headquarters of the 19th District of the US Services of Supply and there was a large storage depot at Norton Fitzwarren. Hestercombe was also the Headquarters of the 801st Hospital Centre and there were US Army hospitals at Sandhill Park and Norton Camp. The troops were housed in large camps, in huts and in tents, at Crowcombe Heathfield, Doniford Camp, Alfoxton and

Hestercombe (Hawkins 1996). The remains of the camps can be identified on aerial photographs taken shortly after the war ended. At Crowcombe Heathfield there was a large camp, housing about 6,000 men, covering an area of more than 16ha (Fig 6.5). The camp was built on an area of outfield cultivation on the lowland common of Crowcombe Heathfield. There were two main groups of buildings to either side of the road with tracks radiating out to areas for tented accommodation and hard standing for vehicles. Close to the approach to Alfoxton was a smaller camp, covering an area of 6ha, with the concrete bases for some 16 buildings. In the northern corner of the same field are two rather unimpressive circular earthworks. These are all that remains of a searchlight battery (Fig 6.5).

Searchlight batteries

In November 1941 a unit of 493 Battery of the 76th Searchlight Regiment moved into Crowcombe Court. The men, including former employees of Bentley's department store in London and a group of ex-miners from West Yorkshire, were housed in two large Nissen huts to the west of the house, the women, including several from the ATS, lived in the house whose southern wing was used as the Quartermaster's stores. Crow-

combe Court was the centre of the West Somerset searchlight grid: the whole country was covered by a network of searchlight positions that formed part of the Air Defence of Great Britain. At the beginning of this survey a prehistoric settlement with three hut circles and three hut platforms was recorded at Crowcombe Gate. A close look at these sites showed that they could not be prehistoric: the platforms overlay the narrow ridge and furrow ploughing of 16th and 17th date that covers the area (*see* Chapter 5).

The site is actually the remains of a searchlight battery, with a grass-covered circular concrete platform for the searchlight itself, the remains of positions for Light Anti-Aircraft guns and a sound locator emplacement, together with the accommodation buildings (Fig 6.6). The light at Crowcombe Gate was a 1.2m searchlight, with a million candlepower brightness, powered by a Lister diesel engine. The gun position housed a Vickers machine gun, mounted on a wooden post. The searchlight was manned until D-Day, when some members of the battery were sent to the Second Front for 'moonlighting' or lighting the battlefield at night. There were also searchlight batteries to the south of the tank training range at West Kilton Farm, Alfoxton and at Aley Lane, southwest of Marsh Mills, Over Stowey (P White, pers comm).

Fig 6.4
The blast-proof shelter on the coast north of Lilstock. (AA053024) (© English Heritage. NMR)

Fig 6.5
Camps for American troops
at Alfoxton (a) and
Crowcombe Heathfield (c),
and PoW camp at
Goathurst (b). (Based on
an Ordnance Survey map,
with permission.
© Crown copyright.
All rights reserved)

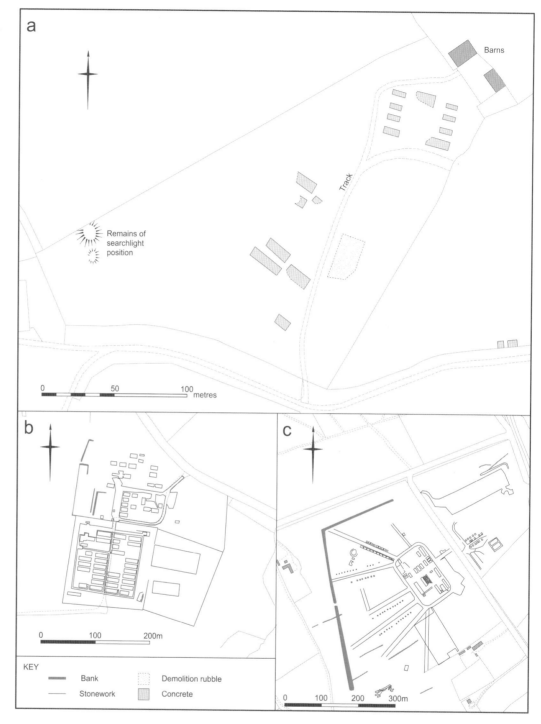

a

Barns

Remains of
searchlight
position

Track

0   50   100
                    metres

b

c

0   100   200m

KEY

—— Bank   ⬚ Demolition rubble

— Stonework   ▨ Concrete

0   100   200   300m

Prisoner of War camps

The main influx of prisoners of war to
Britain was in early 1941 after the capture
of Tobruk in December 1940 when thousands of Italian soldiers were taken prisoner
and eventually brought to this country.
It was not until after D-Day that large
numbers of German prisoners were brought
to this country.

There were Prisoner of War camps at
Bridgwater, Norton Fitzwarren and at
Goathurst Camp, Halswell House (Hawkins
1996). Goathurst Camp, on the southeast
edge of the Quantock Hills, was built in the
park of Halswell House. The camp shows
clearly on aerial photographs taken shortly
after the war. The camp covered an area of
6ha (Fig 6.5). The whole camp was surrounded by barbed wire and the entrance

was guarded by a barrier and guard post. The wooden and corrugated iron buildings included a chapel, a shop and a chicken house, the kitchen was apparently under-ground (D Pusill, pers comm). Many of the men worked on local farms and a local coach firm took the workers out to the farms every day. One of the prisoners, Franz Schmidt from Dusseldorf, made toys from scraps of wood for the children of the owner of the coach firm. These toys were played with for many years and are now treasured family possessions (Fig 6.7).

The Home Guard

The Home Guard began as an organisation of volunteers called the Local Defence Vol-unteers in May 1940. By October of that year the organisation of the Home Guard in Somerset was complete. The Home Guard for the Quantock Hills came from the 1st Somerset (Minehead) Battalion, the 2nd Somerset (Taunton) Battalion and the 10th Somerset (Bridgwater) Battalion (Wilson 2004). The Home Guard manned the coastal defences between Minehead and Blue Anchor as well as road blocks across west Somerset. The Quantock Hills were used for training the Home Guard: the Bat-tle of Staple Plain is commemorated in the menu cover for the 'Stand-down sit-up, or Sit-down stand-up, Farewell Dinner' of the Williton Platoon (Hawkins 1996, 140). On the western slopes of Beacon Hill there are four trenches, each 4m square and 0.75m deep, with mounds of spoil giving some pro-tection on their east sides. One of these has been constructed on the edge of a prehis-toric cairn (Fig 5.14). These may have been dug as part of a Home Guard training exer-cise, perhaps as gun positions or fox holes.

The strength of commitment shown by the Home Guard is demonstrated by the Auxiliary Units, sometimes called the Secret Home Guard. These units were not attached to the normal Home Guard units but they operated in small isolated cells, training undercover, and covering different parts of the country. This was the last phase of the nation's defence: the main job of the Auxiliary Units was to disrupt an enemy occupation by sabotage and assassination. The units had underground bunkers as their base for sabotage operations in case of an invasion. These contained bunks, food and water stores, and separate storage for ammunition and explosives (Osborne 2004). At least one of these units, under the

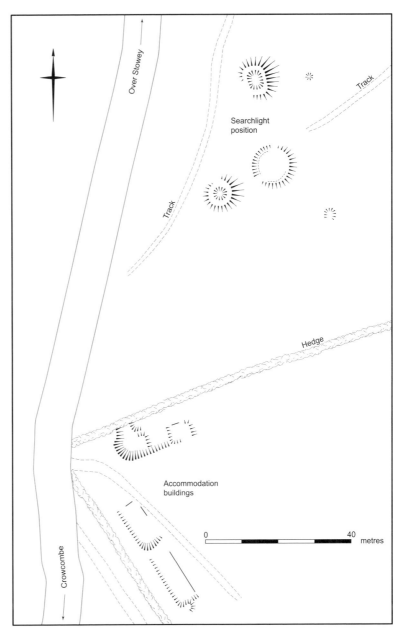

local command of Colonel Ingram at Pight-ley House, Spaxton, was active on the Quantock Hills (Hawkins 1996, 137). The 18th-century ornamental tree ring on the southwest side of Cothelstone Hill (see Chapter 5) was used to construct one of these bunkers. It was camouflaged by the large beech trees growing in the tree ring (Fig 5.15). The entrance to the bunker has been infilled but part of it can still be seen, dug into the northwest edge of the tree ring (Fig 6.8).

The threat of invasion was still very real after the invasion scare of 1940. Villages or groups of villages formed Invasion Commit-tees and Colonel Ingram was the chairman

Fig 6.6
The searchlight battery at Crowcombe Gate.

Fig 6.7
One of the toys made by
a German PoW at
Goathurst. (Hazel Riley)

of the one centred on Spaxton; in his speech at the first public meeting of that committee he advised the people of the district, in the face of an invasion, to stand firm and not abandon their homes. Men were detailed to dig slit trenches for the safety of their women and children, while women were encouraged to hide food in 'a place where it will not be spoilt and where it is well concealed [as] if the enemy is in the neighbourhood it is one of the first things he will look for' (M Treharne, pers comm).

The eyes and ears of the RAF: the Royal Observer Corps

During the Second World War the Royal Observer Corps (ROC) constantly watched the skies of Britain. The ROC identified and tracked all aircraft, both hostile and friendly and also helped with the organisation of air-raid warnings. Their observation posts, usually simple wooden huts or brick buildings,

Fig 6.8
Cothelstone Hill: entrance
to the Auxiliary Scout Unit
bunker. (Hazel Riley)

were located on open or high ground with good views. The network of 29 posts in Somerset included two on the east edge of the Quantock Hills: one north of Holford and one at Dancing Lane, North Petherton. These were part of No 22 Group whose headquarters was at Yeovil. The Second World War observation posts at Holford and North Petherton have been demolished. A satellite post to the North Petherton post was opened at Yards on the boundary between the parishes of Broomfield and Kingston St Mary in October 1942. At the end of the Second World War the ROC was stood down. In 1947, however, the Cold War was already beginning and the ROC was re-formed.

By the late 1950s the threat of nuclear attack on Britain was very real and the ROC was tasked with locating the site of a nuclear detonation and monitoring the passage of radiation fallout. For this task underground bunkers were required and these were often built at or close to the sites of the ROC posts built during the Second World War. Underground bunkers were built at Holford and Yards. At Yards the old brick observation post was demolished in the 1980s as it was deemed too dangerous to walk under it to get to the underground bunker. Both underground bunkers survive in apparently good condition. At Holford the entrance hatch, ventilators and pipe for fixed survey meter probe (*see below*) can be seen (Fig 6.9), at Yards only the entrance hatch shaft is visible through the bramble thicket that covers it. The underground monitoring posts were all built to a similar specification (Cocroft and Thomas 2003) and Mr R A Lawry, who manned the post at Yards from 1973 until the end of the Cold War confirms this. The chamber, accessed by a vertical ladder, contained a drainage sump, chemical lavatory, bunk beds as well as the monitoring instruments and communication equipment. The posts were linked to other posts in the group by open telephones. The monitoring equipment consisted of a ground zero indicator or shadowgraph, which was used to determine the position of the detonation; a bomb power indicator, which recorded the maximum power of the blast; and a fixed survey meter, which recorded levels of gamma radiation. Training and yearly examinations kept the men up to scratch and Mr Lawry seems to have had one of the best jobs: he had to check regularly that a Geiger counter kept behind the bar of a pub in Spaxton was working.

Fig 6.9
Holford: Entrance to the Cold War ROC underground monitoring post, with pipe for fixed survey meter (centre) and ventilators (right). (AA053026) (© English Heritage. NMR)

A changing landscape? The historic landscape of the Quantock Hills in the 21st century

The historic landscape of the Quantock Hills is truly that: it spans millennia and contains the story of the people who lived and worked in this magical place. The hills themselves are perceived by many as never changing, a place that is always the same no matter what life may throw at us. The hills can be a place of comfort and solace, many wish their ashes to be scattered over them, echoing one of their primary functions in the 2nd millennium BC. The hills are also a place for congregation and celebration: witness the beacons and bonfires on the hills for the Queen's Golden Jubilee in 2001 and read the accounts of similar fires lit in celebration of Queen Victoria's Diamond Jubilee on Wills Neck in 1897. But the fairs, festivals and carnivals at Glastonbury and Bridgwater are now the focus of communal celebrations and have replaced the old gathering places on the hilltops.

We have seen how much the landscape has changed: from tangled forest to open heath, from wood and forest to a deer park or ploughed field. The buildings in that landscape have also changed. Prehistoric round houses built of wood with wattle and daub walls and thatched roofs were replaced by country houses of stone with mosaic floors and tiled roofs. The distinctive and durable local stones were used to build medieval church towers, the tallest structures the Quantock Hills had yet seen. Imposing manor houses of local stone, wood and thatch were replaced with mansion houses, often of some pretension, with their own grounds, reflecting the very latest fashions and tastes. Brick and tile houses have replaced the cob and thatch cottages of the agricultural workers and many of the 18th- and 19th-century farm buildings are now themselves residential accommodation. The resulting mix is a challenging landscape, not only to the landscape archaeologist, tasked with telling its story, but to the landscape manager, who must balance this rich heritage against social, financial and environmental constraints.

The Quantock AONB Service is already engaged with this process. A project initiated by the team to manage the beech hedge banks of the hills embraces nature conservation (beech trees), heritage (the artificial banks on which the trees were planted) and addresses the aesthetic of landscape (how will this restoration work change the way the

Fig 6.10
The stable block at Friarn,
built in the 1950s to
accommodate visiting
hunts. (Hazel Riley)

hills look?). Quantock Common is now in an agri-environment scheme, which not only ensures its ecological well being but also benefits its archaeology. The Bronze Age barrows on Wills Neck and Beacon Hill have been carefully restored as part of English Heritage's Monument Management Scheme, following many years of erosion caused by the magnetic attraction between visitors and Ordnance Survey triangulation pillars. A large scar on the Iron Age ramparts of Dowsborough Camp, the result of strenuous activity on mountain bikes, has also been restored as part of this scheme. The enhanced knowledge and understanding of the historic environment of the Quantock Hills gained as a result of this survey is already informing management and conservation decisions. It is also raising awareness, in both local residents and visitors to the hills, of the long history of man's intervention with what is often perceived as a natural landscape, enhancing their enjoyment of, and engagement with, their landscape.

Adscombe Chapel has recently become visible again. The scrubby trees that were beginning to damage the remaining medieval fabric have been removed and new access to the site created as part of an agri-environment scheme. During our survey work at Adscombe Chapel one of us (EJ) spotted a concrete building just below the woods at Friarn through the telescope of the theodolite (Fig 6.10). A brief examination and some local enquiries made us think that this was some long-forgotten building from the Second World War – but what was it for? The nearest recorded military sites were the searchlight batteries at Crowcombe Gate and Marsh Mills, too far away to be associated with this building at Friarn.

Photographs were sent to tame experts but headshaking replies came back. The building at Friarn was put to the back of the file marked 'Query' and was forgotten about until I was shown around the site by local residents, who also showed me examples of iron rations for the troops (tea tins) that they had found in the area. So I conducted a measured survey of the building and took a portfolio of record shots. Then it was time for lunch with some of the AONB team in Nether Stowey, to whom I recounted my morning's work. There was a short pause in the conversation and one of the team (IP) explained to me that the building was put up by the hunt in the 1950s as a stable block to accommodate horses and their grooms comfortably for the odd night if they had travelled some distance to hunt on the Quantock Hills with the Somerset and Devon Staghounds. That explained the concrete mangers in the corners of the building.

It also made me think about the forgotten landscape of hunting on the Quantock Hills, and that is not the only question that this archaeological survey has raised. There are so many questions to ask of this precious resource: 'how old is the heath?', 'where *did* people live in the Bronze Age?', what was the Trendle *for*?', 'how old is the earliest mining on the hills?'. Such a survey can only be the beginning of the story of the historic landscape of the Quantock Hills. I hope that this book goes some way to providing the impetus to ask these questions and to informing the process of answering them.

Appendix 1: Site gazetteer

The major sites discussed in the text are listed below with their National Grid references and NMR (National Monuments Record) numbers (in brackets). Reference numbers for the Register of Parks and Gardens are also given where appropriate. Detailed records for the sites are available using these numbers from the NMRC Swindon, and online via the English Heritage website. Most of the sites in this list are on privately owned land and permission for access should be sought.

Chambered tombs and standing stones
Battlegore ST 0744 4162 (ST 04 SE 140)
The Long Stone ST 1403 4065 (ST 13 SW 35)
Edge set stone on Longstone Hill ST 1397 4026 (ST 13 SW 159)
Triscombe Stone ST 1637 3590 (ST 13 NE 35)

Major barrow groups
Cothelstone Hill ST 1883 3263 (ST 13 SE 5)
Lydeard Hill ST 1816 3416 (ST 13 SE 3)
Wills Neck ST 1651 3516 (ST 13 NE 7)
Great Hill, Fire Beacon and West Hill ST 1565 3625 (ST 13 NE 10)
Hurley Beacon ST 1421 3807 (ST 13 NW 16)
Black Hill ST 1466 3820 (ST 13 NW 23)
Withyman's Pool ST 1530 3813 (ST13 NE 13)
Bicknoller Hill ST 1285 3987 (ST 13 NW 6)
Beacon Hill ST 1243 4100 (ST 14 SW 21)
West Hill ST 1232 4157 (ST 14 SW 20)
Greenway ST 1351 4134 (ST 14 SW 18)
Higher Hare Knap ST 1484 3952 (ST 13 NW 8)

Possible Bronze Age settlements and field systems
West Hill ST 1270 4190 (ST 14 SW 174)
Greenway ST 1337 4090 (ST 14 SW 173)

Hillforts
Dowsborough Camp ST 160 391 (ST 13 NE 2)
Ruborough Camp ST 228 335 (ST 23 SW 1)
Bicknoller Hill ST 122 396 (ST 13 NW 29)

Hill-slope enclosures (earthwork sites)
The Trendle Ring ST 118 394 (ST 13 NW 3)
Higher Castles (Broomfield Camp) ST 216 320 (ST 23 SW 4)
Plainsfield Camp (Cockercombe Camp) ST 184 362 (ST 13 NE 17)
Rooks Castle ST 254 323 (ST 23 SE 14)

Linear earthworks
Higher Hare Knap ST 1495 3924 (ST 13 NW 27)
Dead Woman's Ditch ST 1613 3812 (ST 13 NE 21)
Wills Neck ST 1640 3546 (ST 13 NE 111)
Cothelstone Hill ST 1897 3262 (ST 13 SE 101)

Roman villas
Spaxton ST 2417 3622 (ST 23 NW 12)
Yarford (grid reference withheld)

Castles
Nether Stowey ST 1866 3957 (ST 13 NE 4)
Stogursey ST 2028 4258 (ST 24 SW 8)

Deserted medieval settlements
Deak's Allers ST 1317 4247 (ST 14 SW 175)
Durborough Farm (grid reference withheld)

Post-medieval landscape parks and gardens
St Audries ST 1105 4233 (ST 14 SW 82) (Parks and Gardens 2159)
Weacombe ST 1096 4061 (ST 14 SW 42)
Crowcombe ST 1410 3690 (ST 13 NW 36) (Parks and Gardens 2146)
West Bagborough ST 1686 3370 (ST 13 SE 28)
Terhill ST 1762 3304 (ST 13 SE 118)
Cothelstone House ST 1768 3243 (ST 13 SE 119)
Cothelstone Manor ST 1813 3180 (ST 13 SE 13) (Parks and Gardens 2144)
Tetton House ST 2079 3044 (ST 23 SW 11)
Fyne Court ST 2227 3218 (ST 23 SW 8)
Quantock Lodge ST 1878 3750 (ST 13 NE 112)
Alfoxton ST 1480 4140 (ST 14 SW 177)
Over Stowey ST 1860 3864 (ST 13 NE 68)
Court House ST 1362 4368 (ST 14 SW 178)

Deserted farmsteads
Combe Farm ST 1527 3613 (ST 13 NE 114)
Muchcare Farm ST 1868 3393 (ST 13 SE 93)

Relict field systems
Beacon Hill ST 125 410 (ST 14 SW 49)
Bicknoller Hill ST 120 395 (ST 13 NW 122)
Thorncombe Hill ST 127 395 (ST 13 NW 122)
Higher Hare Knap ST 147 395 (ST 13 NW 126)

Catch water meadows
Ivyton Farm ST 205 310 (ST 23 SW 73)
Stream Farm ST 245 326 (ST 23 SW 43)

Lime kilns (good structural remains)
Kilve ST 1444 4436 (ST 14 SW 64)
East Quantoxhead ST 1368 4419 (ST 14 SW 58)
Aisholt ST 1955 3527 (ST 13 NE 113)
Hawkridge Common (restored) ST 2018 3560 (ST 23 NW 53)

Charcoal burning platforms
Slaughterhouse Combe ST 140 396 (ST 13 NW 129)
Somerton Combe ST 144 395 (ST 13 NW 129)
Frog Combe ST 152 388 (ST 13 NW 129)
Lady's Combe ST 156 388 (ST 13 NW 129)

Tanneries
Holford ST 1514 4051 (ST 14 SE 113)
Nether Stowey ST 1908 3978 (ST 13 NE 115)
Tanyard Farm ST 2156 3071 (ST 23 SW 86)

Textile industry
Holford ST 1548 4104 (ST 14 SE 45)
Marsh Mills ST 1906 3836 (ST 13 NE 52)

Engine houses and mining remains
Glebe engine house ST 1754 4006 (ST 14 SE 100)
Beech Grove engine house ST 1731 4032 (ST 14 SE 108)
Raswell Farm ST 2130 3158 (ST 23 SW 85)
Cothelstone Park ST 1795 3220 (ST 13 SE 120)

20th-century sites
Crowcombe Gate, WWII searchlight ST 1504 3760 (ST 13 NE 65)
West Kilton, WWII tank training range ST 1621 4387 (ST 14 SE 66)
Holford, Cold War ROC bunker ST 1619 4285 (ST 14 SE 114)
Yards, Cold War ROC bunker ST 2327 3039 (ST 23 SW 87)

Appendix 2: English Heritage Quantock project reports

Jamieson, E 2003 An early medieval manor house and landscape at Kilve, Somerset
AI/8/2003

Jamieson, E 2003 Fyne Court, Broomfield, Somerset. An 18th-century landscape park
AI/21/2003

Jamieson, E & Jones, B V 2004 Court House, East Quantoxhead, Somerset. A Jacobean manor house and its surrounding landscape
AI/01/2004

Jones, B V 2003 Chantry Cottage, Priory Cottage and the remains of Chantry, Kilve, Somerset
B/005/2003

Newman, P 2002 The Trendle Ring hill-slope enclosure and the Bicknoller cross-ridge dyke, Bicknoller, Somerset
AI/27/2002

Newman, P 2003 Dodington Mines, Holford, Somerset
AI/17/2003

Riley, H 2002 Dowsborough Camp, Holford, Somerset
AI/23/2002

Riley, H 2002 Crowcombe Gate, Over Stowey, Somerset
AI/36/2002

Riley, H 2002 Adscombe Chapel, Over Stowey, Somerset
AI/38/2002

Riley, H 2003 Earthworks at Parsonage Farm and Castle Field, Over Stowey, Somerset
AI/1/2003

Riley, H 2003 Cothelstone Manor and Cothelstone Hill. An archaeological survey
AI/23/2003

Riley, H 2004 Higher Castles, Broomfield, Somerset. An Iron Age hill-slope enclosure
AI/13/2004

Riley, H 2004 Rooks Castle, Broomfield, Somerset: Iron Age and medieval enclosures and medieval quarry pits
AI/14/2004

Riley, H 2004 Ruborough Camp, Broomfield, Somerset. An Iron Age hillfort and outwork
AI/15/2004

Riley, H 2004 Nether Stowey Castle, Nether Stowey, Somerset. A motte and bailey castle in its medieval and post-medieval landscape context
AI/16/2004

References

Abdy, R A 2002 *Romano-British Coin Hoards*. Princes Risborough: Shire

Acland, T D and Sturge, W 1851 *The Farming of Somersetshire*. London: John Murray

Aldhouse-Green, S (ed) 2000 *Paviland Cave and the 'Red Lady'. A Definitive Report*. Bristol: Western Academic and Specialist Press

Allan, J 1998 'Cleeve Abbey: the pottery'. *Somerset Archaeol Natur Hist* **142**, 41–75

Allen, M 1983 'Frances Hamilton of Bishops Lydeard'. *Somerset and Dorset Notes and Queries* **31**, 259–72

Anon 1908 'Cothelstone Manor, Somerset, the property of Mr C E J Esdaile'. *Country Life* **23**, 54–61

ApSimon, A M 1949–50 'Gorsey Bigbury, the second report'. *Proc Univ Bristol Spelaeol Soc* **6**, 1861–99

Aston, M 1988 'Land use and field systems' *in* Aston, M (ed) *Aspects of the Medieval Landscape of Somerset*. Somerset County Council, 83–97

Ayres, J 1984 *Paupers and Pig Killers. The Diary of William Holland*. Gloucester: Alan Sutton

Ballard, R 1977 *The Priory Church of St Andrew, Stogursey*. Stogursey Parish Council

Barber, M 2003 *Bronze and the Bronze Age. Metalwork and Society in Britain c2500–800 BC*. Stroud: Tempus

Barnwell, P S and Giles, C 1997 *English Farmsteads 1750–1914*. Swindon: RCHME

Barrett, JC, Freeman, P W M and Woodward, A 2000 *Cadbury Castle, Somerset. The later prehistoric and early historic archaeology*. London: English Heritage

Barton, N 1997 *Stone Age Britain*. London: Batsford

Bates, E H 1887 'Leland in Somersetshire; 1540–1542'. *Somerset Archaeol Natur Hist* **33**, 60–136

— 1889 *The Cartularies of the Benedictine Abbeys of Muchelney and Athelney in the County of Somerset*. Somerset Record Soc **14**

— 1900 *The Particular Description of the County of Somerset. Drawn up by Thomas Gerard of Trent 1633*. Somerset Record Soc **15**

Bell, M G 1990 *Brean Down Excavations 1983–1987*. London: English Heritage Archaeol Rep **15**

Bettey, J H 1986 *Wessex from AD 1000*. London: Longman

Billingham, R M 1977 'A Somerset Draw for Painters. Victorian Artists at Halsway Manor'. *Country Life* **August 1977**, 428–30

Billingsley, J 1797 *General View of the Agriculture of the County of Somerset*. Bath: Cruttwell

Blackburn, M A S 1974 'The mint of Watchet'. *Brit Numis J* **44**, 13–38

Bond, J 1994 'Forests, chases, warrens and parks in medieval Wessex' *in* Aston, M and Lewis, C (eds) *The Medieval Landscape of Wessex*. Oxford: Oxbow Monogr **46**, 115–58

— 1998 *Somerset Parks and Gardens, a Landscape History*. Tiverton: Somerset Books

Bowden, M (ed) 2000 *Furness Iron*. Swindon: English Heritage

Bradley, R 2005 *Ritual and Domestic Life in Prehistoric Europe*. London: Routledge

Bradley, R, Entwistle, R and Raymond, F 1994 *Prehistoric Land Divisions on Salisbury Plain: the Work of the Wessex Linear Ditches Project*. London: English Heritage Archaeol Rep **2**

Britnell, W J and Savory, H N 1984 *Gwernvale and Penywyrlod: Two Neolithic Long Cairns in the Black Mountains of Brecknock*. Cardiff: Cambrian Archaeol Monogr **2**

Broadmead, W B 1891 'Our Lady of Addiscombe'. *Somerset and Dorset Notes and Queries* **2**, 239

Burrow, I 1980 'Broomfield, Rooks Castle'. *Somerset Archaeol Natur Hist* **124**, 114

— 1981 *Hillfort and Hill-top Settlement in Somerset in the First Millennium AD*. Oxford: BAR **91**

— 1982 'Hillforts and hilltops 1000 BC-1000 AD' *in* Aston, M and Burrow, I (eds) *The Archaeology of Somerset: A Review to 1500 AD*. Somerset County Council, 83–97

Buxton, J (ed) 1953 *Poems of Michael Drayton*. London: Routledge and Kegan Paul

Calder, M 2003 'Early ecclesiastical sites in Somerset: three case studies'. *Somerset Archaeol Natur Hist* **147**, 1–28

Carew, T 1735–1750 'Unpublished papers relating to the history of Somersetshire'. SRO DD/TB **19**

Catling, H W 1950 'A medieval site in Broomfield, Somerset: an interim report'. *Somerset Archaeol Natur Hist* **95**, 179–80

Churchill, DW 1962 'The stratigraphy of the Mesolithic sites III and V at Thatcham, Berkshire, England'. *Proc Prehist Soc* **28**, 362–70

Cocroft, W D 2000 *Dangerous Energy. The Archaeology of Gunpowder and Military Explosives Manufacture*. Swindon: English Heritage

Cocroft, W D and Thomas, R J C 2003 *Cold War. Building for Nuclear Confrontation 1946–1989*. Swindon: English Heritage

Coles, B and Coles, J 1986 *Sweet Track to Glastonbury. The Somerset Levels in Prehistory*. London: Thames and Hudson

Collinson, R J 1791 *The History and Antiquities of the County of Somerset*, 1983 reprint. Gloucester: Alan Sutton

Costen, M 1988 'The late Saxon landscape' *in* Aston, M (ed), *Aspects of the Medieval Landscape of Somerset*. Somerset County Council, 33–47

Costen, M 1992 *The Origins of Somerset*. Manchester: University Press

Countryside Agency 2003 *The Quantock Hills Landscape. An Assessment of the Area of Outstanding Natural Beauty*. Countryside Agency Publications

Cox, J and Thorp, J R L 2001 *Devon Thatch*. Tiverton: Devon Books

Cresswell, B F 1904 *The Quantock Hills: Their Combes and Villages*. Taunton: Barnicott and Pearce

Cunliffe, B 2003 *Danebury Hillfort*. Stroud: Tempus Books

— 2005 *Iron Age Communities in Britain*, 4 edn. London: Routledge

Daniel, G E 1950 *The Prehistoric Chamber Tombs of England and Wales*. Cambridge: University Press

Davies, J A 1924 'Fourth report on Aveline's Hole'. *Proc Univ Bristol Spelaeol Soc* **2**, 104–14

Dawson, D, Langdon, M, Murless, B, Newsom, M, Ponsford, M and Webster, C J 2001 'Archaeology and the M5 motorway: the gazetteer of sites in Somerset'. *Somerset Archaeol Natur Hist* **145**, 39–51

Dennison, E 1987 'Broomfield, Broomfield Hill'. *Somerset Archaeol Natur Hist* **131**, 207–9

Dickinson, F H 1889 *Kirby's Quest for Somerset*. Somerset Record Soc **3**

Dilks, T B 1940 'Bridgwater Castle and Demesne towards the end of the fourteenth century'. *Somerset Archaeol Natur Hist Soc* **86**, 86–113

Dilks, T B (ed) 1938 *Bridgwater Borough Archives 1377–1399*. Somerset Record Soc **53**

Dunning, R W 1981 'The origins of Nether Stowey'. *Somerset Archaeol Natur Hist* **125**, 124–6

— 1985 *A History of the County of Somerset*, vol 5. Oxford: Oxford Univ P

— 1992 *A History of the County of Somerset*, vol 6. Oxford: Oxford Univ P

— 2001 *Somerset Monasteries*. Stroud: Tempus

Edmonds, E A and Williams, B J 1985 'Geology of the country around Taunton and the Quantock Hills', *Memoir for 1:50 000 geological sheet* **295**, NS. London: HMSO

Edwards, C 1999 'Quantock Hills AONB Management Strategy'. Quantock Hills AONB Joint Advisory Committee

— 2004 'Quantock Hills Area of Outstanding Natural Beauty, Management Plan 2004–2009'. Quantock Hills AONB Joint Advisory Committee

Elkington, H D H 1976 'The Mendip lead industry' *in* Branigan, K and Fowler, P J (eds), *The Roman West Country. Classical Culture and Celtic Society*. Newton Abbot: David and Charles, 183–97

Ellis, P 1986 'A possible henge monument from aerial photographic evidence in Norton Fitzwarren parish'. *Somerset Archaeol Natur Hist* **130**, 164–5

— 1989 'Norton Fitzwarren hillfort: a report on the excavations by Nancy and Philip Langmaid between 1968 and 1971'. *Somerset Archaeol Natur Hist* **133**, 1–74

Feltwell, J 1990 *The Story of Silk*. Stroud: Alan Sutton

Ferris, I M and Bevan, L 1993 'Excavations at Maidenbrook Farm, Cheddon

Fitzpaine, in 1990'. *Somerset Archaeol Natur Hist* **137**, 1–40

Field, D 1998 'Round barrows and the harmonious landscape: placing early Bronze Age burial monuments in south-east England'. *Oxford J Archaeol* **17**, 309–26

Fitzpatrick, AP, Butterworth, C A and Grove, J 1999 *Prehistoric and Roman sites in East Devon: the A30 Honiton to Exeter Improvement DBFO Scheme 1996–9.* Wessex Archaeol

Fleming, A 1988 *The Dartmoor Reaves. Investigating Prehistoric Land Divisions.* London: Batsford

— 1994 'Medieval and post-medieval cultivation on Dartmoor: a landscape archaeologists view'. *Proc Devon Archaeol Soc* **52**, 101–17

Fowler, P J, Gardner, K S and Rahtz, P A 1970 *Cadbury Congresbury, Somerset, 1968.* Univ Bristol

Fox, A 1948 'The Broad Down (Farway) necropolis and the Wessex Culture in Devon'. *Proc Devon Archaeol Soc* **4**, 1–19

— 1952 'Hill-slope forts and related earthworks in south-west England and South Wales'. *Archaeol J* **109**, 1–22

Fox, H S A 1972 'Field systems of east and south Devon. Part I: East Devon'. *Trans Devonshire Assoc* **104**, 81–135

— 1973 'Outfield cultivation in Devon and Cornwall: a re-interpretation' *in* M Havinden (ed), *Husbandry and Marketing in the South West 1500–1800.* Exeter: Univ Exeter, 19–38

Francis, P T H 1984 'A survey and description of the 'catch meadow' irrigation systems found in the Exmoor region of west Somerset'. Unpublished BA dissertation, University of Durham

Fulford, M, Champion, T and Long, A 1997 *England's Coastal Heritage. A Survey for English Heritage and the RCHME.* London: English Heritage and RCHME

Gathercole, C 2003 *An Archaeological Assessment of Watchet.* English Heritage Extensive Urban Survey

Gibson, A 1992 .The timber circle at Sarn-y-bryn-caled, Welshpool, Powys: ritual and sacrifice in Bronze Age mid-Wales'. *Antiquity* **66**, 84–92

— 1994 'Excavations at the Sarn-y-bryn-caled cursus complex, Welshpool, Powys, and the timber circles of Great Britian and Ireland'. *Proc Prehist Soc* **60**, 143–223

— 2005 *Stonehenge and Timber Circles.* Stroud: Tempus

Gray, H St G 1903 'Ruborough Camp in the parish of Broomfield, Somerset'. *Somerset Archaeol Natur Hist* **49**, 173–82

— 1908 'Report on the Wick Barrow excavations'. *Somerset Archaeol Natur Hist* **54**, 1–78

— 1931 'Battlegore, Williton'. *Somerset Archaeol Natur Hist* **77**, 7–36

— 1943 'Stone axe found at North Petherton, Somerset'. Somerset Archaeol Natur Hist **23**, 52

Green, T 2004 *Holworthy Farm, Parracombe.* Exmoor National Park Authority Historic Environment Review 2004

Greswell, W H P 1900 'The Quantocks and their place-names'. *Somerset Archaeol Natur Hist* **46**, 125–48

— 1903 *The Land of Quantock: A Descriptive and Historical Account.* Taunton: Barnicott and Pearce

— 1905 *The Forests and Deer Parks of Somerset.* Taunton: Barnicott and Pearce

— 1922 *Dumnonia and the Valley of the Parret. A Historical Perspective.* Taunton: Barnicott and Pearce

Griffith, F M 1994 'Changing perceptions of Dartmoor's prehistoric context'. *Proc Devon Archaeol Soc* **52**, 85–100

Griffith, F M and Horner, W 2000 'Aerial reconnaissance in Somerset' *in* C Webster (ed), *Somerset Archaeology.* Taunton: Somerset County Council, 7–14

Grinsell, L V 1953 *The Ancient Burial-Mounds of England.* London: Methuen

— 1969 'Somerset barrows, part I: west and south'. *Somerset Archaeol Natur Hist* **113**, 1–43

— 1970 *The Archaeology of Exmoor.* Newton Abbot: David and Charles

— 1976 *Prehistoric Sites in the Quantock County.* Taunton: Somerset Archaeological and Natural History Society

— 1994 *The Megalithic Monuments of Stanton Drew.* Privately Printed

Grove, J 2002 'Dead Woman's Ditch 11127/SM24015'. Somerset HER: Archive Report

Hamilton J R and Lawrence, J F 1970 *Men and Mining on the Quantocks.* Bracknell: Town and Country Press

Harding, J 2003 *Henge Monuments of the British Isles.* Stroud: Tempus

Hardy, T 1887 *The Woodlanders*, 1986 reprint. London: Penguin

Harford, C J 1803 'An account of some antiquities discovered in the Quantock Hills, in Somersetshire, in the year 1794'. *Archaeologia* **14**, 94–8

Harris, A 2000 'The Quantock Common. Continuing Management 2000–2010'. Quantock Common Management Group and the AONB Joint Advisory Committee

Haverfield, F 1902 'Two hoards of Roman coins found in Somersetshire in 1666'. *Archaeol J* **59**, 342–5

Hawkes, C F C 1931 'Hill forts'. *Antiquity* **5**, 60–97

Hawkins, M 1996 *Somerset at War 1939–1945.* Bridgwater: Hawk

Hill, A G (ed) 1981 *Letters of Dorothy Wordsworth.* Oxford: Oxford Univ P

Hill, J D 1996 'Hill-forts and the Iron Age of Wessex' *in* Champion, T C and Collis, J R (eds), *The Iron Age in Britain and Ireland: Recent Trends.* Univ Sheffield, 95–116

Hinton D J 1999 *An Illustrated History of Bishops Lydeard and Cothelstone.* Bishops Lydeard: Rocket Publishing

Hollinrake, C and Hollinrake N 1994 *Parsonage Farm, Over Stowey.* Archaeological Landscape Survey Rep **52**

Hollinrake, C and Hollinrake, N 2003 'Williton, Doniford'. *Somerset Archaeol Natur Hist* **147**,196

Homer *The Iliad* translated by E V Rieu 1950. London: Penguin

Hood, A A 1873 'Note on the Stogursey hoard'. *Proc Soc Antiq* **5**, 427–8

Houlder, C H 1968 'The henge monuments at Llandegai'. *Antiquity* **42**, 216–21

Hurley, J 1978 *Exmoor in Wartime 1939–45.* Dulverton: Exmoor Press

Jamieson, E 2002 *Cosgate Hill, Countisbury, Devon.* English Heritage Archaeol Investig Rep **AI/15/2002**

Johnson, N and Rose, P 1994 *Bodmin Moor: An Archaeological Survey, I: The Human Landscape to* c *1800.* London: English Heritage and RCHME

Jones, B V 2001 The *Manor Tannery, Fore Street, Grampound.* English Heritage Hist Building Rep

Kemeys-Tynte, D M 1920 'Cothelstone Tower and its founder'. *Somerset and Dorset Notes and Queries* **16**, 295–7

King, T 2004 *Yarford 2004 Interim Report.* University of Winchester website

Lawrence, B 1952 *Quantock Country.* London: Westaway

— 1970 *Coleridge and Wordsworth in Somerset.* Newton Abbot: David and Charles

Leach, P 1977 'Excavations at North Petherton, Somerset 1975'. *Somerset Archaeol Natur Hist* **121**, 9–39

— 1984 *The Archaeology of Taunton.* Western Archaeol Trust Monogr **8**

— 2001a *Roman Somerset.* Wimborne: Dovecote Press

— 2001b 'Excavations at Hillyfields, Upper Holway, Taunton'. *Somerset Archaeol Natur Hist* **145**, 57–82

— 2002 'West Bagborough, Lydeard Hill'. *Somerset Archaeol Natur Hist* **146**, 142–4

Leech, R H 1980 'Religion and burials in south Somerset and north Dorset' *in* Rodwell W (ed), *Temples, Churches and Religion in Roman Britain.* Oxford: BAR **103**, 329–66

Lynch, F 1993 *Excavations in the Brenig Valley. A Mesolithic and Bronze Age Landscape in North Wales.* Cambrian Archaeol Monogr **5**

Lynch, F, Aldhouse-Green, S and Davies, J L 2000 *Prehistoric Wales.* Stroud: Sutton

MacDermot, E T 1973 *A History of the Forest of Exmoor.* Newton Abbot: David and Charles

McAvoy, F 1986 'Excavations at Daw's Castle, Watchet, 1982'. *Somerset Archaeol Natur Hist* **130**, 47–60

McCann, J and McCann, P 2003 *The Dovecotes of Historical Somerset.* Somerset Vernacular Building Research Group

McCrone, P 1994 'Carhampton, Eastbury Farm'. *Somerset Archaeol Natur Hist* **138**, 177

McDonnell, R R J 1990 *The Quantock Hills Area of Outstanding Natural Beauty. Summary Report of an Archaeological Survey.* Somerset County Council

— 2003 *Great Wood, Quantock Hills. A Preliminary Archaeological*

Field Assessment of Eleven Acres Prior to Clear Felling. Somerset County Council

McNeil, R 1973 'A report on the Bronze Age hoard from Wick Park, Stogursey, Somerset'. *Somerset Archaeol Natur Hist* **117**, 47–64

McOmish, D, Field, D and Brown, G 2002 *The Field Archaeology of the Salisbury Plain Training Area.* London: English Heritage

Manley, J 2002 *AD 43. The Roman Invasion of Britain.* Stroud: Tempus

Manning, W H 1976 'The Conquest of the West Country' *in* Branigan, K and Fowler, P J (eds), *The Roman West Country. Classical Culture and Celtic Society.* Newton Abbot: David and Charles, 15–41

Marshall, W 1796 *The Rural Economy of the West of England*, 1970 reprint. Newton Abbot: David and Charles

Mayberry, T 1998 *The Vale of Taunton Past.* Chichester: Phillimore

— 2000 *Coleridge and Wordsworth. The Crucible of Friendship.* Stroud: Sutton

Mead, A and Worthy, D 2001 *Images of the Quantocks and their Villages.* Friends of Quantock

Moorman, M (ed) 1971 *Journals of Dorothy Wordsworth*, 2 edn. Oxford: Oxford Univ P

Moysey, C F 1918 'A flint implement factory site near Milverton'. *Proc Prehist Soc East Anglia* **2**, 521–3

Nesbitt, R R 1970 'Nether Stowey'. CBA Groups 12 and 13, *Archaeol Rev* **5**, 35

Newman, R, Cranstone, D and Howard-Davis C 2001 *The Historical Archaeology of Britain, c 1540–1900.* Stroud: Sutton

Nicholas Pearson Associates 1998 *Cothelstone Park: Historic Landscape Survey and Management Proposals.* Tiverton: Nicholas Pearson Associates

Nichols, W L 1891 *The Quantocks and Their Associations*, 2 edn. London: Sampson Low, Marston and Co

Norman, C 1975 'Four Mesolithic assemblages from west Somerset', *Somerset Archaeol Natur Hist* **119**, 26–37

— 1978 'Two flint artefacts from the gravel cliffs at Doniford'. *Somerset Archaeol Natur Hist* **122**, 157–8

— 1980 'Timber structures to the south of Chedzoy: Moor Drove'. *Somerset Archaeol Natur Hist* **124**, 159–63

— 2001 'Mesolithic to Bronze Age activity at Parchey Sand Batch, Chedzoy'. *Somerset Archaeol Natur Hist* **145**, 9–38

Norman, C and Clements, C F 1979 'Prehistoric timber structures on King's Sedgemoor: some recent discoveries'. *Somerset Archaeol Natur Hist* **123**, 5–18

Odlum, M J 1974 *The History of the Church and Village of Spaxton in the County of Somerset.* Privately printed

Ordnance Survey 1802 Three Inch Drawing No 43, part 1

Osborne, D 2004 *Defending Britain. Twentieth-Century Military Structures in the Landscape.* Stroud: Tempus

Oswald, A, Dyer, C and Barber, M 2001 *The Creation of Monuments. Neolithic Causewayed Enclosures in the British Isles.* London: English Heritage

Owoc, M 2001 'Experiencing continuity and development in the early Bronze Age funerary rituals of southwestern Britain' *in* Bruck, J (ed), *Bronze Age Landscapes, Tradition and Transformation.* Oxford: Oxbow, 193–206

Page, J L W 1890 *An Exploration of Exmoor and the Hill Country of West Somerset with notes on its Archaeology.* London: Seeley and Co

Page, W (ed) 1906 *A History of the County of Somerset, vol 1.* London: Univ London

— 1911 *A History of the County of Somerset, vol 2.* London: Constable

Palmer, M and Neaverson, P 2005 *The Textile Industry of South-West England. A Social Archaeology.* Stroud: Tempus

Papworth, M 2004 *Trendle geophysical survey report.* National Trust

Patourel, H E J le 1968 'Documentary evidence and the medieval pottery industry'. *Medieval Archaeol* **12**, 101–26

Phelps, W 1836 *The History and Antiquities of Somersetshire.* London: J B Nichols

Pollard, S H M 1967 'Seven prehistoric sites near Honiton, Devon. A Beaker flint ring and three flint cairns'. *Proc Devon Archaeol Soc* **25**, 19–39

— 1971 'Seven prehistoric sites near Honiton, Devon. Part II. Three flint rings'. *Proc Devon Archaeol Soc* **29**, 162–80

Ponsford, M W and White, B 1971 'Nether Stowey, Over Stowey'. CBA Groups 12 and 13, *Archaeol Rev* **5**, 6 and 42

Ponting, K G 1971 *The Woollen Industry of South-West England.* Bath: Adams and Dart

Pytches 1964 'Excavation at Broomfield Hill, near Broomfield, Somerset'. *Somerset and Dorset Notes and Queries* **28**, 187–9

Quinnell, H 1997 'Excavations of an Exmoor barrow and ring cairn'. *Proc Devon Archaeol Soc* **55**, 1–39

— 2003 'Devon Beakers: new finds, new thoughts'. *Proc Devon Archaeol Soc* **61**, 1–20

Rack, E 1782–1786 'Topographical notes for the history of Somerset'. SRO A/AQP G/1968

Radford, C A R and Hallam, A D 1955 'The history of Taunton Castle in the light of recent excavations'. *Somerset Archaeol Natur Hist* **98**, 55–96

Rahtz, P 1969 'Cannington hillfort 1963'. *Somerset Archaeol Natur Hist* **113**, 56–68

— 1979 *The Saxon and Medieval Palaces at Cheddar.* Oxford: BAR **65**

— 1993 *Glastonbury.* London: Batsford

Rahtz, P, Hirst, S and Wright, S M 2000 *Cannington Cemetery.* English Heritage: Britannia Monogr **17**

Reed, S J 2003 'Hillfarrance Flood Defence Scheme'. *Somerset Archaeol Natur Hist* **147**, 195

Riley, H 2003 *Mill Hill, Oare, Somerset.* English Heritage Archaeol Investig Rep **AI/3/2003**

Riley, H and Wilson-North, R 2001 *The Field Archaeology of Exmoor.* London: English Heritage

Robinson, S 1992 *Somerset Place Names.* Wimborne: Dovecote Press

Roffey, S, Wilkinson K and Webster, C 2004 'Kingston St Mary, Ivyton Farm'. *Somerset Archaeol Natur Hist* **148**, 107–8

Ross, C D (ed) 1959 *Cartulary of St Mark's Hospital, Bristol.* Bristol Record Society **21**

Royal Commission on Common Land 1957 *Minutes taken before the Royal Commission on Common Land.* London: HMSO

Sabin, D 2003 *Geophysical survey at Over Stowey, Somerset.* Stratascan **1809**

Sandford, E 1888 *Thomas Poole and his Friends*, 1996 reprint. Over Stowey: Friarn Press

Seaby, W A 1950 'Mesolithic chipping floor at Fideoak Farm, Bishops Hull'. *Somerset Archaeol Natur Hist* **95**, 169–70

Silvester, R J and Quinnell, N V 1993 'Unfinished hillforts on the Devon moors'. *Proc Devon Archaeol Soc* **51**, 17–31

Simpson, S J and Noble S 1993 *Archaeological survey and management study of areas on Gittisham Hill, Farway Hill, and Broad Down, East Devon.* Exeter Mus Archaeol Field Unit Rep **93.38**

Siraut, M, Dunning, R and Brown, K 1992 *The Quantocks. A Past Worth Preserving.* Tiverton: Somerset Books

Smith, C 1992 *Late Stone Age Hunters of the British Isles.* London: Routledge

Smith, N 1999 'The Earthwork remains of enclosure in the New Forest'. *Proc Hampshire Field Club Archaeol Soc* **54**, 1–56

SRO 1609 'A plot of Quantock belonging to the right honourable the earle of Northumberland'. DD/SAS C/923

— 1687 'A True Plott of the Manner of East Quantoxhead belonging to the Honorable Francis Luttrell of Dunster Castle'. DD/X/LTR1

— 1724 'Maps of Crowcombe'. DD/TB

— 1750a 'A view and plan of Nether Stowey by Thomas England'. DD/SAS (a) C/1207

— 1750b 'Plan and view of Nether Stowey by Thomas England'. DD/AH 66/27

— 1767 'A Plan of the Park, House and gardens with part of the Demesne Lands, Crowcombe'. DD/TB 51/2

— 1776 'A Map of the New Inclosures in the Parish of Crowcombe, Somerset'. Q/RDe 138

— 1778 'A plan of the manor of East Bagborough'. DD/ES C/2217

— 1792 'Plan of the lands of Edward Jeffries Esdaile'. DD/ES C/2217

— 1797 'Survey and descriptive particulars of several manors of Crowcombe Biccombe'. DD/TB 51/3

— 1801 'Survey of the Earl of Egremont's manors'. DD/WY C/306

— 1825 'Plan of Estates, Manors and Lands in the Parishes of Spaxton, Stogursey, Over and Nether Stowey, Kilve, Stockland Bristol and

Fiddington in the County of Somerset, the property of Henry Harvey Esq'. DD/SAS C/549
— 'Esdaile Manuscripts'. DD/ES
Stafford, D forthcoming *An Amble through St Audries. The History of West Quantoxhead*
Stanier, P 2003 *Somerset in the Age of Steam*. Tiverton: Somerset Books
Stawell, G D 1910 *A Quantock Family. The Stawells of Cothelstone and Their Descendants, the Barons Stawell of Somerton, and the Stawells of Devonshire, and the County Cork*. Taunton: Barnicott and Pearce
Straw, A 1999 'Palaeolithic: the earliest human occupation' *in* Kain, R and Ravenhill, W (eds) *Historical Atlas of South-West England*. Exeter: Univ P, 43–50

Thorndycraft, V R, Pirrie, D and Brown, A G 2004 'Alluvial records of medieval and prehistoric tin mining on Dartmoor'. *Geoarchaeology* **19**, 219–36
Thorpe, N 2002 'Kingston St Mary, Vollis Hill'. *Somerset Archaeol Natur Hist* **146**, 139
Timberlake, S 1992 'Prehistoric copper mining in Britain'. *Cornish Archaeology* **31**, 15–34
— 2001 'Mining and prospection for metals in Early Bronze Age Britain' *in* Bruck, J (ed), *Bronze Age Landscapes, Tradition and Transformation*. Oxford: Oxbow, 179–92

Vancouver, C 1808 *General View of the Agriculture of the County of Devon*, 1969 reprint. Newton Abbot: David and Charles
Virgin, P 1994 *Sydney Smith*. London: HarperCollins
Vyner, B 1994 'The territory of ritual: cross-ridge boundaries and the prehistoric landscape of the Cleveland Hills, north-east England'. *Antiquity* **68**, 27–38
— 1995 'The brides of place: cross-ridge boundaries reviewed' *in* Vyner, B (ed), *Moorland Monuments. Studies in the Archaeology of North-east Yorkshire in Honour of Raymond Hayes and Don Spratt*. York: CBA Res Rep **101**, 16–30

Wainwright, G J and Smith, K 1980 'The Shaugh Moor Project: second report – the enclosure'. *Proc Prehist Soc* **46**, 62–122
Waite, V 1969 *Portrait of the Quantocks*, 2 edn. London: Hale
Ward, A H 1989 'Cairns and 'cairn fields'; evidence of early agriculture on Cefn Bryn, Gower, West Glamorgan'. *Landscape History* **11**, 5–18

Warren, D 1996 *Somerset's Industrial Heritage. A Guide and Gazetteer*. Somerset Indust Archaeol Soc Survey **8**
Watts, M 2000 *Water and Wind Power*. Princes Risborough: Shire
Webster, C J 2000 'South East Quantocks Archaeological Survey'. *Somerset Archaeol Natur Hist* **144**, 225–6
Webster, C J and Brunning R A 2004 'A seventh-century AD cemetery at Stoneage Barton Farm, Bishops Lydeard, Somerset and square-ditched burials in post-Roman Britain'. *Archaeol J* **161**, 54–81
Wedlake. A L 1950 'Mammoth remains and Pleistocene implements found on the west Somerset coast'. *Somerset Archaeol Natur Hist* **95**, 167–8
— 1973 *A History of Watchet*. Dulverton: The Exmoor Press
Wedlake, A L and Wedlake D J 1963 'Some palaeoliths from the Doniford gravels on the coast of west Somerset'. *Somerset Archaeol Natur Hist* **107**, 93–100
Wessex Archaeology 1994 *The Southern Rivers Palaeolithic Project Report No 3 1993–1994: The Sussex Raised Beaches and the Bristol Avon*. Salibury: Wessex Archaeology
Wilkinson, K and Thorpe, N nd 'The Southern Quantock Archaeological Survey Project Design'. Winchester: King Alfred's College Dept Archaeol
Wilkinson, K, King, T, Marter, P, Stoodley, N, Turner, A and Webster, C 2003 'Southern Quantocks Archaeological Survey'. *Somerset Archaeol Natur Hist* **147**, 191–2
Williams, M 2002 *Ward's Silk Factory, Evercreech, Somerset*. English Heritage Archit Investig Rep **B/048/2002**
Williams, R 2004 *Limekilns and Limeburning*, 2 edn. Princes Risborough: Shire
Williamson, T 1995 *Polite Landscapes. Gardens and Society in Eighteenth-Century England*. Stroud: Alan Sutton
— 1997 'Fish, fur and feather: man and nature in the post-medieval landscape' *in* Barker, K and Darvill, T (eds) *Making English Landscapes*. Oxbow Monogr **93**, 92–117
Wilson, J 2004 *The Somerset Home Guard. A Pictorial Roll-call*. Bath: Millstream Books
Worthy, D 1998 *Quantock Tragedy: the Walford Murder of 1789*. Over Stowey: Friarn Press
Wright, G N 1967 'By Kilve's smooth shores'. *Country Life* **142**, 1077–9
Wright, B 2002 *Somerset Dragons*. Stroud: Tempus
Wymer, J 1962 'Excavations at the Maglemosian sites at Thatcham, Berkshire, England'. *Proc Prehist Soc* **28**, 329–61

Index

Figures in **bold** refer to illustrations.

A

Acland, Sir Thomas Dyke 135
Addison, Robert 21
Adscombe 87, **93**, 94–5, 113
Adscombe Chapel **93**, **94**, 94–5,
    95, 160
aerial photography
  catch water meadows
      135, 135
  coastal strip **85**
  cropmarks **61**, 67
  Doniford valley **16**
    and enclosures 60
  English Heritage survey 14
  henge footprints 25
  Higher Castles **65**, 65
  Neolithic sites 21, 22
  Nether Stowey 90
  north from Vale of Taunton **1**
  Rooks Castle **63**, 63
  Slaughterhouse Combe
      and Black Ball Hill **6**
  transcription of features
      13
  Wills Neck **40**
agriculture
  Bronze Age field systems
      43, 44, 45
  on common land 110–11,
      127–31
  and geology 5
  improvement 115
  Iron Age 51, 72
  medieval 91, 108–12
  medieval crops 109
  Neolithic 19–20
  outfields 131
  relict field systems 127–31,
      128, **130**, 133
  Roman 73, 75–6
  rye 131
  use of lime 135–6
Aisholt 3, 104–5, 136, **137**, 152
Aisholt Common 10, 105–6,
      106, 113
  relict field system 127, 130
  trial pits 147, 148
Alderley Edge, Cornwall 29
Alfred, King 79
Aley 3, 97
Aley Lane 155
Alfoxden Manor 12
Alfoxton 10, 154, 155, **156**
Alfoxton Park 147
Alfred d'Espaignes 92
Anglo-Saxons
  burhs 79, 81–2

coins **82**, 82
estates 77, 79–81, 83, 84–5
  hunting grounds 82–4
  landscape 79–81, 84–5
  sites 80
animals, wild 15, 15–16, 16,
      19, 21, 22
annual regeneration rites 25
antiquarians
  accounts 10–12
  and barrows 10, 12, 31–2
archaeology 12–14
*Archaeology of Exmoor,
      The* (Grinsell) 13
Area of Outstanding Natural
      Beauty (AONB) 1, 7
artefacts
  Bronze Age 30, 43–4
  Dark Ages 79
  Mesolithic 18–19
  Neolithic **20**, **21**, 21, 22, 23
  Palaeolithic 15, 16–18, **17**, **18**
  Roman 54
Athelney Abbey 94, 95
Avebury 26
Aveline's Hole 18
Avill Sandstones 4
Avill Slates 4
Axe Valley, Devon 15

B

Bagborough 86
Bagborough Hill 127
Bagborough Plantation 30
Bagley, Exmoor 61
Baker's Farm (now Court Farm)
      132
barns 108, **131**, **132**
barrows: *see also* cairns;
  chambered tombs; Lydeard
  Hill; Wills Neck
  antiquarian investigations
      10, 12, 31–2
  Battlegore 10, 22–3, **23**,
      24, 32
  cemeteries 31, 37–8, **38**, **39**,
      41, 50
  cone 36
  dating 32
  dimensions 34, 38
  distribution 30–1, **31**, **49**
  ditches 33–4, 38
  Dowsborough Camp 56–7
  flat topped 36
  Greenway group 27
  Grinsell's survey 13
  groups **35**
  and linear earthworks
      47, 48, **49**, 50
  Mendip Hills 24

numbers 30
  paired with platform cairns
      36, **37**, 38, 41
  restoration 160
  round **33**, 33–4
  satellite cairns 34–5
  signs of disturbance 10
  Sling Camp Group 36
  Thorncombe 33–4, 128
  tradition begins 19
  triple 38, **39**
  truncated 35–6
  use for beacon fires 32–3
Barton, Nick 18
Bats Castle, Exmoor 52
Battlegore
  barrows 10, 22–3, **23**, 24, 32
  cemetery **23**
  Gray's excavation 12
  Neolithic tombs 22–4, **24**
  sanctuary area 19
  standing stones 10
Beacon Hill
  barrow and cairn pair
      36, 37, 41
  barrows 33, 34, **36**, 160
  beacons 32
  outfields 131
  practice trenches 157
  relict field system 127, 128,
      130, **130**
Beacon Tower 126, **126**
beacons **32**, 32–3
Beech Grove mine 147, **148**,
      149, 149–50
bench ends 88, 110, **111**, **112**
Bicknoller
  antiquarian investigations 11
  common land 110
  drainage 3
  enclosed field strips 109, **109**
  grazing rights 7
  outfields 131
  tanning industry 142
Bicknoller Combe 4, 35,
      35, 129
Bicknoller Hill
  hillfort 58–9, **59**, 60
  linear earthwork 47, 58–9, **60**
  outfields 131
  relict field system 127, 129
Bicknoller Post 1
Bin Combe 139, 143
Bincombe Farm 143
Binfords 11
Bishops Lydeard 3, 12
  boundaries 85
  church 88, 110, **111**
  cropmark sites 67
  manor 87
Bishpool Farm 135

numbers 30
Black Ball Hill **6**, 35, **111**, 111
Black Death, the 89
Black Hill
  barrow cemetery 37–8, **38**,
      39, 50
  barrows 19, **49**
  cairns 37
  mine workings **147**, 147
  relict field system 127
Blackdown Hills 7
Bodmin Moor 35, 60, 128–9
boroughs 88
bowling greens 118, 120
Brean Down 29, 43, 76
Brecon Beacons National Park
      7
Brendon Hills 1, 22
Brenig Valley, Wales 35, 38,
      40, 43
Brent Knoll 76, 77
Bridgewater 1, 90, 113,
      142, 156
Bridgewater Castle 10, 113
Bristol Channel, bombing
      range 154
Bronze Age
  artefacts 30, 43–4
  burial monuments 30–2, 45:
      see also barrows; cairns
  burials 29, 40–1
  chronological framework 28
  field systems 43, 44, 45
  funeral rituals 38, 40–1, **42**,
      43, 45
  hoards 29–30
  landscape 28, 43, 45, 50
  linear earthworks 46–8, **48**,
      49, 50
  metalworking 28–9, 30
  pottery **29**, 29, 43
  settlements 43–5, **44**, **46**, 52
Broomfield
  catch water meadows 135
  common land 8, 110
  copper mines 147, 150
  geology 4
  hill-slope enclosure 12, **69**
  medieval landscape 113
  Rack's description 11
  royal connections 83
Broomfield Consols Copper
      and Silver-Lead Mining
      Company 150
Broomfield Hill 1, 99
Brydges, James, duke of
      Chandos 142
Buckingham Mines 148–9, 150
building materials, stone 4, 4, 5
buildings: *see also* castles
  Adscombe Chapel **93**, **94**,
      94–5, **95**

barns 108, **131**, **132**
changing styles 159
Chapel House 95
charcoal burners **139**, 139,
   140, 142
Cothelstone House 93, 94
Cothelstone Manor **116**, 117
Court House **102**, 102,
   131, 132
engine houses **149**, 149–50
farm and farmstead 104, **108**,
   108, **131**, **132**, 132
Friarn stable block **160**, 160–1
garden 117
gatehouses **102**, 102, **116**
Holford Glen dye house
   146, 146–7
hunting lodges 83
lime burner's shelters
   136, 136
Manor Cottages **100**, 102
manor houses 91, 102,
   103, 104
Marsh Mills silk factory
   146, 146
medieval fabric 88
outbarns **132**, 132
on relict field systems 128–9
ROC observation posts
   158, **159**
Roman 71, 73–4
Rooks Castle 63–4
Ruborough Camp 56
St Audries 125
tanning industry 143–4,
   144, 145
Terhill House 122
Terhill Park grotto 122, **124**
Tom Poole's Bark House
   143–4, **144**
Trendle Ring 62–3
Buncombe Farm 134
Buncombe Wood 134
Burghal Hidage, the 79
burhs 79, 81–2
burials
   associated with ringed cairns
      37
   Bronze Age 29, 40–1
   Dark Ages 77, 78–9
   and henge monuments 25, 26
   Mesolithic 18
   Neolithic 19, 22–4, **24**, 25, 26
   Palaeolithic 18
   pot 71
   ritual 26
   Roman 76
Burrington Combe 18
Burrow, Ian 63, 67

C

Cadbury Castle 29, 52, 76, 77
Cadbury Congresbury hillfort
   57, 77

cairns: *see also* barrows,
   Lydeard Hill
   antiquarian investigations
      12, 31–2
   clearance 45, **46**
   dating 32
   distribution 30–1, **31**, 34, **49**
   embanked platform 37, **37**,
      38, 45
   Grinsell's survey 13
   groups **35**
   and linear earthworks 48, 50
   numbers 30
   platform 35, **36**, 36–7, 37,
      38, 40, 41
   and relict field systems 130
   ring 19, 37, **37**, 38, 40–1, **41**
   Roman coins 75
   satellite 34–5
   signs of disturbance 10
   stone 34
   truncated 35–6
   West Hill 30, **34**, 34, 37,
      46, 130
Camden, William 10
canals 115
Cannington
   Anglo-Saxon estate 77, 80, 83
   cemetery 78–9
   minster church 81
   nunnery 87
   quarry 79
   Roman 56, 76
Capton 75
Caratacus Stone, the 77
Carew Cottage 108
Carew, Sir John 120, 121
Carew, Thomas 10–11, 120
Carhampton 77
Castle Ditches, Wiltshire 55
castles
   Nether Stowey Castle 11, **90**,
      91, 91–2, **92**
   Norman construction 86
   Over Stowey 92
   roof tiles 113
   sites **89**
   Stogursey **86**, 86
catch water meadows **128**,
   134–5, **135**, 152
Catling, Dr H W 65
cemeteries
   barrow 31, 37–8, **41**, 50
   Battlegore **23**
   Dark Ages 77, **78**, 78–9
   Roman 76
Centwine, King of Essex 82
chambered tombs 19, 23–4, **24**:
   see also barrows
chapels 87
charcoal
   burning 138–40, **139**, **140**,
      141, 142, 150, 152
   from funeral pyres 40–1
Charterhouse 72

Charter of Privileges 83
Cheddar 79
Christianity 77, 81
churches
   Anglo-Saxon 81, 81–2
   early Christian 77
   foundation 87
   Kingston St Mary **87**, 88
   medieval fabric 88
   St Decuman's Church 77, **81**,
      81, 82
   St Mary's Church 80
   West Quantoxhead 125
Clavelshay, enclosures 69, **70**
Cleeve Abbey 87, 97, 112
Clovelly Dukes, Devon 60, 61
coastal strip
   abandoned farms 132
   medieval landscape 113
   settlements **85**
Cockercombe 3, 4, 47–8, 139
Cockercombe Tuff 4
coins
   Anglo-Saxon **82**, 82
   Roman 32, 54, 74, 74–5,
      75, 79
Cold War, the 158, **159**
Coleridge, Samuel Taylor
   1, 12, 143, 150
Collinson, John 11
Combe Farm 4, 131, **132**,
   132–3, **133**
Combe Florey 1, 151
combes 1, 3, 5
Combwich 75
common land 7–8, **8**, **9**, 10
   cultivation 26, 110–11,
      127–31
   medieval landscape 113
   relict field systems 127
   water supply **111**, 111–12
Commons Registration Act
   of 1965 8
Congresbury 77
Congyer Hill 98
Cooksleigh 84
copper and copper-mining
   4, 28–9, 57, 140, 142,
   147, 147–50, **148**, **149**
Cornwall 60
Cosgate Hill, Exmoor 34
Cothelstone
   antiquarian investigations 12
   Church of St Thomas of
      Canterbury 87
   copper mines 150
   deer park 97
   holy well of St Agnes 79
   landscape 1
   landscape park 151
   manor 86
   Manor Cottages 88, **100**, 102
   medieval **100**
   rabbit warren 98
   settlements 3

Cothelstone estate, Bronze Age
   metalwork hoard 30
Cothelstone Hill
   Auxiliary Unit bunker
      157, **158**
   barrows 48
   Beacon Tower **126**, 126
   cairn **36**
   deer park 97, 99
   height 1
   lime industry 137
   linear earthwork 48, 48
   pillow mound **99**, 99
   quarry 34
   Roman shrine 79
   Seven Sisters 37
   tower 48
   tree rings **126**, 126
Cothelstone House 93, 94
Cothelstone Manor
   conspicuous consumption 102
   deer park 118
   garden **117**, 117–18
   gatehouse **116**, 117
   layout **116**
   mine workings 147
   pillow mounds 99
Countryside Agency 7
Countryside Stewardship
   scheme 13
Court Farm (formerly Baker's
   Farm) 132
Court Farm (now Court
   House) 132
Court House, East
   Quantoxhead **88**, 88,
   102, 102, **131**, 132
   gardens 118, **119**, 119–20
Courtway 92, **93**
Cow Castle, Exmoor 52
Crandon Bridge 75
Chedzoy 110
Creech St Michael 145
Cresswell, B F 12
Crocker, Philip 11
cropmarks 13–14, 25, 45, 60,
   61, 67–70, 70–1, 73, 76
Crosse, Andrew 11, 150
Crosse, Richard 121
Crowcombe
   Black Death deaths 89
   Carew's description 10–11
   catch water meadows 135
   Combe Cottage 113
   common land 110, 113
   deer park 97
   dovecote 102
   farmstead buildings 108
   fish ponds 102
   settlements 3
   tanneries 142
Crowcombe Biccombe Manor
   132–3
Crowcombe Church, dragon
   bench end **58**, 58

Crowcombe Court 10, **11**, 118, **119, 120**, 120, 155
Crowcombe Gate
    cairn **36**, 37
    searchlight battery 155, **157**
    tree ring 125–6
Crowcombe Heathfield 8, 15, 154, 155, **156**
Crowcombe Park **120, 121**, 121, 127, 151
Crowcombe Studley estate 132
Currill 97
Currill Common 8
cursus monuments 22, 26

D

Danish raids 23
Dark Ages
    cemeteries 77, **78**, 78–9
    landscape 77–8
Dartmoor 24, 43, 48, 60, 130, 131
dating
    barrows and cairns 32
    of early Palaeolithic sites 15
    hill-slope enclosures 62
    radiocarbon 19, 28
    relict field systems 129
Daw's Castle
    burh 81–2
    minster church 81
    Roman burials 76
Dead Woman's Ditch 13, 37, 47, **49**, 50
Deadmanswell 83
Deak's Allers 88, 107, **132**, 132
deer 84, 97
deer parks **89**, 91, 95, **96**, 97, 98, **98**, 99, 118
Dene Cross **67**, 68
Dens Combe 1, 127
Denscombe 132
Derbyshire Old Workings 147
deserted medieval farmsteads 104–6, **105**
Devil's Ring **126**, 126
Devon 131
Dissolution of the Monasteries 115
Dodington, copper mines 57, 147, **148**, 148–50, **149**
Domescombe 107, **107**
Domesday Book 51, 80–1, 83, 84, 104–5
Doniford
    artillery range 153
    mammoth teeth 16
    Mesolithic artefacts 19
    Palaeolithic artefacts 15, 16–17
    Roman settlement 76
    valley **16**
Doniford Camp 154
Doniford Stream 3
Dorset 47, 90

Dorset Cursus 22
dovecotes 100, 102, 104, 120
Downs Farm 114
Dowsborough Camp
    antiquarian investigations 11, 11–12
    barrow 56–7
    dragon tales 10
    entrance 11–12
    hillfort **56**, 56–8, **57**, 78
    Julius Caesar at 1
    restoration 160
    trial pits 148
Dowsborough Wood 140
dragon tales 10, **58**, 58
drainage 1, 3, 5
Duke's Plantation 112
Dumnonii, the 51, 72
Dunning, R W 92
Dunster Castle 132
Dunster deer park 97
Dunster Priory 87
Durborough Farm **105**, 105, **106**
Durotriges, the 51, 72
Durrington Walls 25
Dyche 67
Dyffryn Ardudwy 24

E

earthworks: *see also* burhs;
        hillforts; pillow mounds
    agricultural enclosures 45
    castles **91**, 91
    circular ditched 38
    decay 60
    deer parks 97
    hut circles 43–4
    linear 45, 46–8, **48, 49**, 50, 58–9, **60**
    manorial 92–4, **93**
    medieval 63
    mining **147**, 147–8
    Neolithic 21–2
    shooting butts 127
    windmills **110**, 110
East Bagborough **93**, 93–4
East Devon AONB 7
East Nurcott Farm 135
East Quantoxhead:
        see also Court House
    common land 7, 110, 111
    Deak's Allers 88, 107, **132**, 132
    deer park **96**, 97, **98**, 99
    dovecote 102
    drainage 3
    farmsteads 106–7, **107**
    fish ponds **100**, 102
    geology 4
    lime kilns 136, 137
    manorial enclosures **101**, 102
    medieval manor 85, 90
    rabbit warren **98**, 98, 99
    settlements 3
    windmills 109–10, **110**

eastern scarp 3
Ebsley Farm 113
Ellis, Peter 25
Elworthy Barrows, Brendon Hills 58
enclosure 7–8, 108–9, **110**, 110–11, 115
enclosures 60: *see also* hillforts;
        hill-slope enclosures
    Adscombe Chapel 95
    Clavelshay 69, **70**
    cropmark sites 67–70, 70–1
    Iron Age 71–2, 73
    manorial **101**, 102, **103**, 104
    pounds 83–4
    Rooks Castle **83**, 83–4
    survival of 113–14
England, Robert 92
English Heritage 14
English Heritage Aerial Survey
        team 14
English Heritage Monument
        Management Scheme
        13, 160
Esdaile, Edward Jeffries 117, 118
European Commission Habitats
        and Species Directive 6
Exeter 72, 73, 145
Exeter, Bishop of 95
Exmoor 1, 4, 26, 34, 44, 57, 60, 60–1, 82, 84, 130, 131
Exmoor National Park 7

F

farms and farmsteads
    antiquarian investigations 11
    buildings 104, 108, **108**, **131**, 132, **132**
    deserted 131–4, **132, 133, 134, 135**
    deserted medieval 104–6, **105**
    dominant form of settlement 104
    East Quantoxhead 106–7, **107**
    Higher Aisholt Farm **106**
    and the landscape 113–14
    location 3
Farway Downs, Devon 40–1
Farway Hill 38
Fideoak Park 19
field systems
    Bronze Age 43, 44, 45
    on common land 111
    Dene Cross 67
    enclosed field strips 108–9, **109, 110**
    Iron Age 68, 72
    medieval 108–9
    Plainsfield Camp 99
    relict 58, 98, 105–6, 127–31, **128, 130**, 133
    Upper Cheddon **68**
Fire Beacon Hill 32, 34, 127
Firebeacon 130

First World War 153
fish ponds **100**, 102, 104
Flaxpool 102, 112
Flaxpool Cottage 108
Fleming, A 130
flint 18–19, 21
Follies **121**, 121
Forbes-Leslie, Dr W 152
Forge Cottage 108
Friarn **160**, 160–1
Friends of Quantock, The 12, 27
Frog Combe 148
Fuller-Palmer-Acland,
        Sir Peregrine 125
funeral pyres 40–1, **42**, 43
funeral rituals, Bronze Age 38, 40–1, **42**, 43, 45
Fyne Court 11, **121**, 121, 151

G

Garden Mine 148, 149
gardens 115, **117**, 117–20, **118**
Gay, Robert 10, 23
Gay's House Combe 107, 127
geology **3**, 3–5
Gerard, Thomas 10
Gittisham Hill 38
glass making 142
Glastonbury Abbey 82, 86, 89, 97
Glastonbury Lake Village 51
Glebe engine house **148, 149**, 150
Goathurst 67, 69, **70**
    Prisoner of War camp **156**, 156–7
Goods Farm 138
Goose, Matthew 150
Gorsey Bigbury 26
Gough's Cave, Cheddar Gorge 18
Gouz, Willelmo 107
Grabburrowes: *see* Battlegore
Gray, Harold St George 12, 23, 32, 54
grazing rights 7, 8
Great Bear 125
Great Hill 34, 34, **35, 49**, 127, 130, 133, 147
Great Ormes Head, Wales 28–9
Great Wood 4, 6, 7, 99, 142
Greenway 27, 127
Greenway Farm 18–19
Greenway Spur 34, **44**, 45
Greswell, Rev William 12
Grinsell, Leslie 13, 33, 38, 63, 65
gunpowder works 142

H

Halford Combe **138**
Halsway 3, 135
Halsway Hill 127

Halsway Manor 12, **147**, 147
Halsway Post 35
Ham 134
Ham Hill, Somerset 21, 52
Hamilton, Francis 124
hamlets 3, 104, 113–14,
133–4, **134**
Hamme 105, 148
handaxes 15, 16, **18**
Hangman Grits 4
Hare Knap 1
Hawkridge Common 8, **136**
Hazelmere Farm 68
Head deposits 5
Heathfield 111
heathland 5–6, **6**, 44
Heddon 8, 111
Hembury Castle, Devon 21
henge monuments 19, 25–6
Heron, HMS 154
Hestercombe 68, 114, 155
Hestercombe House 154
Higher Aisholt Farm **106**
Higher Castle, Exmoor 55
Higher Castles **64**, 64–5, **65**,
66, 67, 68
Higher Hare Knap 37, 38, 41,
127, 128
linear earthwork 47, **48**, 48,
49, 50
Higher Holworthy 45
Higher Ivyton 133
Hill Farm, Kingston St Mary 88
hill-slope enclosures 60–1:
see also enclosures
associated with farms 113–14
Broomfield 12, **69**
dating 62
excavations 65, 67
Higher Castles **64**, 64–5,
66, 67
Plainsfield Camp **62**, 63
Rooks Castle **63**, 63–4, **64**, 69
Ruborough Camp 55
Trendle Ring, the 61–3, **62**
Hillfarrance 45
hillforts: *see also* enclosures
Bicknoller Hill 58–9, **59**, **60**
Cadbury Castle 29, 52, 76, 77
circular hollows 57–8
classifications 55
Dowsborough Camp **56**,
56–8, **57**, 78
earthworks 54–5, 56–7, 58
entrances 55, 57
function 52, 55–6
incomplete 58
Iron Age 45, 51–2, 71, 160
post-Roman occupation 77–8
ritual activity 52
Ruborough Camp 12, 47, 52,
54, 54–6, **55**, 78
size 52
Hillyfields 73, 76
Hinkley Point 32, 76, 77

*History and Antiquities of the
County of Somerset*
(Collinson) 11
*History of the Antiquities of
Somerset* (Phelps) 11–12, 30
hoards
Bronze Age metalwork 29–30
Roman coins 74–5, **75**
Hodder's Combe 1, **139**, 139
Holcombe 104–5, **106**
Holford 3, 143, **144**, 144–5,
158
Holford Combe 1, **139**, 139,
144
Holford Common 8
Holford Glen 4, **146**, 146–7
Holland, William 12
Holway 73, 76
Home Guard 154, 157–8
Hugh de Bonville 92, 94
Hugo le Helier 113
Hull, Sir Edmund 105
Hulle 105
human activity, earliest evidence
15
human remains
Dark Ages 78
Mesolithic 18
Palaeolithic 18
hunting 19, 82–4, 126–7, 161
Huntstile 67
Hurley 84
Hurley Beacon **32**, 32, 33, 35,
37, 38, **39**, 130

I
ice ages 5, 15–16, 16
Ifracombe Beds 4, 5
Ifracombe Slates 4
Ingram, Colonel 157–8
Iron Age: *see also* enclosures
definition 51
enclosures 71–2, 73
field systems 68, 72
hillforts 45, 51–2, 71, 160
landscape 51, 71–2
pottery 65, 70, 73
settlements 45, 60, 71, 71–2
sites **53**
tribal areas **73**
iron-working 4, **66**, 72, 73, 77,
113, 140, 142
irrigation 134–5
Ivyton 76, 113, 133, 152
Ivyton Farm 45, 71, 114, 133,
134

J
Jeffries, Edward 122, 150
Jenkin, William 148
John de la Linde 99
John de Neville 82
Julius Caesar 1

K
Kahlmeter, Henrik 147
Kenley 135
Kenley Copse 132
Kiln Close 136
kilns 4, 112: *see also* lime kilns
Kilton
deer park 97
location 3
medieval agriculture 108, 109
medieval manor of 85, 90
Roman coin hoard 75
Kilton Park Wood 153
Kilve
chapel 87
church font 88
common 7, **8**
deer park 97, 99
dovecote 102, 104
fish ponds 102, 104
foreshore **5**
geology 4
lime kilns 136, 137
mammoth teeth 16
manorial enclosures **101**, 102,
103, 104
medieval building remains 88
medieval manor **5**, 85, 90
Neolithic artefacts 21
oil fields **152**, 152–3
rabbit warren 98
settlements 3
standing stones 27–8
tanning industry 143
Kings Cliff Cottage 69
King's Cliff stream 63
Kingscliff 125
Kingshill 83
Kingslands 83
Kingston Beacon 68
Kingston St Mary 3, 4, 86
church **87**, 88
iron-working 113
tanning industry **144**, 145
textile industry 145
Knackers Hole 37

L
Lake Meadow 30
Lake Villages 51
landscape
21st Century 159–61
and abandoned farms 132
Anglo-Saxon 79–81, 84–5
Bronze Age 28, 43, 45, 50
contrasts 1
Dark Ages 77–8
deer parks 97
early 20th century 152
geology and 3
heritage 159–60
impact of man on 6–7
Iron Age 51, 71–2
management 7

medieval 85–90, 113–14
medieval manors influence
on 91
Mesolithic 18, 19
Neolithic 19–22
ornamental **125**, 125–7, **126**
post-medieval 150–1
relief **3**
ritual 50
Roman 75–6
settlement 3
landscape parks
Crowcombe Park **120**, **121**,
121, 127, 151
Dorothy Wordsworth on 151
Fyne Court 11, **121**, 121, 151
sites **118**
Terhill Park 122, **123**, 124–5
water features 121, 124
landuse **9**
Langford, timber circle **25**, 25, 26
Larkbarrow Association, the 5
Lawrence, Berta 12, 94
Lawry, R A 158
Lay Subsidy (1327) 105, 107
lead 4
legends 10, 32, 54, **58**, 58
Leigh 84
Leland, John 10
Lexworthy 113
Lilstock 108, 154, **155**
lime industry 135–8, **136**, **137**
lime kilns **128**, 135–8, **137**, 152
limestone 136, **137**, 137, 138
Little Hangman sandstones 4
Little Quantock Farm 112,
131, 135
livestock
cattle 97, 109
pigs 83, 97, 109
sheep 84, 90
location 1, **2**
Locke, Anthony 37, 63, 65
Lodes Lane 72
Long Stone, the 26–8, **27**
Longstone Hill 26–8
Lonlay Abbey 87
Lower Hare Knap 127, 128,
129, 140
Lower Ivyton 133, **134**
Lower Palaeolithic 15
Lower Weacombe 70
lowland commons 8
Lowsey Thorn 83, 84
Luttrell family 97
Luxborough Farm 136
Lydeard Farm 114
Lydeard Hill
barrow **33**, 36
beacon 33
cairns 32, 34, 37, 75, 79, **129**
deserted medieval farmstead
104
field systems 105, 127, 128,
129

shelters **129**
Lydeard St Lawrence 67
  Roman coin hoard 75
Lyf, Lucia de 95
Lyf, Walter de 95
Lynch, F 38
Lynton Slate 4

M
McDonnell, Richard 13
Maidenbrook Farm 51, 73,
  76, 77
mammoth teeth 16
management 7, 10
market towns 88
Marrow Hill **126**, 126, 127,
  130, 147
Marsh Mills 142, 145–6, **146**
Marshall, W 12
Marshwood 97
Meare Lake Village 51
medieval
  agriculture 91, 108–12
  common land 7
  conspicuous consumption
    97–102
  deer parks 95, **96**, 97, **98**, 98, 99
  earthworks 63
  farmsteads 104–8
  field systems 108–9
  growth in prosperity 88–9
  industry 112–13
  landscape 85–90, **100**, 113–14
  manor houses **5**, 85, 90, 102,
    103, 104
  manorial earthworks 92–4, **93**
  manors 85, 86–7, 90–1
  population change 88–90
  sites **89**
  windmills 109–10, **110**
Melcombe 83
Membury Castle, Devon 21
Mendip Hills 7, 16, 24, 58,
  72, 82
Merridge 3, 8, 92, 113, 150
  lime industry **137**, 137–8
Merridge Hill 85
Mesolithic, the 18–19
Middle Halsway Farm **108**
Middle Hill 104, **105**, **106**, 127
Middle Palaeolithic 16
Middlehill House 104, 105
Milber Down, Devon 61
Milford Association, the 5
military sites
  American Camps 154–5, **156**
  bombing range 154
  Home Guard 154, 157–8
  practice trenches 57, **125**, 157
  Prisoner of War camps **156**,
    156–7
  Royal Observer Corps 158
  searchlight batteries 130,
    155, 157

training ranges 57, 153–4, **154**
Mill Hill, Exmoor 128–9
mills 88, 113
Milverton 21, 22
Minchin Buckland Priory 87
Minehead 90, 97
minerals 4, 72, 147
Mines Royal 148
mining and miners
  copper 4, 28–9, 57, 140, 142,
    147, 147–50, **148**, **149**
  medieval 113
  Roman 72
  sites **128**
  trial pits 57–8, 72, **147**, 147–8
monasteries 86–7, 115
Money Field 54
Morte Slates 4, 5, 113
Mounsey Castle, Exmoor 56
Moysey, C F 21
Muchcare Farm 132, 133, **133**
Muchcare Wood 30, 37
Myrtleberry Camp, Exmoor 55
Myrtleberry North, Exmoor
  57–8

N
name, origin of 1
National Mapping Programme
  14
National Monuments Register
  (NMR) 14
National Parks Commission 7
Neanderthals 16
Neolithic, the
  artefacts **20**, **21**, 21, 22, 23
  burials 19, 22–4, **24**, 25, 26
  landscape 19–22
  monuments **25**, 25–8
  ritual killing 26
  settlements 21–2, **22**
  sites **20**
  temperatures 21
Nerrols Farm 22, 76
Nether Stowey
  aerial photograph **90**
  Coleridge and Wordsworth at
    12
  deer park 97, 99
  enclosed field strips 109, **110**
  location 3
  pottery industry 112
  rabbit warren 98
  tannery **143**, 143, 143–4, **144**
  textile industry 113
  vicarage garden 118–19
Nether Stowey Castle 11, **90**,
  91, 91–2, **92**
New Forest, Hampshire 83
New Hall Mine 148, 149
Newbolt, Sir Henry John 152
Newton Park 95, 97
Nichols, Rev William 1
Norman, Chris 18

Normans, the 85–7, 97
North, John William 12
North Petherton
  Anglo-Saxon estate 80, 81, 83
  deer park 95, 97
  minster church 81
  pigs 83
  ROC observation post 158
  settlement 3
  St Mary's Church 80
North Stream **135**
North Yorkshire Moors 47, 48,
  50
northern plateau 4, 7, **8**
Norton, John 125
Norton Camp 154
Norton Fitzwarren
  American camp 154
  Bronze Age metalwork hoard
    30
  Bronze Age site 43, 45
  deer park 95
  dragon tales 10, 58
  earthwork 22
  henge monument 25
  hill **22**, 22
  Neolithic settlement 22
  Prisoner of War camp 156
  Roman finds 76
  sanctuary area 19
  settlements 52
Norton Fitzwarren Camp 58

O
Oggshole 83
Oggshole Farm 114, 133
oil production **152**, 152–3
Old Minster Field 81–2
Old Rectory, the 108
outbarns **132**, 132
outfields 131, 140
Over Stowey
  building material **4**
  Castle Field 92, **93**
  charcoal burning 139
  common land 7
  gardens 118
  location 3
  manor 94
  mining 148
  pottery industry 112
  searchlight batteries 155
  silk industry 146

P
Page, Rev J L W 12, 23, 32,
  54, 75
Parrett, River 3, 54, 84
Parsonage Farm 118, **119**, 119
*Particular Description of the
  County of Somerset, The*
  (Gerard) 10
Paviland 16

peat 21
Penn, battle of 78
Perry 3, 102, 110, 135
Perry Combe 1
Perry Farm 132
Perry Hill 148
Petherton Park 10, 135
Phelps, William 11–12, 30
Philip de Cauntelo 98
Philip de Columbers 91, 99
photograph collections 12
pigeon houses 99–100
pillow mounds 63, **89**, 98–9,
  99, 121, **125**, 130
Pilot's Helm 21
Pinwell, G J 12
Pitt Rivers, Augustus Henry
  Lane-Fox 12
Pixies Mound: *see* Wick Barrow
Plainsfield
  deer park 97, 99
  dovecote 102
  location 3
  rabbit warren 98
Plainsfield Camp **62**, 63, **99**,
  99, 148
Plainsfield Manor 87, 99
Poly-Olbion, The (Drayton) 10
Poole, Matthew 145
Poole, Tom 1, 139, 143, 145,
  146, 148–9, 150
Porlock Common 26
portal dolmen 23–4, **24**
post holes, henge monuments
  25
post-Roman shrine 56
pottery
  Beaker 29, 32, 43
  Bronze Age **29**, 29, 35
  Grooved Ware 25
  Iron Age 65, 70, 73
  medieval 112
  Neolithic 22
  North African 77
  Roman 71, 73, 76
  Saxon 80
  Trevisker 43
Poundisford, deer park 95
pounds 83–4
Price, S H 21
Priddy Circles, the 26, 58
Prisoners of War **156**, 156–7, **158**
prospecting 4
Putsham 75

Q
Quantock Combe 3, 139
Quantock Common 82–3, 84,
  160
Quantock Common
  Management Group 10
Quantock Forest 82–3, 84
Quantock Hills AONB Service
  7, 14, 159

Quantock Lodge 4
Quantock ridge, the 1
Quarkhill Farm 108
quarries and quarrying 4, 34, 79, 113
   limestone 136, **137**, 137, 138

R

rabbit warrens 63, **89**, 91, 97–8, **98**
Rack, Edmund 11
Raddon, Devon 21
railways 115, 152–3
Rams Combe 3
Ramscombe 130, 139
Raswell 133
Raswell Farm 150
Raswell House 133
Red Lady of Paviland 16
relict field systems 58, 98, 105–6, 127–31, **128**, **130**, 133
Rich family 95
Rich's Holford 67
ritual pits 41
Roadwater Limestone 4
Robert de Odburville 83
Robert Waleraund 83
Robin Upright's Hill 47, 147
Roborough, Exmoor 61
Rogero de Comb 133
Romans, the
   artefacts 54
   coins 32, 54, 74, 74–5, **75**, 79
   conquest of Britain 72
   fortifications 72, **73**
   landscape 75–6
   mosaics **74**, 74
   occupation of hillforts 52
   pottery 71, 73, 76
   roads **73**
   settlements 51, 60, 72–3, 75–6
   sites **53**
   temples 76
   villas 71, 73–4, **74**
   withdrawal 77
Rooks Castle
   cropmark sites 68–9
   enclosures **83**, 83–4
   hill-slope enclosure 63, 63–4, **64**, 69
   medieval and prehistoric sites 114
   quarries 4, 113
Rooks Castle Farm 114, 134
Rows Farm 114
Royal Commission on Common Land 8
royal forests and parks 82, 84, 97, 114
Royal Observer Corps 158, **159**
Ruborough Camp 12, 47, 52, **54**, 54–6, **55**, 78

'rycroft' fields 8
rye cultivation 131

S

St John's Hospital, Bridgewater 94
St Michael's Chapel 91
Salisbury Plain 47, 48
salt production 76
Sandhill Park 154
Sarn-y-bryn-caled, Powys 26
sea level, rises in 20–1
Seaby, W A 19
searchlight batteries 130, 155, **157**
Second World War
   American Camps 154–5, **156**
   Auxiliary Units 157, **158**
   bombing range 154
   Home Guard 154, 157–8
   practice trenches 57, **125**, 157
   Prisoner of War camps **156**, 156–7
   Royal Observer Corps 158
   searchlight batteries 130, 155, **157**
   training ranges 57, 153–4, **154**
Selwood Forest 82
settlements
   Bronze Age 43–5, **44**, **46**, 52
   coastal strip **85**
   common field villages 108
   Dark Ages 79
   Dene Cross **67**, 68
   deserted 104–6, **105**, 131–4, **132**, **133**, **134**, **135**
   hill-slope enclosures 61, 62, 63–4, **66**, 67
   Iron Age 45, 60, 71, 71–2
   in the landscape 3
   Neolithic 21–2, **22**
   Roman 51, 60, 72–3, 75–6
   Upper Cheddon **68**, 68
Shalime Company, the 153
Shervage Wood 83
Shervage Wood, the Great Worm of 58
shooting butts **118**, 127
Short Combe 34, **140**
Shoulsbury Castle, Exmoor 58
Sidbury 47
silk industry **145**, 145–7, **146**
silver 4
Simon de Furneaux 104
Site of Special Scientific Interest (SSSI) 5–6
Skinner, Rev John 10
slaked lime 135–6
Slaughterhouse Combe **6**, 127, **140**, **141**
Slocombe, Thomas 122, 124
Smith, John 125
Smith, Sydney 1, 151
Smith's Combe 1, 4, 126, **127**

soils 4, 5
Somerset 7, 72
Somerset Archaeological and Natural History Society 32
Somerset County Council 14
Somerset Historic Environment Record (HER) 14
Somerset Levels, the 51
Somerset moors 3
Somerton 83
Somerton Combe **140**
South Cadbury, Somerset 21
South Downs 47
South Ivyton **134**
Southern Quantocks Archealogical Survey (SQAS) 13–14, 45, 60, 70, 73
Spaxton 12, 97, 102, **112**, 113, 158
Spaxton Roman Villa 73
Special Area of Conservation 6
standing stones 10, 26–8, **27**, 34
Stanton Drew 26
Stawell family 84
Stawell, Elizabeth **87**, 87
Stawell, Sir John 117
Stawell, Sir Matthew de **87**, 87
Stawell, Robert 87
Stert Combe 126, 127
stock ponds **111**, 111–12
Stockland 10
Stogumber 72
Stogursey 7, 110
Stogursey Priory 87
Stolford 21
stone circles 19
Stoneage Barton 71, **78**, 78–9
Stonehenge 22, 25
Stowborrow Hill 98, 98–9
Stowey 10, 147
Stream Farm **134**
Stringston 8, 10, 83
Stringston Heathfield 8
Stogursey Castle **86**, 86
swaling (controlled burning) 7, **7**
Sweet Track, the 21
Swinage Wood 142

T

tanning industry 142–5, **143**, 143–4, **144**
Tanyard Farm 143, **144**
Taunton
   Anglo-Saxon estate 80, 83
   Bronze Age metalwork hoards 30
   castle 86, 113
   foundries 142
   minster church 81
   royal hunting lodge 83
   textile industry 145

timber circle 19
Taunton, Vale of 67
Taunton Deane 86
Terhill House **122**, 122
Terhill Park 122, **123**, 124–5
Tetton 135
textile industry 89, **112**, 112–13
   silk **145**, 145–7, **146**
   woollen 88, 145
Thorncombe Barrow 33–4, 128
Thorncombe Hill 127, **129**
Tilbury Farm 133
timber circles 19, **25**, 25–6, 26
tin 28, 29
Tiverton 145
tools
   Mesolithic 18–19
   Neolithic **21**, 21, 22, 23
   Palaeolithic 15, 16–18, **17**, **18**
topography 1, **3**
Toulton 71
Townsend Farm 132
tree rings **118**, 125, 125–6, **126**
Trendle-castle 11
Trendle Ring, the 58–9, **59**, 61–3, **62**
Trentishoe Grits 4
trial pits 57–8, 72, **147**, 147–8
Triscombe 3
Triscombe Farm 131
Triscombe Quarry 4
Triscombe Stone, the **27**, 28
Trotts 138
Tuck's Barn 136, 138
turf cutting 44, 110

U

Upper Cheddon **68**, 68
Upper Palaeolithic 16–18, **17**, **18**
urns **29**, 29, 35

V

Vancouver, Charles 131
vegetation 5–6, **6**
Victoria County History 12, 90
Viking Club 32
Viking raids 82
Vinny Combe 1, 98, **99**
Volis Farm 45, 114
Volis Farm North 68
Volis Hill 43, **71**, 71

W

Waite, V 12
Walford, John 47, 139
Walford's Gibbet 149
Walker, Frederick 12, **13**
Ward, Thomas 146
Warman, Simon 88
Watchet
   Anglo-Saxon 82

burh 79
handaxes 15
mammoth tusks 16
military sites 153
St Decuman's Church 77, **81**, 81, 82
water supply **111**, 111–12, 124, 134–5, 143, **144**, 144–5, 146
Waterman's Wood 142
Weacombe 3, 127
Weacombe Hill **35**, 36, **125**, 127, 128, 130
Wedlake, A L 15
Wells, Bishop of 87
Wessex, Kingdom of 79
West Bagborough 3, 97
   Roman coin hoard 74–5, **75**
West Hill
   Bronze Age settlement 45, **46**
   cairns 30, **34**, 34, 37, **46**, 130
   mine workings 148
   relict field system 127
West Holcombe 105
West Kilton Farm 155
West Kilton Farm tank training range 153–4, **154**

West Monkton 145
West Quantoxhead
   church 125
   common 7, **8**
   deer park 97
   lime kilns 136
   local history publications 12
   mammoth teeth 16
   medieval manor 85, 90
   outfields 131
   St Audries 125
   valley 3
western escarpment 1, 3, **40**
Westleigh Farm 19, **29**, 29, 133
Wheatley, W W 102
Wick 7
Wick Barrow 12, 29, 32
Wick Fitzpayn 82
Wick Moor 32
Wick Park, Bronze Age metalwork hoard 30
William I, King (the Conqueror) 85
William de Falaise 82, 87
William de Mohun 87
William de Roumare 87
Williton 15, 19, 76, 80, 83

Willoughby Farm 55
Wills Neck
   aerial photograph **40**
   barrow cemetery 38, **41**
   barrows 7, 19, **33**, 33–4, 37, 41, **49**, 160
   beacon 33
   common land 10
   height 1
   linear earthwork 48, **49**
   ringed cairn **37**, 37, 38, **41**
   trial pits 147
Wiltshire 35, 36, 90
Winchester, Bishop of 86, 95
Wind Hill, Devon 52
windmills 109–10, **111**
Winton, Helen 67
Withyman's Pool
   barrow cemetery 50
   barrows **39**, 41
   pond **111**, 111–12
   ringed cairn **37**, 37, 38, 41
   satellite cairns 34
Wivelsicombe 72
Woodhenge 25
woodland 5–6, **6**, **9**: *see also* Quantock Forest; tree rings

bark stripping 142
conifer plantations **127**
coppiced 58, 138, 140
Dowsborough Camp 58
industries 138–45
landscape parks 121, 124–5
Mesolithic 18
Neolithic 19–21
oak **138**, 138
pollards 140
tree clumps 126–7
Woodlands Hill 10, **111**, 111, 127, 128, 140, 147
Woodward, John 147
woollen cloth industry 88, 145
Wooston Castle, Dartmoor 55
Wordsworth, Dorothy 12, 150, 151
Wordsworth, William 1, 12
Wort Wood 150

Y
Yalway Farm 68
Yards 158
Yarford **61**, 70–1
Yarford Roman Villa 73–4, **74**, 77